LINCOLN CHRISTIAN P9-CPX-824

The missionary children, like the Lisu children, were carried on people's backs when they became tired, or when the road was too difficult.

Everyone looked forward to reaching a good camp site in the evenings, relaxing beside the fire, and having a hot meal, as Eugene's family is doing here, January, 1966, en route to Junction Camp.

The Eugene Morse family at Green Water Flats. Left to right: Front row, Ronnie, Marilyn, Margaret, Jeannette; Back row, Eugene, David, Helen, Tommy. February, 1966.

Drema Esther and Lucy Yangmi in front of the Yangmi shelter beside the river in Empty Valley. February, 1966.

Robert and Betty, February, 1966, in Green Water Flats. Robert's beard was the envy of the Lisu men, for they have little or no beard.

At Green Water Flats camp, the tents were in a row along the river, at the base of the mountain. The Lisu people camped nearby in small huts made of bamboo poles, with walls and roofs of banana and other jungle leaves.

Sunday morning church services at Green Water Flats, with Robert preaching. In the background are the tents and shelters which served as "home."

Following a rough animal trail through the jungle, these men pause to rest a moment before moving on with their heavy loads.

Gertrude and carriers safely crossed this bridge over a rushing mountain stream.

During a rest stop, Helen and Tommy enjoyed the wild beauty of Empty Valley.

Often the only trail through the jungle was a small footpath, almost hidden by jungle undergrowth.

The Lisu people traveling to Hidden Valley took most of their worldly possessions with them in baskets carried on their backs.

Streams such as this had to be crossed several times daily. Occasionally someone slipped and loads got wet. Note the small child sitting in the basket in the foreground.

Bridges across the many streams were usually nothing but a few poles lashed together and laid across rocks in the streams. Balancing with a heavy load was tricky.

The slender poles of the bridges became wet from the splashing of the rapids, and very slippery.

Unaccustomed to the rough trails, and having only smooth-soled shoes for walking, Helen needed assistance in getting over the rocks along the riverbed in order to keep up with the rest of the party.

The scenery was beautiful, but picking one's way over the stones beside the river could be extremely tiring.

Gertrude Morse and some of the Lisu Christians at Rice Field Camp, February, 1966. Behind them Russell and Gertrude's tent.

Binuzup settlement, made up of about five families who had moved there several years before the "exodus" of so many from the Putao area.

Gertrude Morse taught at an open-air church service held at Rice Field Camp. A box propped up on poles served as a "pulpit."

Sammy and Jesse Yangmi display the langur killed for their evening meal, while Lucy looks on. February, 1966, in Empty Valley.

Gertrude Morse with load carriers as they take a break to rest along the jungle trail.

In the bamboo forests, the carriers sometimes had to hack a path through the almost impenetrable barrier formed by intertwined branches.

At noon the load carriers stopped and built a fire, rested and had some hot tea.

The Lisu carried with them their most valuable possessions: their children and their crossbows.

Eugene (in helmet) and Helen arrived at Rice Field Camp early in March, 1966. Margaret (barefoot) seated in front, Tommy behind Eugene.

Robert, Betty, and family arrived at Rice Field Camp in April, 1966. Like many others, they used strong walking sticks to help them along the rugged trail.

At Rice Field Camp, Eugene preached from a fallen tree, while the ground or logs served as seats for the congregation.

Margaret, DeeDee and Marilyn enjoyed playing with the three tiger cubs brought into camp by a hunter.

A Lisu family beside their hastily constructed temporary home in Rice Field Camp.

Getting ready to break camp. Eugene and Ron stand beside the tent which sheltered the supplies. In the background is one of the housing tents made of plastic sheeting. April, 1966.

The eleven Morses in Bangkok soon after arrival from Burma in June, 1972. Left to right: Eugene, Helen, Gertrude, Russell, Jeannette, Ron, Margaret, Tom, David, Marilyn, Robert.

Exodus to a Hidden Valley

Eugene Morse was four months old when his
parents left Oklahoma, in 1921, to become missionaries in the Himalayas. His brother Robert was
born in Tibet in 1923. During World War II they
and a younger brother helped flyers who crashed
while carrying supplies over the 'Hump'.

After the war they returned to the United States
to study and to marry, and then followed their
parents as missionaries. The Morses were forced
out of China by the Communists (their father was
imprisoned for fifteen months) and settled in
Burma. The author, his brother Robert and some
of their children are at present missionaries in
Thailand.

EXODUS TO A HIDDEN VALLEY

Eugene Morse

Published as a private edition for the benefit of North
Burma Christian Mission

Published by William Collins+World Publishing Co.
2080 W. 117th Street, Cleveland, Ohio 44111

First published in the United States of America in
1974 by Reader's Digest Press, New York.

The scripture quotations in this publication are
from the Revised Standard Version of the Bible,
copyrighted 1946, 1952 and © 1971, 1973 by the
Division of Christian Education of the National
Council of the Churches of Christ in the USA and
are used by permission.

Copyright © 1974 by Eugene Morse

ISBN 0-529-05393-4
Library of Congress Catalog Number 77-82017

Printed in United States of America

TO MY PARENTS
J. Russell and Gertrude Morse,
whose faith and courage
have been an example
to their children
and an inspiration
to all who know them.

The author wishes to acknowledge the
contributions to this book from all the
members of the Morse family, particularly
his wife, Helen, who took over the chore
of editing the final draft when he
returned to Thailand, and to his brother,
Robert, who freely offered all of his
recollections and reactions to enrich the
story. In addition, the author wishes to
acknowledge the encouragement and
editorial assistance of Reader's Digest
staff members Noel F. Busch, S. A.
Schreiner, Jr, and Edward W. Ziegler.

76345

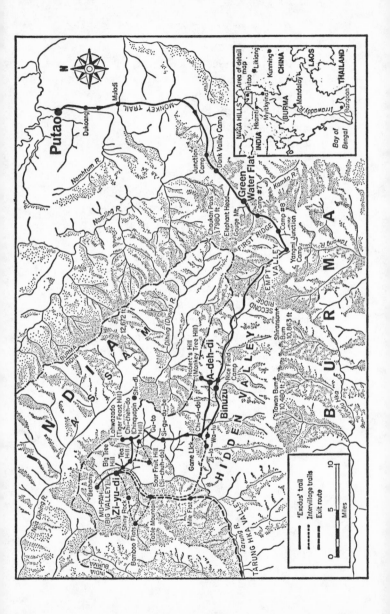

FOREWORD

This book is the story of one six-year period in the life of a family which for three generations has been involved continuously in Christian missionary work in Asia — first in Tibet and China, then in Burma, and more recently in Thailand. The events recorded here are typical of their experiences over a period of more than sixty years, as they have traveled hundreds of miles, endured physical hardships and political instabilities, and even imprisonment. But through it all they have been upheld by faith in God, and have found their greatest joy in serving Him. Their continuing service is a witness to the power of God to keep and bless those who trust Him.

CHRONOLOGY

1921 — On August 13, J. Russell and Gertrude Morse, with four-month-old son Eugene, left the U.S., and on December 23 arrived at Batang, the remote mission station on the Tibetan border.

1923 — Second son Robert born April 8.

1926 — Resigned from Batang mission; began work in Yunnan Province (southwestern China) as "independent" missionaries, trusting God for support.

1927 — Morses ordered by U.S. Consul to leave China due to political unrest; spent 70 days traveling through trackless jungle into Burma, then on to U.S.

1929 — Returned to Yunnan, China, established mission station in Yea Chi.

1930 — Began teaching among Lisu tribe.

1931 — Adopted two Tibetan girls — Anzie Ruth, age 9, and Drema Esther, age 4 — orphaned by death of parents. Both girls grew up to become a great help in the work. (Anzie Ruth died from typhus in 1949, while working with Dorothy Sterling as a translator. Drema Esther remained with the senior Morses until her marriage to Jesse Yangmi in 1963.)

1939 — More than thirty churches had been established, with over two thousand Christians.

1940 — Mission home at To-ba-lo destroyed by flood on October 23. In December the family moved into the Salween Valley where they remained for the next six years, during World War II.

1942–45 — World War II years, family cut off from outside world. Eugene and Robert worked with Allied forces, organized ground search and rescue service to aid downed airmen. Mission work continued, number of Christians increased to almost 6000.

1946 — Returned to U.S. for furlough after 9½ years of uninterrupted service in China.

1948 — Eugene and Robert both married, returned to Yunnan with brides and senior Morses.

1949 — Communist take-over in China forced evacuation of all mission personnel except J. Russell Morse, who was caught in sudden Communist take-over of Kunming.

1950–52 — J. Russell Morse still behind Communist lines. Arrested in March, 1951, and imprisoned in solitary confinement. No word received from him until his sudden release and arrival in Hong Kong in June, 1952, for an unexpected reunion with wife Gertrude and son LaVerne who were en route to the U.S.A. J. Russell and Gertrude returned to Burma in July, 1953.

1950–64 — Base of mission operation moved to Putao area, N. Burma. Morses helped resettle some 20,000 Lisu and Rawang Christians who moved down to plains from famine-stricken mountain areas. More than thirty Christian villages established. It became one of the most prosperous and progressive areas in Burma.

1965 — In December, Morses ordered to leave Burma by Gen. Ne Win's socialist government. Unable to leave by usual routes due to illness and other circumstances, the group traveled overland to India border, together with several thousand Lisu Christians who had fled from rule of the apparently Communist government. Refused permission to cross into India, the people settled in undemarcated, unadministered border area. More than twenty Christian villages established. The Morse families remained in this "Hidden Valley" area for over six years.

1972 — Burma/India Border Commission completed their work, "Hidden Valley" area determined to be within Burma; Morses once again ordered to leave, and escorted to Rangoon; from there they flew to Bangkok, Thailand, and on to U.S.A. after absence of eleven years.

1973 — In June, Eugene and Robert, each accompanied by two sons, began work in Thailand. Based in Chiang Mai, outreach was directed toward the estimated 20,000 Lisu living mostly in the northern part of the country.

1985 — After twelve years, there are around 3000 Lisu Christians in Thailand, scattered in some seventy villages. Eight of the brothers' twelve children are serving with them as missionaries and the others are in training. Family members, now joined by newcomers, continue to be involved in evangelism, preparation of literature, tape ministry, leadership training, church planting, and village development. Contact has been maintained with Christians in north Burma, and advice and assistance given as needed and possible.

NOTE: Mr. & Mrs. J. Russell Morse had two other children, neither of whom were involved in the events described in this book:

R. LaVerne Morse, the third son, was born January 4, 1929 in Los Angeles. After completing his education, he and his wife worked with his parents and brothers in north Burma until 1964. Since that time he has served as a professor at Cincinnati Bible Seminary, Cincinnati, Ohio, and has also been involved in several missionary efforts. He has four daughters and one son.

A daughter, Ruth Margaret, was born February 25, 1935, in Hong Kong. Ruth Morse Johnson lives in Joplin, Missouri, and has two sons and three daughters.

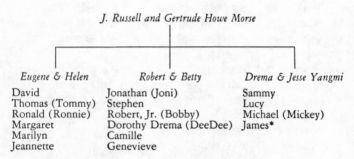

J. Russell and Gertrude Howe Morse

Eugene & Helen	*Robert & Betty*	*Drema & Jesse Yangmi*
David	Jonathan (Joni)	Sammy
Thomas (Tommy)	Stephen	Lucy
Ronald (Ronnie)	Robert, Jr. (Bobby)	Michael (Mickey)
Margaret	Dorothy Drema (DeeDee)	James*
Marilyn	Camille	
Jeannette	Genevieve	

* James was not born until after the Yangmis left Hidden Valley

–*–*–*–*–*–

Listing by families of those who took part in the experiences described in this book.

Chapter 1

So they made the people of Israel serve with
rigor, and made their lives bitter with hard
service, in mortar and brick, and in all kinds
of work in the field; in all their work
they made them serve with rigor.

EXODUS I : 13–14

As so often happens in life, our great adventure in the
wilderness came to us unsought. We loved working and
living on the fertile plain of Putao, in northern Burma,
where we had spent more than fifteen years teaching and
helping the local tribes create what was, for them, a
paradise. We had entertained no thoughts of leaving –
that is, not until 3 December 1965, which was the day my
brother Robert went to the post office in Putao to pick up
the week's mail and found that it included the following
government order:

THE REVOLUTIONARY GOVERNMENT OF THE UNION OF BURMA
OFFICE OF IMMIGRATION AND NATIONAL REGISTRATION

Subject: Presidential Order and Instruction to Leave the Country

The Chairman of the Revolutionary Government of the
Union of Burma hereby orders Mr/Mrs/Miss [list of all
our names] of the North Burma Christian Mission
Station at Muladi Village, Putao, Kachin State, North
Burma, to leave the Union of Burma by air or by sea,
before midnight, Friday, 31 December 1965.

[*Signed*]
Immigration Officer
Rangoon

We were all stunned. But the letter was real enough, and
so was the situation that must be faced. We were reminded
of the Old Testament king Hezekiah, who, when he

7

received a disturbing letter from his enemies, took it to the temple, spread it before the Lord, and asked his guidance and help in that time of distress. So we decided to follow the kingly example and take the expulsion order to the church, even though it was nearly midnight. My parents, my brother Robert, my wife, and I went out of my parents' house, where we had gathered, into the starlit winter night. The gravel on the path crunched under our feet as we walked between the rows of citrus trees my father had planted. We were silent during the short walk to the church, except for an occasional whispered comment. Somehow it seemed more appropriate to whisper, even though no one would have heard our normal voices.

At the church we paused while I got out the key to unlock the door, fumbling just a bit because of the cold. Then I pushed open the door and we entered the darkened church. I felt the thrill that swept over me every time I entered this building, for this was the only church of its kind in the country. Most of the church buildings of the Lisu and Rawang Christians were simple structures, made up of a wooden framework, with bamboo walls and a .hatch roof. But this one, which I had designed and helped erect, was built in the shape of a cross and was 100 feet long, 40 feet wide, and 80 feet wide at the transept. With its high, steep roof and wooden arches, it always reminded me of a cathedral. The five of us walked down the long centre aisle and stopped in front of the communion table. My father took the expulsion letter from his pocket, unfolded it, and then, both literally and in prayer, we spread the letter before the Lord, asking for wisdom, guidance, and help in this difficult and distressing situation. We were torn between our obligation to obey the government order and our longing to remain with our flock. The Bible instructs Christians to obey the laws of the land, and this we had always tried to do. The situation we now faced could be no exception. Only a miracle could prevent our leaving.

Though the reality of this expulsion order was a shock,

it had not come entirely without warning. Three years earlier General Ne Win had taken control of the government in a coup, and since then the country had been moving steadily further and further to the left. It had become a full-fledged socialist state and was using methods of discipline that had become all too familiar to us during our last years in China in the late 1940s. The day-to-day affairs of Putao had been placed under the rigid control of a five-man Security and Administrative Council. Through this group flowed a steady stream of orders and propaganda from the central government to the tribesmen.

Tribal people who were used to wandering at will through thousands of miles of mountain ranges found their freedom suddenly curtailed. They had to get official passes for travel between villages less than ten miles apart. Because they knew the hills, they were pressed into service as porters and guides when the Burmese army made forays against the 'insurgent' Kachins. A truckload of troops would arrive in a village at night and rout out every able-bodied man at gunpoint; if there weren't enough men available, they would take women in their place. These arduous expeditions could last anywhere from a few days to a few months, and the nominal wages that were promised to the tribesmen were not always paid.

The plain around Putao, some seven hundred and fifty miles north of Rangoon, was settled by about fifteen thousand members of the Lisu and Rawang tribes, most of whom were Christian. These tribes are two of those included in the general term *Kachin*. There are some two million Kachins living a nomadic life in the mountains of Burma's Kachin state, and others in India, and China. Strife between tribal peoples and central governments is as old as the history of South-East Asia. The Kachins had never really been subjugated; even when Burma was part of the British Empire they had effectively maintained their independence. In 1948, when Burma became a republic, a Kachin state was established in the northern part of the country and given a great deal of local autonomy.

But within a few years the Jinghpaw Kachins began to feel oppressed, and they reacted by forming the formidable Kachin Independence Army (KIA). The people of the Putao plain, among whom we lived and worked, were mostly peaceful and prosperous settlers, with houses, cows, oxcarts, gardens, and paddy fields. They found themselves caught between the insurgent tribesmen and the central government. Elements of the KIA, many of whose members had fought in World War II, often staged raids in the valley. The Burmese army would come out to meet them. One such encounter occurred in our village of Muladi, about ten miles south of Putao, on the Namling River. In the course of the battle several villagers were killed and ten houses were burned.

The Burmese government, of course, suspected the tribal people in the Putao plains of collusion with their cousins in the hills. Every so often they would try to force some young man or woman to go into the hills as a spy. My Tibetan foster-sister Drema Esther and her family were at breakfast one morning when they heard a commotion outside. They saw a squad of soldiers trying to drag off two boys from the congregation. The boys resisted, and the soldiers beat them with rifle butts until they sank to the ground with blood streaming from their cheeks and noses. Later, they were tied up and taken away.

The pressure on native Christians was particularly harsh. In Burma's new socialist society, citizens were forced into co-operating on public works projects such as roads, bridges, and public buildings. Sunday was a favourite day for 'recruiting' labour, because soldiers could surround a church where a service was being held and easily corral enough people. When they weren't shanghaiing workers, they would frequently take over the service and turn it into a political indoctrination meeting.

As missionaries, we made every effort to remain politically neutral, though it wasn't always easy. In addition to the danger from stray bullets, we were beginning to encounter some personal harassment. On the night of 4 July 1965 – a rather significant date – arsonists crept into my brother Robert's house, a few miles from our family compound. While Robert's family was asleep, the men poured kerosene on the floor and set it afire. The bamboo structure went up like a torch. Fortunately, Robert was able to get his family out; but his papers, records, and household goods were all consumed in the flames.

In view of all this, we could well understand why some of the more adventurous Lisu had already left Putao and moved westwards across the mountains into India. Though others had begun to follow them, we felt it our plain duty to stay. We were hopeful, until we got the expulsion order, that our neutrality might help to mitigate the lot of the majority of our fellow-Christians, who also wanted to stay in Putao.

Now, however, the time had come for us to leave Burma. The hardest job was telling our friends. We decided to do that publicly at a service in our thatch-roofed cathedral in the village of Muladi. The task fell to my father, J. Russell Morse, the spiritual leader of the whole community. But news of our expulsion must already have spread along the valley grapevine, because all of the five hundred seats were taken, and some people were standing outside, in spite of the chilly winter weather, hoping to see and hear what was going on. The Lisu women wore their best black velvet jackets and the colourful beads that proclaim their wealth and station; the men were wearing a variety of shirts and jackets, some of them remnants of service in various armies, and many wore wide wrap-around pants. If not festive, the occasion was at least impressive.

My father, grey-haired at sixty-nine and a little stooped, was the perfect picture of a patriarch. Speaking softly in Lisu, he chose a text that had become his guiding light during more than forty years of being harried by war and political persecution from one part of Asia to another: 'When they persecute you in one town, flee to the next; for truly, I say to you, you will not have gone through all the towns of Israel, before the Son of man comes' (Matt.

10 : 23). Moving on, he suggested, was for us, the Morses, God's will, and he could only pray for God's blessing on those we left behind. When the sermon was over, the congregation joined in a familiar hymn that, in Lisu and in the same four-part harmony found in American hymnbooks, sounded like the swell of a great organ:

> *He leadeth me: O blessed thought!*
> *O words with heav'nly comfort fraught!*
> *Whate'er I do, where e'er I be,*
> *Still 'tis God's hand that leadeth me.*
>
> *He leadeth me, he leadeth me;*
> *By his own hand he leadeth me:*
> *His faithful follower I would be,*
> *For by his hand he leadeth me.*

After the service, the congregation lingered in the bright winter sun to shake our hands and to offer help. A few of the village elders, we noticed, hung back; when the crowd thinned, they surrounded us. If we were leaving Putao, they said, they and their families were leaving too. Their plan was to follow the other Lisu who had trekked over the great snow-capped ranges to the west into India. They particularly wanted us to go with them. Some of the more recent travellers had sent word back that the Indians had closed the border. Perhaps we could help them negotiate with the Indian authorities.

One man named Khisu, a little over forty but prematurely aged by the rigours of an adventurous life, was especially persistent. I had first known him as a boy in China, and he had always been wild and looking for excitement. As a young man, he had left home and joined the Burmese army. He was an inveterate gambler and had won his wife in payment of a gambling debt. He had such a fierce temper that no one dared cross him. He was known to have killed an enemy or two in former times, and his fights with both men and beasts had cost him most of his teeth. This, coupled with his hooked nose, gave him something of the look of a pirate. One time, on a hunting expedition, he was badly mauled by a tiger, and the accident resulted in a broken shoulder and a dislocated neck, which caused him to hold his head at an odd angle. However, the dislocation was healed in answer to prayer, and as a result he became a Christian.

It was just shortly afterwards that he moved to our village of Muladi. Because of his past reputation, village people were sceptical of his conversion, and tended to give him a wide berth. But since we had known each other as boys, he came to visit me fairly often, and we did a lot of talking about the many places where he had been, including the country to the west of Putao where he had made many hunting trips. We even studied the maps of the area, and he described the different valleys he had visited. He was able to give such glowing accounts of the advantages and joys of life in the jungle that his hearers were almost convinced that he was telling the truth.

But the idea of walking out to India was so novel to us that we could only promise Khisu and his friends to give it some thought. To that end, we had a family conference that very afternoon. Sitting there in the peace of the familiar compound, we gazed out over the park-like yard and acres of thriving fruit trees that my father, long an admirer of Johnny Appleseed, had grafted from cuttings sent to him from Florida and California and so lovingly nurtured. Talk of leaving by any means whatever seemed unreal. All around us were evidences not only of the work we had done but of work yet to be done. More and more families were learning from my father how to grow their own trees; Robert and his wife, Betty, were little more than halfway along on a great project to translate the New Testament into Rawang; I, for whom engineering was a vocation, had already laid out a dozen villages, supervised the survey of roads, designed and built several bridges across the Namling, and, ironically, helped in the improvement of the airstrip by which we would probably have to leave. The main reason we had persuaded the government to let us

13

help with the airstrip was so we could bring in equipment and supplies, because there was no railway north of Myitkyina, and much of the year the roads were impassable due to washouts and landslides during the monsoon rains. Several of the Lisu and Rawang young men had been trained as tractor drivers and had been taught to maintain the tractors in good working order. With three tractors in operation, some seventeen hundred acres of new farmland had been opened up.

'We've got to go down to Rangoon by air and then on back home', I said. 'It's the only thing that makes sense. Drema Esther is eight months pregnant, you know, and Helen won't vouch for what might happen if she starts scrambling up and down those trails. Of course, we could leave her until the baby comes and . . .'

'Abandon her and Jesse? Never!' my father roared. 'She might make it out, but we have no idea what they would do to Jesse, who is, after all, a Burma national, and to little Lucy and the new baby. No, whatever we do, we all do together.'

Robert reminded us of the fact that Drema Esther's little daughter, Lucy, and his own son Stephen had come down with chicken-pox, and that his daughter Deedee had contracted mumps. 'Not very serious now,' he said, 'but what might happen with the kind of exposure they would suffer in the jungle?'

'And what about the women?' I asked. 'Mother is a wonderful traveller, but after all, she is almost seventy, and jungle travel would be pretty strenuous for her. In fact, it would be pretty rough for Helen and Betty, even though they are much younger. Betty's arthritis has been so bad, and Helen's back has been giving her a lot of trouble too. Then there's Drema Esther and her condition. With that sort of rough travel and who knows what kind of places to sleep – well, do you think they could get through all right? Or would it be asking too much of them?'

'Oh, I don't think you need worry about any of our women', Robert said. 'They're all the pioneer type, and they'll keep going even if it is pretty rugged. And besides, if it really becomes necessary to go that way, surely the Lord will give them the strength they need.'

'That's right', my father interjected. 'After all, remember, long before you were born your mother was facing hardships women aren't even supposed to know about. As you say, if it's necessary, they will be given the strength they need. And if there are difficult spots along the way, there would surely be a helping hand available from someone.'

'Well, whatever the case,' said Robert, 'I know two who are all in favour of the overland route. Joni and Steve are just dying to go on a long trip through the jungle.'

I knew what he meant. Joni and Steve were already wise beyond their years in the ways of the wild. As recreation, Robert had taken the boys camping and hunting in the jungle; they were good trackers and crack shots. They weren't big, but, like their Lisu friends, they were hard-muscled. Their idea of fun was to stop on the way home from school and, with the aid of the masks, spears, and fins they had recently ordered from the States, catch a few fish in the swift, clear Namhtum River. To them the prospect of a long trip through the jungle was like the thought of heaven.

'That's all right', I said. 'But what about the younger boys and the little girls? They're certainly going to slow us down. And if anything were to happen to his glasses, our David would be literally lost in the jungle.'

'Huh!' my father snorted. 'Sounds like we're a bunch of weaklings, the way you talk. Surely it isn't all that bad!'

'Dad, it sounds like you really want to go with the Lisu', I said.

'I don't know', he replied. 'I am worried about them. What if they don't get across the border? You know what will happen to them if they try to come back. If we don't go with them just because of our own weaknesses, we ought to be ashamed. Remember John, chapter ten, verses eleven to twelve: "The good shepherd lays down his life for the sheep. He who is a hireling and not a shepherd, whose own the sheep are not, sees the wolf coming and leaves the sheep and flees; and the wolf snatches them and scatters them." '

We were silent for a while after that, each busy with his own thoughts in the drowsy quiet of that Sunday afternoon. Then my father spoke again. 'But it's God's will we seek. We have applied to get on the aeroplane. If they take us, we'll go; we're meant to go. If not, it's got to be the jungle. I think we should pray for a sign.'

The first sign was not long in coming. We were told that Burmese and international airline regulations forbade carrying either women in such an advanced stage of pregnancy or any passengers suffering from contagious diseases. We therefore applied to the local Security and Administrative Council for a delay in our departure until Drema Esther's baby arrived and our children recovered. One prominent member of this SAC was a Marxist doctor whose arrogance towards my father had been honed to a fine edge by professional jealousy. Though my father was not a physician, he had studied practical medicine on home leave. One reason we had been able to persuade the Lisu and Rawang tribespeople to come down from the hills and settle in the semi-tropical, lush Putao valley was that we had been able to virtually wipe out malaria, the traditional scourge of the plains, with chloroquin and a British product called Gammexane which we used for spraying homes. Understandably, villagers often came to my father instead of to the doctor at the government civil hospital in Putao for medical advice.

As if this were not enough, we had recently experienced an incident that further antagonized the doctor. The son of one of our preachers had cut his foot while playing around a pigsty. A few days later he developed convulsions, and his head drew back rigidly so that his mouth was frozen in a tight grin. My wife, Helen, a trained nurse, immediately suspected tetanus. The boy was rushed to the hospital. They had no vaccine, and the doctor said there was no hope for him. Well, we managed to scrounge some outdated anti-tetanus medicine from the local military hospital, and the doctor administered it. I went to the telegraph office and sent a telegram to Rangoon for more. Before and during the administration of the medicine, we held a prayer service for the boy right there in the hospital. The doctor quoted one-in-a-thousand as the usual rate of cure for people so gravely afflicted with tetanus, but the boy recovered, and the doctor evidently felt we had somehow held him up to ridicule. Thereafter, he banned Christian prayers in the hospital. And now he used his considerable influence on the SAC to see that our request for a delay in departure was refused.

Indeed, the doctor took an almost sadistic pleasure in our plight. Having made it clear that the alternative to departure by 31 December was jail for all of us, he suggested, 'Bring the Tibetan girl round to the hospital and I'll take care of the whole thing by performing a Caesarean section.'

Drema Esther, who had worked for many years with my father as a medical assistant, knew there were no medical grounds for recommending such a procedure. She was, naturally, horrified. Moreover, both she and my father knew that the Putao hospital did not really have the proper facilities for such an operation, so we refused to agree to it. At this point we had no other recourse but to appeal to the central government in Rangoon through the American ambassador, Henry A. Byroade.

We set about the arduous and dismal chore of dismantling our homes and packing. It reminded us of previous years when, on a smaller scale, we had gone through our belongings and had them packed, ready to leave at a moment's notice if the threatened Chinese Communist invasion of North Burma materialized. We had even sent loads of supplies up into the mountains for safe keeping. Fortunately, during the past two years of strife, we had all sent quite a few mission supplies, such as books and hymnals and copies of some of Robert's records and papers that were lost in the fire, into the hills for safe keeping against a more peaceful day. We assumed that if we were ever forced to leave, the Burmese government would confiscate our compound and whatever they found in it. Now, uncertain as to how we would depart, we began assembling not only our personal effects but some of the things we might need for survival in the jungle.

The list of needs included: medicine; basic food supplies such as salt, sugar, dried milk, seasonings, and whatever canned foods we had on hand; clothing and, since it was the cold season, all the bedding we could manage to carry; camping items like a number of sixteen-by-twenty-four-foot heavy-gauge polyethylene plastic tarpaulins that could be used for makeshift tents; books, paper and printing supplies, small typewriters, transistor radio receivers (we had no transmitters, since privately owned equipment of this type was not allowed in Burma), a tape-recorder, and D-cell torch batteries. Indeed, we put together enough material to set up a temporary mission station if we were granted permission to stay in India.

Assembling these loads was not easy. One of the first problems was the fact that all loads had to be compact and light enough to be carried – the average burden would be sixty to sixty-five pounds for men and forty-five to fifty pounds for women. Moreover, aside from the sheer physical labour and the problem of selection, there was the emotional strain of meeting and trying to comfort the hundreds of Lisu and Rawang who crowded into our two-acre home compound daily, either to wish us goodbye or to urge us to come with them to India. We estimated that in all there were several thousand of these well-wishers. We could not work when they were around, not only out of courtesy, but because we had decided that any preparations for an overland departure towards India would have to be made in utmost secrecy, and the contents of our loads would have been a plain give-away.

There were several reasons for this secrecy. One was that we would obviously be violating the government edict to go 'by air or by sea', although not by choice. And we knew, of course, that many in the government felt that because we worked with hill people, we must be sympathetic with their insurgent relatives. So, if they knew we were intending to go into the mountains, they would assume we were planning to join or at least help the insurgents, and would simply arrest and imprison us to prevent our leaving.

We also had to think of those we were leaving behind, since many of the Lisu and most of the Rawang were staying in Putao. If the government learned that any of these people had prior knowledge of our plans and failed to divulge it, things would go hard with them. And, sad to say, even in a Christian community there were those few who might purposely betray us to advance their own plans. The Lisu and Rawang, ethnically related but culturally dissimilar tribes, had settled into a fairly amicable relationship under the Christian umbrella in Putao. But the Burmese had recently taken to playing cleverly on their differences by raising a Rawang to the high rank of head of state in Kachin state, with offices in Myitkyina, the state capital. This alienated the Lisu but tended to give the government some measure of grudging acceptance among the Rawang. To further complicate the already complex picture, there was the matter of ancient feuds between the Rawangs and other Kachins, with both sides trying to solicit sympathy and support from the Lisu, whose chief desire was to be left in peace to work their fields and carry on their usual way of life.

Time was clearly running out when, on 21 December, my son David drove into town on our tractor, taking with him the last of our flock of chickens to be sold in Putao. At the government office there he was given a telegram. The tractor was roaring wide open when David pulled into our compound. I knew at once something important had happened, otherwise a boy with David's respect for machinery would never have so abused the engine. I ran out and snatched the telegram from his hand. By then, Robert, whose family had moved into our compound to expedite preparations for leaving, was by my side.

I tore open the envelope and scanned the lines:

NO ACTION TO POSTPONE YOUR DEPARTURE DATE WILL BE TAKEN HERE STOP PRIME MINISTERS OFFICE REFERS YOUR REQUEST TO LOCAL AUTHORITIES STOP BYROADE

When I passed the message to Robert, he said quietly, 'Well, this means the jungle.'

I nodded. No more words were needed.

Chapter 2

And Moses said, 'We will go with our young
and our old; we will go with our sons
and daughters . . .'
EXODUS 10 : 9

Between Putao and the Indian border lie seventy miles of some of the most awesome topography on the face of the earth. Like a wooded sea, the mountain ridges rise in wave after wave, each cresting higher than the one before. In the valleys between them nest jungles so dense that the foliage obscures the sun at noon; and the peaks are often shrouded in cloud or frosted with snow. Winds sweeping up all the way from the Indian Ocean break against these ridges and swoop down into the valleys and up again in draughts that create extreme atmospheric turbulence. This region is the dreaded 'Hump' that so many American pilots had to cross in World War II. Their wheezing cargo planes could not climb over the thirteen-thousand-foot peaks of the ridge between India and Burma, so they had to seek out the gaps, few of them lower than nine thousand feet. Not surprisingly, some two thousand planes crashed against the mountain flanks during that desperate effort to supply China by air.

The area supports an amazing growth of dense rain forest. But, unfortunately, domesticated crops are less prolific. Rain and melting snow provide the head-waters for five of the great rivers of Asia, including the mighty Irrawaddy, which flows the length of Burma. In the tropical valleys, the lush growth supplies tons of fodder for wild elephants. The rivers abound in fish, and the trees give refuge to birds, monkeys and flying foxes. Tigers still stalk deer and other prey. Snakes, rodents, leeches and lizards thrive, and insects of all shapes and sizes abound

Though the area may be remote and seems to be hostile to man, it is a hospitable home to the most extravagant variety of flora and fauna imaginable.

This, then, was the jungle into which we planned to take our families. There were no roads leading westward towards India, not even a proper foot trail. The people who had gone that way followed, as all hill people do, narrow animal trails, hacking them wider with a machete if necessary, or even chopping their own short-cut through a thicket if it seemed to make sense. Rivers tumbled turbulently down the steep mountainsides and had to be waded, swum, or bridged. New trails then had to be discovered on the other bank. Worst of all, precipitous cliffs had to be scaled or crossed, and there were to be many narrow escapes.

Because the mountains run north and south, the whole way west would entail climbing one ridge – four thousand feet straight up from the Putao plain to begin with – then going down and up the next, still higher range. And all of this would have to be accomplished while carrying packs or basketloads of supplies. With a pregnant woman. With ageing parents. With children too small to walk. Furthermore, the area was virtually uninhabited, so we would not have a ready source of food supply. It wasn't a pleasant prospect.

Fortunately, events allowed us little time to dwell on what was ahead of us. Now that the telegram had arrived and all possibility of an extension was ruled out, we knew we had less than forty-eight hours in which to complete our preparations for departure. Still thinking we were going by plane, the Lisu and Rawang Christians had planned to help move our loads to the airport on Thursday, 23 December, and hold a great parting feast for us. We let them go ahead with these plans as a kind of cover but alerted some of the most trusted Lisu to the fact that we were going to depart for the mountains after dark on Wednesday. Many hundreds of Lisu had already moved up into the surrounding hills, the first stage in the migratory trek westward. Our Lisu confidants promised to send us porters and guides, and we went to work.

By mid-afternoon, Lisu whom we recognized as the promised porters began drifting in and mingling with the constant crowds of well-wishers. As darkness fell, these Lisu stayed on and more came out of the hills, stealing up from the river-bank a hundred yards away and through our back door. They began stuffing our loads into the huge baskets used by the tribespeople on jungle trails. Woven of strong bamboo or rattan and held on the carrier's back by a head strap and shoulder board, each basket was designed to hold a load of seventy or eighty pounds. During the next four hours, more than a hundred of these baskets disappeared silently across the lawn and down over the bank.

Because we were receiving so many visitors, the lights had been burning late in our houses for a week or more. As a result, the feverish activity that carried us through almost the entire night of 22 December went unnoticed. However, early in the evening something happened to make us think our plans might be doomed. Three Burmese officials, an immigration officer and two police officers, arrived to make an inventory of everything we planned to leave behind. Fortunately, they were friends of ours who could be convinced that we were too tired and busy that evening – which was indeed true – and we asked them to wait until the next morning. As they departed, they told us cheerfully, 'That's all right. We'll just spend the night at the military police post.'

This news left us feeling rather uncomfortable, for even though the post was located at the opposite end of the village, it was still only a half-mile away from our compound. Moreover, it stood at the village bridgehead, which made it impossible for us to leave by way of the bridge. Therefore we made arrangements to go downstream instead and cross the river by raft. We knew that any commotion surrounding our departure would be bound to alert the post's permanent garrison. With the additional official reinforcement, they could easily round us all up.

There were a few tense moments around ten o'clock, when one of our sons came in looking very disturbed and told us there were people moving about in the orchard. Robert and I slipped out into the yard, where we could get a view of the orchard. Our compound consisted of two cleared acres, with three houses and a garage, adjoining some ten acres of orchard on the north and east sides. As we stood there trying to assess the situation, we could see a number of torches moving erratically through the trees like giant fireflies. It was the last thing we wanted to see. The lights had to be in the hands of soldiers, since it was well after the nine-o'clock curfew the authorities had clamped on the citizens of Muladi. Watching the movements of the lights, we could tell that the soldiers were busy picking fruit, and we could only hope and pray that this diversion would draw their attention away from all the activity around our compound long enough for us to get away.

As midnight approached, we all assembled at our house, which was closest to the river. The small girls were placed on the backs of their carriers, Lisu-style, still drowsy, having just been awakened from a sound sleep.

'Let's go', I said. My father called for a short prayer and then we all started, single file, into the night. The last to leave was Robert, who had been busily penning a note to what we hoped would be the surprised authorities. Without revealing exactly where we were going, Robert reassured officials of our appreciation for the courtesies many of them had shown us. He informed them that we were leaving this way, not to join the insurgents, as some might suggest, but because we had no other alternative. He left the letter prominently displayed on the table in the dining room, where it couldn't be missed.

If we could make it out of the Putao plain, we were fairly certain of getting away. We estimated that we should pass through the KIA-held territory by the following night, and we felt reasonably sure that the Burmese army would not follow us except in a large force. There was a chance that the KIA would turn us back, since we had objected strongly in the past to some of their tactics in reprisal raids on the villages. But our Lisu friends assured us that we would be welcomed by any Kachins. We could only take their word for it and trust the Lord to keep us safe.

Fortunately, Wednesday, 22 December, was a moonless night. It was also the height of the dry season, and the river level had dropped to the point where we could walk along the rocky bank. We stumbled along the rough path down the jungle-covered hundred-foot embankment behind the house and were hidden from view. There was no moon, but once we reached the open area along the river the starlight was so bright we could see well enough to pick our way carefully and silently around the boulders and through the rubble of the river-bed. Venus, lying low in the south-west, was so brilliant that its light actually cast a reflection. I don't know about the others, but I thought that this burning planet was as welcome a sign as the biblical fire by night or the star in the East.

The staging-area where we were to meet the raft was about a quarter of a mile downstream from our house. We all negotiated the distance over the rocky beach without incident. Under the cover of darkness, the Lisu had hastily thrown together a couple of bamboo rafts to get us across the river. They were still busily ferrying our loads and porters when we arrived at the crossing. For a nervous hour or so we had to wait, and the young people, who were either unaware of our peril or too tired to care, took full advantage of the time. They sank down against the loads and fell sound asleep. We envied them, because none of us had had much rest for two hectic weeks. But tired as we were, we were determined to push on through what was left of this night and as much of the next day as might be necessary to put at least the first great ridge between us and any pursuers from Putao.

At last we crossed the river but there was still one more

crisis to face. On the opposite bank a string of houses stood right beside the road along which we must pass. Their black silhouettes showed plainly that the people, driven indoors by the curfew, had long since gone to sleep. But they kept dogs. As anyone who has ever visited an Oriental village well knows, just one barking dog can set off a chorus to awaken the dead. The village remained silent as the first of our party went by. Then suddenly, out of the corner of my eye, I saw a dark shape detach itself from the darker shadows by the houses. A dog, outlined eerily in the starshine, stood watching us. I held my breath. But there was not a bark, not so much as a whine. At that moment, I knew we were going to make it.

From the river, our guides led us on to what was aptly called a monkey trail. Travelling in the dark, except for the occasional cautious shining of a torch, we climbed almost vertically up the mountain on a path scarcely wide enough for one person. We had to move by first finding safe toeholds and then grabbing roots, vines, branches, or whatever came to hand to pull ourselves up. If we had had tails like monkeys, we could have used them. It was very hard going, even with many helping hands from our guides. One step up was often followed by a slide of several steps back if you got the wrong footing or couldn't find a handhold. Within minutes we were all sweating, even in the cool, forty-degree temperatures of that winter night.

We had no wish to surprise any KIA patrols in the dead of night and so maintained our rule of silence. I have no doubt, though, that our slippings and slidings and involuntary grunts and wheezes must have sounded like a freight train coming through. Meanwhile, the dense forest around us spoke back to us in the darkness. The night was full of the chirpings, cheepings, pipings, and chatterings of hosts of birds, monkeys, and other animals. We knew there were tigers, too, but counted on their being frightened by the movement of our large party and on the fact that they seldom attack a human being unless cornered. Still, it was unsettling to feel that unseen animal eyes were watching us.

What we really feared at night was being unable to see a snake. Around us, we knew, were cobras, kraits and various other deadly vipers. A bite from one of them could mean quick and painful death, and we had to be wary with each step and handhold. On the other hand, the dry winter weather cut down on insects, and especially on leeches, which, while seldom fatal, can drive a person nearly out of his mind.

Although I was accustomed to the rough travel and was not having difficulty myself, I was much concerned for my parents and the women, particularly Drema Esther. I knew Drema Esther would get help from her husband, Jesse Yangmi, a sturdy young man, even though he had their two-year-old, Lucy, strapped to his back. But my parents, in addition to being the oldest of our party, were already physically and emotionally exhausted even before we left our homes, so I wondered how they would stand up to this strenuous travel. I had seen my father fall once just after we started, but knew that he had strong helpers now to keep him from taking any further tumbles. At one rest stop my mother had been so extremely weary that she leaned against Helen and fell asleep immediately. Some of us were so sleepy we found ourselves dozing whenever we stood still to rest a few minutes. Still the column kept moving, and there were no reports of trouble or undue stress.

It was dawn before we covered the ten miles to the top of the first ridge, and even then we kept right on going down the other side. Descending was in some ways more difficult than climbing. A misstep could send you into a bruising slide or a dangerous crash off the trail. For us tenderfeet, just a few minutes of non-stop downhill travel left our knees trembling with weariness.

About 8.00 a.m. we stopped to rest, thinking that would be a good time to have breakfast. However, in all the confusion of our departure from Muladi, the basket con-

27

taining our food had been picked up by someone who had gone ahead faster than the rest of us could travel, so we had to move on without eating. As noon approached, we really began to feel hunger pangs. Some of us had not eaten since noon the day before. The children were actually crying with hunger. About 2.00 p.m. we came upon a small clearing where some Lisu travellers were cooking rice, which they shared with us. Plain rice had never tasted so good before!

About four o'clock we reached a high mountain meadow that local hill people had cleared for growing rice. This clearing was known to the Lisu as Elephant Corral Camp. In one corner it had a threshing floor of hard-packed earth, where we found several dozen Lisu families who had preceded us along the trail. Here at last we caught up with our lunch, which we had for our evening meal, along with rice and tea prepared over the camp-fire. As we ate, we exchanged greetings with many Lisu friends also camped there. Except for the primitive facilities, the social scene would be familiar to many Americans who have camped their way through national parks. Spreading our blankets on piled-up rice straw left over from the harvest a few weeks before, we went to sleep as soon as the sun set, with no need for a roof between ourselves and the stars.

All the physical and emotional strains we had experienced in preparing to leave Muladi, coupled with the strains of unaccustomed travel and loss of sleep, left us feeling exhausted. So it was decided that the next day, 24 December, should be a rest day. That evening all the people camped in the vicinity gathered together, and by the light and warmth of a big bonfire, we held a Christmas Eve prayer service. That service, held out in the open under the bright stars, retains a vivid place in our memories.

Beginning the next day, Saturday, 25 December, we started a kind of leap-frog progression that was to take us all the way to the Indian border. Drema Esther confided to Helen that the exertions of the first long climb had, indeed, brought on some symptoms of impending labour, but they had subsided. Because we were most concerned about keeping Drema Esther and her husband out of the hands of any possible pursuers, we sent them ahead to what our guides called Road Junction Camp – a crossing of two elephant trails – about halfway to the border. The rest of us planned to move in shorter stages, to see that our loads kept pace. Then my family would wait at Road Junction to help the Yangmis, while Robert's family and my parents went on to the border.

It took us about four days to catch up with the Yangmis, and in doing so, we passed what we all realized was the point of no return. It was a peak descriptively called Elephant Head Gouge Mountain. Unlike monkeys or Lisu or even Morses, great, lumbering elephants cannot climb straight up a mountain; their trails zigzag and circle. But the pitch was so steep on this hill, and the trail so narrow, that every time an elephant made a turn his tusks would scrape into the hillside, leaving great scars; hence the name.

Looking back from this point, we could see the whole plain of Putao spread at our feet. About ten miles wide and twenty miles long, surrounded on three sides by high, snow-capped mountain ranges rolling into the distance as far as the eye could see, this area, where we had spent fifteen happy years, looked strangely remote and miniature. For our children especially it was a very poignant moment. They had spent all their lives there, and it was the only home they knew.

My son, Ronnie, then thirteen years old, noted the moment in the diary he was keeping: 'Now, this is the last view I'll have of our former place, probably. And we could even see an airplane coming in, way in the distance; and we could see the different villages, and it was so flat and beautiful-looking back through the crack in the jungle. We could see the plain down below, and beyond, the border of Tibet and China, and fields and settlements below. Once we passed that mountain, it was just like going into another world.'

Joni, Robert's son, was older than Ronnie and a little more articulate about the experience. 'We really didn't want to leave', he commented later. 'We had a sadness. This was where we had grown up, our land that we had known all of our lives, and now we were probably leaving it for good. I remember asking myself, Why does this thing have to happen? Why do we have to be on the move? Why do we have to leave our home? Just a big question mark. It was only after we had crossed that mountain that we were looking forward to the big adventure. After we had crossed that mountain, it was onward, onward.'

At Road Junction Camp we found to our relief that Drema Esther had not yet had her baby. It was agreed that my parents and Robert's family would go on ahead to a place called Green Water Flat Camp. There they hoped to arrange with the Indian government about entering the country. Meanwhile, we settled down to wait, making good use of our plastic tarpaulins as tents. We threw some over a ridge-line rope tied between two trees, secured the sides with stakes, and covered the ends with more tarpaulins to keep out wind and rain. The plastic, although clear enough to see through, was heavy enough to withstand even hail, which turned out to be a good thing. We were now high enough in the mountains to experience the dramatic atmospheric turbulence that had made this area so dreaded by pilots during World War II.

The first thunderstorm that came upon us while we were lying under our clear plastic tent-roof was a truly fearful experience. The wind shook and snapped the tarpaulins and clawed at the straining stakes. The rain came pouring down in buckets, in sheets. The hail beat a sharp tattoo. And then there was the thunder, echoing back and forth between the high mountain peaks and rolling on and on and on. Through it all, lightning flashed or shot brilliant forked streaks right over our heads and down along the great jungle trees.

We lay there watching in awe and with profound

reverence for God's might. When at length the storm passed and left us dry, secure, and again within sight of the stars, we felt once more that his hand was truly leading us.

Chapter 3

All the congregation of the people of Israel
moved on from the wilderness of Sin
by stages, according to the commandment
of the Lord . . .
EXODUS 17 : 1

There have been Morses on the move for more than two
hundred years. The family records go back to the early
seventeenth century, when many of our ancestors were
doctors and ministers in and around Dedham, Massa-
chusetts. Their descendants made their way westward,
often as physicians or pastors, until my Morse grandfather
moved from South Dakota to Oklahoma, not long after the
territory was opened to homesteaders in 1906. My mother
also came from a pioneer family. In 1901, when she was
only five years old, her father, George O. Howe, a Baptist
preacher, took his family from Kansas to the Oklahoma
Territory, travelling through Indian country on the
way.

My mother and father continued moving westward in an
even more emphatic way. They had met while in college
and were married on 27 May 1920. In August 1921, when
I was only four months old, they left Oklahoma and
undertook the long and arduous journey to the Tibetan
frontier of China, as assistants to the renowned missionary
Dr Albert L. Shelton. Just three days before Christmas,
1921, they and Dr Shelton arrived in Batang, now called
Paan, high in the mountains of western China.

Only six weeks after their arrival, Dr Shelton was
murdered by brigands. This tragedy left my parents with
a deep sense of loss and a great loneliness, despite the
presence of other missionaries. Ordered by the Mission
Board to avoid danger by staying within the mission-base
town of Batang, my parents spent two years in language

study. After that it was considered safe for them to work throughout the small surrounding valley. My father travelled about, preaching and teaching to all who would listen, including travellers from inner Tibet. An invitation from one of these travellers resulted in our family's being allowed to make a trip to Gartok to spend a month as the guests of a wealthy Tibetan nobleman. But the Mission Board refused permission for my parents to establish a new mission base outside the valley. As a result, my parents resigned from the Mission Board after their five-year term and became independent missionaries, supported by individual congregations of the Church of Christ (Christian Church) in the United States.

My parents were still at their first post on the China-Tibet border when Robert was born in 1923. We and our younger brother, LaVerne, born in 1929 and now a professor at Cincinnati Bible Seminary, were educated largely by my mother, a Phi Beta Kappa graduate of Oklahoma University. We also took correspondence courses and later attended college in China and the United States, where Robert took a master's degree in linguistics at Indiana University.

In 1927, after only a few months in our new location in the area where China, Tibet and Burma meet, civil war broke out in China, and the American consulate in Kunming ordered all United States nationals to leave the country. Because of the war, all normal exit routes were cut off, and we had to flee through trackless jungles, over high mountain ranges, and across deep gorges of the Hump region of the Himalayas into Burma. Together with two families from another mission, our family walked seventy days before we reached Myitkyina, a railhead in northern Burma.

Two years later we were able to return to our mission work. From 1929 through the Sino-Japanese War, we were able to continue to work among the Lisu and Rawang tribal groups on both sides of the China-Burma border. During World War II, Japanese forces took all of Burma except the extreme northern tip, which was where we were working.

In 1943 my two brothers and I went from the Salween valley across northern Burma in order to visit and teach in some of our congregations there. We had no idea that the Japanese were as far north as they were. While we were on the eastern border of Burma, we received a letter from the commanding officer of the British garrison at Fort Hertz asking us to come there. When we arrived, he talked with us only a short time before deciding to send us on to the Allied headquarters in Assam. There we were interviewed at length and finally asked to formulate a plan for rescuing airmen whose planes had crashed while crossing the Hump. After our plan was accepted, we distributed circulars in the native languages explaining to the tribespeople who the fliers were and what they were trying to do. We also gave them messages written in English to hand to any survivors of the wrecks, assuring them of the friendliness of all the tribes and offering their help in getting the airmen back to their bases.

Through these efforts, dozens of survivors of the many wrecks inevitable in flying this hazardous route were able to get home alive. One group of four came to our mission and stayed with the family for fifty-four days while the Salween valley was snowbound. During the peak period of the airlift to Chungking, as many as eighty planes would cross the Hump within sight of our mission house in the course of a single day and night. However, since many planes that crashed on those steep, jagged peaks and jungle-covered slopes contained no survivors, much of our work consisted of identifying the bodies and providing Christian burial. Assurance of this service, and the prospect of help from the tribespeople if they were lucky enough to live through a crash, served to raise the morale of thousands of fliers. When the war ended, we received treasured letters from Air Force generals H. H. Arnold and George E. Stratemeyer thanking us for our efforts.

Long before the war was over, Robert and I decided to

follow in our parents' footsteps in the missionary calling. During a brief furlough in the mid-forties we both married American girls and, in January 1949, took them with us to China. It was a happy and hopeful period, but it was not to last.

The bitter struggle between Chinese Communist armies under Mao Tse-tung and Nationalist forces under Chiang Kai-shek soon reached our district. We stayed on even after the Communists took power, much as we did later in Putao, in the hopes of helping our people. It was of little use. We were witness to the cold-blooded killing of some three thousand 'traitors to the people' after summary sentences handed down by the so-called People's Courts. And, as the anti-foreign sentiments intensified, we knew our own time might come.

So in October–November 1949, the mission base was shifted across the border into Burma. In the spring of that year, Robert and his wife had gone from Kunming to our northern Salween valley mission station. In mid-September, they, together with several missionary co-workers, fled from that Communist-held area of Yunnan on foot, and made the two-week journey across the high mountains which formed the China-Burma border. Several thousand Lisu Christians also fled about that same time, leaving everything and taking refuge in Burma. My family – only Helen, David and myself at that time – had tried to reach the Salween station but were forced to return to Kunming after being stopped and undergoing about six weeks of house-arrest and harassment by the Communists in Likiang. So we and Drema Esther took the more circuitous route – from Kunming to Hong Kong, Rangoon, Myitkyina and Putao. My mother also accompanied us to Burma, having arrived in Hong Kong on what proved to be the last plane out of Kunming before the Communist take-over.

My father, delayed because of mission business, was to fly to Hong Kong by the next plane, on the following day, but there wasn't any next plane. Remaining in Kunming, he was allowed to continue his missionary work for fifteen months, while all around him he witnessed unbelievable atrocities and killings and watched the destruction of an entire society. Then, in March 1951, he was put into prison, where for another fifteen months he was kept in solitary confinement and subjected to the many tortures for which Chinese prisons have been notorious. In June 1952 he was finally released and deported to Hong Kong. Much later we learned that during the week preceding his release there had been a 'week of prayer' – someone praying for him twenty-four hours a day – in his supporting church in California, and this had ended the very day of his release. To this day, my father has preferred not to discuss the details of his ordeal because it was such a nightmare.

When my father arrived in Hong Kong, he found that my mother and brother LaVerne had arrived there from Burma seeking news of him, for they had no idea of where he was or even if he was still alive. They were in Hong Kong while en route to the United States, and the remarkable timing of this surprise reunion seemed to all of us a special evidence of God's love and mercy and answered prayer.

After this most welcome reunion my parents rejoined Robert's growing family and mine in the Putao valley of northern Burma. I need not dwell on the accomplishments of all the Morses in those work-filled but happy years, other than to say that they were, and remain, a source of great satisfaction to us. Some years later a distinguished Burmese attorney spoke to us about what we and our flock accomplished in our fifteen years in Putao. His words seem to me a brief but eloquent summary and tribute. 'I have never had the pleasure of visiting the region,' said the attorney, 'but I understand that it is green with rice-fields and blooming with fruit trees. A kind of paradise, some say.' But now we had put this paradise behind us, and once again the Morses were on the move.

Our Tibetan foster-sister – her name is taken from the Tibetan goddess Gazen-Drema – had been with us through all these ordeals. Her parents, who worked for mine when we first went to Tibet, were still in our employ when they died. At that point Drema Esther and her older sister were adopted by my parents. The older sister, who had come into Burma with Robert's party, died of typhus in Putao in December 1949. Drema Esther had accompanied my mother and my family to Hong Kong and then to Burma. We were all delighted when she married Jesse in Putao and started a family of her own.

I suppose there are people who cannot understand why we risked taking Drema Esther into the jungle so close to her time. We were putting two lives in jeopardy, and even if the birth went well, the chances for an infant's survival under such difficult conditions might seem slim. The truth is that we could not have gone ahead if all of us had not been sustained by faith. It may sound odd in this day and age, when the Bible is more often displayed than read, but we truly felt there was a good omen in the coming together of the Christmas season, Drema Esther's pregnancy, and our flight.

Fortunately, my foster-sister not only shared our faith but had, ever since she was a small girl, shared the uncertain life that had given us Morses solid grounds for that faith. We all, including Drema Esther herself, accepted her predicament as part of the kind of life to which we had grown accustomed in our work. When we finally arrived at Road Junction Camp, we found her and Jesse and little Lucy comfortably bedded down in their own tent, calmly awaiting events. It hadn't been a Christmas baby after all. We set up our own camp and prepared to wait with them.

As the days went by, we began to have the first inkling of the migration that was taking place. The road on which the well-named Road Junction Camp was located was originally nothing but a rarely used, barely traceable hunting path. Now it had become a jungle superhighway to India. Lisu, travelling in family groups, were filing by in a constant stream. There weren't just a few hundred of them, as we had at first thought, but thousands. They were creating a traffic jam which, for this part of the world, was equivalent to the Los Angeles freeway in the rush hour. Their feet were turning the trail into something like a narrow road, and their overnight camps were proliferating all along the way.

As is their custom when on the move, the Lisu kept going until they got hungry or tired and then simply made their camp at any likely spot along the trail. With their machete-like knives they chopped a small clearing; then they threw the vegetation aside, tied a few likely saplings into a frame for a lean-to, covered it with banana leaves or a plastic sheet, and lo! they had their shelter for the night. Every camp needed a fire for cooking and to keep off stray animals by night, so they made a fireplace of three stones and erected a green-sapling tripod over the fire on which to place the kettles for boiling water for tea and rice. Because wind or rain sometimes played havoc with the lean-to, and the green-sapling tripod turned to ash during the night, it was easier for each family to build a new camp-site than to try to occupy an old one. As a result, the trail to India was soon marked in every convenient place by these tiny clearings.

As far as we could tell from talking to the passing people, this migration was totally unorganized. Nobody, least of all the Morses, had arranged it. Each family group had decided more or less on its own to leave Putao. For most of them it must have been an agonizing decision. Moving out meant leaving homes and fields and often a number of cattle, which in their economy made them relatively rich. Many carried their chickens and what they could in the way of food and bedding, and some drove their pigs. And that was about all their possessions. In a way, it was touching to see that so many people valued their Christian faith and their freedom above material things, but it was alarming, too, in view of the uncertain future.

If we were somewhat surprised at what was happening, the KIA were even more so. It was one thing to let the Morse family and a few faithful porters and guides go through their territory. But what looked like the movement of a whole people was another matter. The KIA were more than happy to have so many of their cousins, Christian or otherwise, earning good livings in the fruitful Putao valley. Undoubtedly they were getting some direct support, and they were probably counting on the settled community in the valley to provide a stable nucleus if and when they ever achieved their aim of establishing an independent state.

Small, uniformed patrols of twenty or so KIA began interrupting the march to try to influence the travellers. Road Junction Camp, with its multitudes of camp-sites, was a favourite spot for them to try to persuade as many people as possible to settle in territory over which they held control, or else to go back to Putao. They obviously did not want so many Lisu travelling further west, away from their influence. There was one young KIA officer who was particularly militant.

'You cannot go beyond here', he would tell whatever Lisu he found encamped near us.

'But we're just escorting our missionary friends to the Indian border', they would reply.

'And then what?' he would ask. 'Your missionary friends will go across the border and home to America and leave you in the jungle. God is not going to drop you manna from heaven like he did for the Israelites. So you had better turn back.'

The Lisu would shrug and then just melt away into the jungle in the night. For the moment we were all carrying enough food, and there was an established Lisu community across the border in India that all of them were looking forward to meeting. Game in the jungle was so plentiful that even the poorest hunter could get a rat or monkey or bird, as needed, to augment his family's diet. So the march kept on, and the small bands of KIA, helpless against such numbers, merely fumed. The Lisu are a very independent people anyway, and because this vast migration was unorganized and spontaneous, there was no head or leader whom the KIA or anyone else could hold responsible.

On 6 January the waiting for Drema's baby came to an

end. About four o'clock that afternoon, Jesse came hurrying from his tent, about a hundred feet from ours, and told Helen that Drema Esther's pains had started. While Helen went to examine her, Jesse constructed an impromptu delivery room beside a nearby bamboo clump, stretching blankets around some saplings to give a semblance of privacy. Fortunately, it wasn't raining. Helen and Drema Esther disappeared behind the blankets, and three-quarters of an hour later, Helen appeared with the new arrival – later to be named Michael Timothy – warmly wrapped but loudly proclaiming his displeasure over the new environment in which he found himself.

It was an occasion for prayer and rejoicing, and in the next ten days, while we waited for Drema Esther to regain her strength, the baby became the centre of attention, both within the family and to outsiders. All the passing Lisu would come to the Yangmi tent to congratulate the parents, and many brought presents for both the baby and his mother. Other gifts were in short supply, so they would offer small delicacies from their food supplies, such as eggs, vegetables or a chicken. Most welcome was a fat grey hen given by a friend who intended it as the main ingredient of a rich soup for the baby's mother. Instead, with her characteristic foresight, Drema Esther decided to keep the lucky fowl alive. Soon it began to lay eggs, and for the next five months it provided one every day to enrich the Yangmi diet.

As soon as Drema Esther was able to travel, the Yangmis decided to move slowly on to join the main party at Green Water Flat Camp. Drema carried the new-born Mickey on her back, Lisu-style, using a long piece of cloth wrapped around and over the baby and then tied in front. Jesse carried Lucy on his back and assisted Drema. Their loads were carried by Lisu friends and relatives. We hated to see them go on, but we had to stay and bring up the rear.

We were eager to get on the trail again and learn at first hand how Robert's family and my parents were faring at the border. Rumours of delay and uncertainty in discussions with the Indians had filtered back, but we were not too concerned. We felt that Robert, with his gift for languages and diplomacy, must surely have worked out something with them by now. On 24 January we left Road Junction Camp and headed west, fully confident that we would be settling down in India long before the rains came at the end of May.

Chapter 4

But the Lord hardened Pharaoh's heart, and
he did not let the children of Israel go.
EXODUS 10 : 20

Before we left Road Junction Camp, we asked about the
road ahead and learned that, because of the many people
passing that way, the trail was well defined. It was now a
fairly easy three-day walk to the encampment at the foot
of the pass to the Indian border. But we were anxious to
catch up with the rest and decided to try to make the trip
in just two days.

The first part of the journey was uneventful and not too
difficult. But the final descent into the valley was by way of
an almost perpendicular trail, which did strange things to
our knees after about an hour or so of travel. As we
descended into the valley and began to draw near to the
encampment, we could hear dogs barking, even though we
could not see anything because of the dense jungle foliage.
However, when we came out of the jungle to a place where
the valley was visible, we just stopped and looked in
astonishment. We knew there had to be a big, flat valley
floor, because of the descriptions we had heard. But none
of the things we had been told really prepared us for the
sight before us. Green Water Flat, as the Lisu called the
place, was at the head-waters of the Kamko River, a
tributary of the Irrawaddy. The stream flowed deep and
clear around the edge of a spacious flood plain which was
almost like an Alpine meadow, at an altitude of about
fifty-five hundred feet. On all sides, towering, jagged
eleven-thousand-foot snow peaks raised their glistening
white heads above the beautifully green jungle-clad slopes,
which dropped suddenly to form a steep embankment on

the south side of the river. As we stood taking it all in, we could again hear the barking of the dogs, mingled with the voices of people calling to one another and the crying of babies. The huge encampment spread out along a stretch of flat, sandy beach on the north side of the stream. For almost two miles upstream the landscape was dotted with lean-tos and bamboo shelters, some roofed with leaves and others with cloth or transparent plastic. The pungent aroma of wood smoke from what must have been more than a thousand camp-fires drifted up to us on the evening breeze.

Word of our coming had gone ahead, and the rest of the family came out to meet us. Tribal leaders were there, too. Some of our boys had arrived ahead of us and, with the help of many willing hands, had already prepared a sapling framework and covered it with our plastic tarpaulins, and had erected a crude shelter where we could cook. Weary as we were, we were glad to be able to walk right in and settle down. It was only when we sat down and relaxed a little that we began to realize fully the effects of the long downhill climb. Once down, it was difficult to get up, and once up, it was even more difficult to walk. But, fortunately, our aches were relieved by liberal application of tincture of iodine, followed by a good night's rest.

During supper we learned from Robert that our situation was uncertain, at best. He had been dealing with a Sikh immigration officer whom the Lisu called Moo-Bee, or Blackbeard, and Robert was at a loss to know what the man thought or intended to do.

'You know those fellows', Robert said. 'They have a shake of the head – it isn't a yes or a no the way we do it – but a kind of wagging that doesn't say anything. Well, every time we ask Moo-Bee whether we're going to get into India, he just wags. I finally gave him a letter to the governor of Assam, but I can't even tell whether he has delivered it. I just get a wag. He's due here again tomorrow; maybe you can understand him.'

We were just finishing our own camp-site when Moo-Bee

arrived. His entrance was an event, and Lisu gathered from all over the area to witness it. Hours before he put in an appearance, an advance guard of bearers, cooks and coolies arrived to erect a tent with a table and bench for his dining and a raised wooden dais on which they placed an enormous bed, complete with mosquito netting. Because we were some twenty miles from his outpost on the other side of the border, Moo-Bee, as usual, planned to spend the night with us. Fortunately for the dramatic effect of his visits, his person more than lived up to the advance preparations. He wore a splendid uniform and an elaborate jewelled turban, sometimes white, sometimes pink or blue, but never the same colour twice running. The turban, of course, was to cover his long hair – Sikhs never cut their hair or shave – which was bound up into a knot. His luxuriant black beard, curled and doubtless delicately scented, was gathered up under a sort of hair-net or snood that hung from his ears.

Everyone was hopeful that this time Moo-Bee would have an answer to our questions.

'Did the governor get my letter?' Robert asked.

Moo-Bee wagged his head. 'And what is his answer?' Robert pursued.

Moo-Bee smiled and wagged again. With an almost visible effort to keep his temper under control, Robert said, 'In other words, you still have nothing to tell us. You must realize we have to do something soon. Even if you do let us into India we'll need a month to clear the land and plant before the April rains start.'

Moo-Bee smiled again, then in a deceptively gentle voice said, 'I would suggest that you go down and try the Ledo Road. That's the *normal* way to enter India.'

'And how do you propose that we get there?'

Moo-Bee unfolded a map and pointed to it. 'You could cross over these first two mountain ranges from here, then travel along the Tarung River valley clear down to the Ledo Road, and go right on into India. It shouldn't take more than three weeks.'

'What!' Robert exploded. 'You expect us to make that trip with our party? You still don't seem to understand the problem. In the first place, all of us could never travel so far. After all, we have little children and old people, and they could never get through that wild jungle where there aren't even any trails. Secondly, that's uninhabited country where we couldn't get any food, and we certainly don't have enough here with us to go so far. Besides, all our Lisu friends are running low on food too. They need to find a place where they can get jungle food while they settle down and start getting their fields cleared so they can have food for next year.'

Moo-Bee wagged his beard in what might have been a gesture of sympathy, then said, 'That *is* still the proper way to enter India, you know.'

'The proper way', Robert repeated. 'A three-week journey through jungles with no trails, with women, children and old people. Not enough food with us, and no place along the way to get more. And to top it all, the path would go right through Naga territory, head-hunter country. Proper way, indeed! No, thanks! There *must* be some other way.'

Moo-Bee laughed a little, then indicated it was time for him to retire. The next day, after further fruitless discussion, he took his leave, but promised to come back another day with more definite word, perhaps even from the governor himself. He kept his word and returned later but once again had nothing to report.

Though we wanted very much to get into India, it would have come as a relief even if Moo-Bee had given us a flat refusal. At least that would have been an answer. By mid-February we realized that something had to be done or all of us might starve. Nearly a thousand Lisu had already camped in Green Water Flat when Robert first got there. By the time the last of the Lisu arrived from the plains, shortly after our own arrival, nearly five thousand people were camped along the river. The food we had all brought with us, enough to last for a journey of a few weeks, was soon exhausted. Daily, nearly every able-bodied man and boy, including the third-generation Morses, went into the jungle searching for edible plants and game. With so many people feeding on them like locusts, the hills around Green Water Flat were soon stripped of food. Hunting parties had to go further and further afield, for days at a time.

The one thing of which there was an ample supply was firewood. All around us were logs that had been swept downstream when the river was at flood stage, then deposited along the banks as the water receded. We had to learn the hard way which kinds of wood to get, because some gave off a hot, bright flame, while others produced little but smoke. All of us began to realize just how much skill is really required to live and travel as the Lisu do.

A food shortage was not the only problem created by the gathering of such a large number of people in so small an area. Sanitary facilities were lacking, but because the people were accustomed to having their own latrines back in the plains, they could readily appreciate the need for strict community cleanliness. It wouldn't do just to find a convenient log and relieve oneself behind it, because there would be many other people travelling the trail, and it had to be kept clean. In Green Water Flat there were other rules, too: don't wash clothes in the stream, to avoid polluting the drinking water; don't merely wound animals and let them escape to die uselessly; don't kill more than you can eat at one time; don't destroy bamboo, trees or leaves, as all are needed for building shelters; don't waste firewood. Right from the first we urged strict rules and reminded people that in Old Testament times God instructed Moses to enforce strict rules of hygiene among the Israelites in their wilderness travels.

But, in spite of rules and attempts to be careful, sickness did come to the camp. There had been isolated instances of sickness along the trail, but at Green Water Flat we were faced with an epidemic of an extremely virulent type of dysentery. It struck all ages – old people, babies, strong young men – with ruthless impartiality. One of the young men travelling with our party, later to become one of our schoolteachers, almost died. A young mother did die. And another woman, who was pregnant, had such a severe case of dysentery that it brought on early labour. Betty and Helen nursed her through a situation that is very difficult to deal with. A delivery where the mother has any type of dysentery almost invariably results in an infection of the birth canal, which sometimes proves fatal. In this case, with good nursing care and the aid of what drugs we had, this young mother lived, but the baby, being premature, died.

This incident marked the beginning of one of the most difficult, and dramatic, of our experiences on the trail – the birth, in one afternoon and evening, of three children. Traditionally, the Lisu man absented himself at the time of childbirth. But this pattern changed in the jungle, where often the husband was the only person available to help the mother. Shortly after the premature child died, there came two other calls so close together that we scarcely knew how to handle them. Helen and Betty were both exhausted by the time the first of these calls came. But Betty went to the woman's shelter, about half a mile upstream, and determined that it would still be a few hours before the child arrived. 'It looks as if the baby won't be born before evening. I'll come back later by lantern light', Betty told the anxious mother, and then returned to our camp. Not much later, while we were eating, the second call came: 'Please come help me, it's desperate. I'm all alone.' Helen was with the woman who had lost her baby, and Betty was too tired to handle things alone, so Robert went with her. As Robert described it:

'I had a torch and Betty had a lantern. She went one way, and I went the other, to check on these two calls. I found the first woman further along than Betty had anticipated. I was reticent about being the main figure to help at a delivery, so went after Betty. She had delivered the other woman's baby and had just finished wrapping it

47

in an old blouse of the mother's. As we rushed back to where the expectant mother was lying by a camp-fire in the open, I stepped into a sort of quicksand bed and lost my shoe. There wasn't time to go back for it, so I rushed along after Betty, with one shoe off and one shoe on. The child was born just as we arrived. We were barely in time to take care of the baby and minister to the mother. We had not really finished, when someone came rushing breathlessly to tell us that a third baby was about to be born. "You go," I said to Betty, "and I'll finish up here." Betty was so tired she scarcely felt she could keep going, but I managed to join her, and together we took care of the third case that evening. All evening we had been running back and forth, a team, though not always side by side, hurrying through a boulder-strewn bed, sand pits, and quicksand – and with one shoe missing part of the time.'

This is a good illustration of the unexpected emergencies that can develop. Two of the babies born that night were first children, so the mothers needed reassurance and ministry to their spiritual as well as their physical needs. So many things can go wrong. If, as in the case of one of these women, there is undue delay in the separation of the afterbirth, the mother may become panicky because she knows that incomplete separation can bring on complications and even death. Our supply of drugs was very limited in these cases, and we depended mainly on prayer, asking God to guide us in deciding the care or treatment to use.

A welcome diversion that relieved the tensions of the constant struggle for survival showed up in the form of a daring flying fox. At 6.10 every evening, give or take not more than a minute or two, he would soar out from the slope above our encampment, plane down the steep incline about twenty feet above the treetops, swoop over our heads, and land in a tree across the river several hundred feet away. The fox's flight was great entertainment for the children, who would run screaming after him, and invariably some adult would seize his rifle or crossbow and try to bring him down. Surprisingly, no shot found the mark, and the fox became a sort of jungle clock that signalled the time, just after dinner, when the Lisu elders would often get together for a conference.

It was soon after the flying fox's sunset show one evening in mid-February that some forty or fifty tribal leaders began to gather for a conclave to decide what, in the absence of any definite word from Moo-Bee, we should do next. These men gathered in a leisurely way around a row of five or six flickering camp-fires a few yards back from the river-bank. Balanced somewhat precariously on the three-stone makeshift tripods, cauldrons of green tea were simmering. Youths old enough to take an interest in the proceedings took on the job of pouring the scalding hot brew into the bamboo tubes used as teacups and passing them out to their elders. The older men sat cross-legged on the ground or squatted in a wide circle around the fires, some in the shadows, some where the light of the flames intermittently lit up a head or a profile.

On this evening, as I recall it, a man named Sukin, well known as a former musk-deer hunter and prosperous merchant in the Putao area, opened the meeting, raising his voice loud enough to be heard by the whole group.

'Well, here we all are', Sukin began. 'We are running low on food, as you all know, and we still can't find out whether or not the Indians are going to let us cross the border. What we have to decide soon – this evening, if we can – is what to do next; whether to go back or stay here or go somewhere else. If we don't go back, we will have to find a better place than this particular area. Game is running short in the jungle around here already, as are the sago and other jungle foods. This altitude is too high for planting. So what shall we do? Who has any ideas?'

Several voices were raised in answer, but the one that carried most firmly came from somewhere in the shadows, and I could not make out whose it was.

'One thing is for sure. We don't want to go back to Putao. We've had enough of the fighting and other troubles there. Life in the jungle may be hard, but at least we're free to do what we can about it. No one here can pen us up in a refugee camp or make us work on Sunday so we can't go to church. And we know how to live in this kind of jungle – if we can just find a good valley with enough jungle food and game, and good land for rice fields.'

A murmur of assent greeted this speech, and another leader, whom I knew well – Wafoo by name – spoke up from beside the fire near me.

'The next valley to this on the west, the one we call Empty Valley, might be a good spot to try. There is a big salt-lick over there – that much I already know – and so there is sure to be plenty of game, especially deer. I don't know much about how the land will be for farming, but it doesn't look too bad – though of course landslides during the big earthquake in 1950 ruined most of the flood plains along the river.'

As leader of one of the first groups to reach the area – and one that had tried to cross into India but had been turned back before our arrival – Wafoo had more knowledge of the vicinity than most of the rest of us. Also, as one of the earliest arrivals, he and his group would have a priority claim in choosing where to settle. His views, therefore, received serious attention. A buzz of comment followed his contribution before another man spoke up:

'There's nothing very promising in this Kamko valley or south of us here. I know that country well from a hunting trip I made some years ago. The jungle down that way is so thick you have to cut your way, step by step.'

A moment's silence and then a new speaker:

'How about that valley two ridges further to the west – the one they call Hidden Valley? That runs along right next to the border-line ridge, so if we ever do get permission to cross into India, we won't have far to go. Khisu says the Tarung River there has plenty of fish, and there's lots of farmland once we cut and burn off the jungle. Khisu is hunting over there now because he thought there ought to be plenty of game, too.'

So that's where Khisu had gone! Remembering his

efforts to enlist us back in Muladi, I had wondered where he was. It was interesting to hear the respectful way in which his views were now cited by men who had scorned this hunter in civilization.

'Doesn't he know that valley is under a curse?' asked one voice from the shadows. 'Why, one time a few years back, a whole party of fifty hunters went over there all the way from Putao because they had heard there was plenty of game. Only two of them ever came back alive.'

'We Christians don't need to fear those curses now as we did before', Sukin reminded the group.

'Well, the Naga head-hunters consider the whole valley their territory', the former speaker went on. 'That probably explains what happened to the hunting party, curse or no curse. The only two that survived were captured by the Nagas too, but they finally managed to escape.'

This was followed by a somewhat grisly discussion of the various tortures and ceremonies favoured by the renowned Naga tribespeople, reputed to be cannibals as well as head-hunters.

'There are no Nagas there any more', someone volunteered. 'They never did really live there. They just claimed the area. Now they have all settled far to the south-west – and they have pretty much given up head-hunting, I've been told. The Hidden Valley has been unsettled for years and years. It could be ours for the taking.'

'Yes, that's true', another seasoned frontiersman agreed. 'But we should remember', he went on, 'that some say the reason no one has dared live in that valley is that it's sort of a buffer zone between the Nagas and other tribes to the north and east, all of whom lay claim to it. I'm willing to give it a try, but once there we'd have to keep a sharp eye out for Nagas and others who might resent our presence.'

'But even if there were no disputes with anyone about our living in the area,' someone else queried, 'how would we ever get there? The highest ridges we crossed coming here from Putao were only about seven thousand feet high, and we had enough trouble getting over those.

Between here and Hidden Valley there are only two ridges, but both of them are over eleven thousand feet high. And both still have snow near the top! Maybe hunters can get across, but not us with our heavy loads and our families to think about.'

'Oh, we could make it all right,' another speaker countered, 'if we had to. There are lower passes only about nine thousand feet high where we could cross over.'

'Yes, and there must be elephant trails that cross both ridges. If we can find elephant trails to follow, it shouldn't be too hard.'

While the boys kept refilling the teacups, the talk went on like this for the better part of five hours. The view that gradually emerged was that, while some thought the so-called Empty Valley, just across the next ridge to the west, was the likeliest refuge because of its proximity and the abundance of game, a majority favoured the Hidden Valley, if we could gain access to it. From reports of scouts who had seen it, there were better possibilities there for permanent settlement. An additional advantage was that it ran east and west along the tongue of Indian territory in which the Lisu settlement had been established ten years before. Some members of our group had already made contact with these original settlers, crossing the unpatrolled border line. They felt that being near this large Lisu village might prove to be a valuable asset in case of some future emergency.

As the meeting continued, many other matters came up for discussion. An urgent one was the question of what to do about the many orphaned children and widows among us. When I myself asked why they had been allowed to come with us to begin with, I was promptly and properly put in my place by an elderly tribesman, who mildly replied:

'They wanted to come – and, as Christians, we could not leave them behind. They were the most anxious of all to escape from the terror in Putao, because most of them are children whose parents, or women whose husbands, were killed in the fighting between the KIA and the Burmese. Surely it was our duty to bring them, just as it is our duty now to find families who are willing to care for them when we get ready to settle down.'

I had no answer to that, and soon others spoke up in a similar vein. Families who were now caring for these helpless ones, it developed, could continue to do so until others became able to share the burden.

Most such gatherings broke up around nine or ten o'clock, but on this occasion it was well past eleven before some of the leaders began to move away from the fires in groups of two or three. By midnight only a dozen or so were left, still squatting down around the dying embers. Most of the major items on the agenda had been more or less satisfactorily settled. As to where to move from Green Water Flat, no true consensus was really necessary or desirable. It would clearly be better for us all if we were split into two parties. This would mean more game and more jungle food for both; and if either were to meet with especially adverse or especially favourable conditions, the good fortune could be shared or the hardships relieved. The upshot of the whole session was that some fifty families, led by Wafoo, would settle in the Empty Valley (Mugo) near the salt deposits. The remaining four thousand or so of us would try to cross both high ridges and reach the area of Hidden Valley called Binuzu – a name that in Kachin means something like 'river junction' or 'confluence'. We all agreed that the move would start as soon as the first few families were ready to go.

The morning after the conclave, the Morse families were confronted once more with a difficult decision. We had come to the border from Putao confidently expecting to be able, after a brief period of negotiation, to cross over with a few hundred Lisu brethren. As things developed, however, we now found ourselves not only stalled on the Burmese side of the line, but the responsible leaders of a much larger migration.

Our total of some five thousand migrants amounted to

53

about a quarter of the whole population of the Putao area. The departure of so many people could scarcely pass unnoticed by the authorities there or go unreported by the SAC to their superiors in Rangoon. As the spiritual leaders of the Lisu community, we would be suspected of having planned the entire exodus in advance, perhaps as part of a mass defection to the independence forces in the jungle.

Ironically, all the time we were in Green Water Flat, we were conducting almost daily negotiations, mostly through Robert, with KIA leaders. They were still understandably reluctant to see so many prospective supporters leave that part of the country. Though they knew they couldn't stop the Lisu by force, they attempted to persuade them to go back to Putao and tried to get us to join them in this effort. Here, they were more subtle than the militant young officer had been at Road Junction Camp. Instead of a military man, they sent a tactful young political officer, a tall, light-skinned college graduate who spoke English well. When he argued that his movement needed the support of prosperous farmers in the Putao valley, we countered with stories of the raids and reprisal killings by insurgent bands that had contributed to sending the Lisu on their way to India. He claimed to have known nothing of these killings and seemed so genuinely shocked by our accounts that we believed him. We heard later that one result of the great exodus was an easing off of the civil war in Putao.

The young political officer seemed happier when people began talking about settling in Binuzu and other parts of Hidden Valley, instead of attempting to cross over into India. It would, in effect, mean a possible extension of his territory. But we knew it would be viewed differently by the Burmese government. If we made no further effort to leave the country, we could be accused of wilful and premeditated violation of the expulsion order. On the one hand, there was no reason to hope that we could solve our problems by a return to Putao; but on the other hand, there was still no indication from Moo-Bee that we would be allowed to enter India on any terms, even without our

Lisu brethren and as mere transit travellers *en route* first to Calcutta and then back to the United States.

After much prayer, meditation and family discussion, we decided that it was too late for us to hope to get out of Burma by any other route until the next dry season, six months later. Meanwhile, our only practical course would be to settle in Hidden Valley at least until the end of the rainy season. There we would be near the border, and if permission to cross were granted, we would be in a position to receive the message and act on it as soon as feasible.

In practical terms, this meant that within the next few days, we would join the overland trek to Hidden Valley with the thousand or so Lisu families who had also chosen this destination. We would then be within a few hours' walk of the border – actually, owing to the odd configuration of the boundary line, closer than we were now at Green Water Flat.

This decision was confirmed the next day by the receipt of an unexpected invitation. While Hidden Valley was largely untenanted – either because of the legendary curse on it or because of uncertainty as to its tribal ownership – there was one small Lisu Christian hamlet known as Binuzu, barely inside the Burmese side of the border with India. This hamlet had been settled by a few families from the original group that had migrated to the Indian side ten years before. For reasons of their own – perhaps just to get away from it all, in the Lisu tradition – they had crossed back to Burma. They were probably unaware at the time that they were doing so, since the boundary line was totally devoid of demarcation. These families remembered my parents from earlier years in the Salween valley in China; and they sent word through hunters from our encampment who had visited their village that if we entered the Binuzu area, they wanted the J. Russell Morses to come to their village and live with them.

On the Sunday following the big conclave, everybody in the encampment, except for the youngest children, gathered for services. Robert and I were scheduled to preach. As we stood in the shade of a huge rock, looking at some four thousand people squatting down in the dry, rocky stream bed strewn with big boulders, women on one side and men on the other, in a semicircle that spread out for a hundred yards or more, we decided to tell them the blunt truth, as we knew it.

Referring to the biblical story of Exodus and drawing the obvious analogy between our Kamko River and the Red Sea, I preached the message that we had no assurance of help from any hand but God's and that together we were going to try to find peace and happiness in a new land. To succeed in this venture, we must undertake it, as the children of Israel had done, with pure hearts and with minds totally committed to God's will. I emphasized some of the trials we would surely encounter – hunger, fear, hardships of every sort – and the strains that these might put on our Christian ideals of charity and neighbourly love. I also stressed the fact that in our new land we would have freedom and an opportunity to show what good use we could make of it. 'Where we are going', I said, 'there will be no government but God.'

Robert also referred to Moses and touched on the concern which that great leader had shown for the simple practicalities of settling in a new country. We must take care to separate widely enough to be able to live off the jungle game and other sustenance – into settlements of ten or twenty families each, at least two to five miles apart from each other. In Exodus, Moses makes mention of the strict rules of hygiene that his followers must be prepared to observe, and Robert tried to do the same. (We had, of course, stressed these rules at Green Water Flat.) Each family must take care never to pollute the streams on which others further down would necessarily depend for drinking water. Game should be killed as sparingly as possible and shared as far as practical in each community. Anyone not prepared to come with a pure heart and the resolve to adhere to Christian principles should turn back now and not cross the Kamko River. Robert especially warned everyone that we had no outside sources to look to for supplies, that we would have to depend on God to help us find food in the jungle, and that we must work hard to plant fields. But even so, no one expressed any desire to turn back.

Later – much, much later – we learned that someone had started the rumour that, since we were trying so hard to tell people of all the difficulties and disadvantages, almost trying to dissuade them from going, there must be some choice spot that we wanted to share with only a select few. We had hoped that our words would have the effect of impressing upon people the seriousness of the situation, the magnitude of the problems, so that the weak, the faint-hearted and the fearful might turn back before it was too late. But instead, it seemed to do just the opposite, and people seemed even more determined than before to push on to Hidden Valley.

After we had both finished our sermons, and while one of the Lisu pastors was addressing the congregation, I noticed a commotion in the rear of the crowd. The cause of it soon became apparent: two runners had arrived from the Indian border carrying some sort of message from Moo-Bee. The crowd parted enough to allow the messengers to find their way to Robert and me, just below the rocky outcrop we had used as a pulpit.

Thinking that this must, at last, be news of some decision about allowing us to cross the border, I hurriedly tore open the envelope and read the contents aloud for all to hear. Incredibly enough, the letter so dramatically delivered at this tense moment provided neither the long-awaited permission to cross nor a firm refusal. It was, in fact, merely one more ambiguously worded literary head-wag, stating that no word from Assam had yet arrived and that as soon as one did, Moo-Bee would get in touch with us.

It was not until years later that we were all to learn – from sources that cannot even now be safely divulged – that all of Moo-Bee's elaborate 'negotiations' had been merely a charade. No messages had in fact ever been sent to the governor of Assam, let alone to New Delhi. The pretence of a protracted effort to reach a decision was merely a smoke-screen devised to keep us on the Burmese side of the border without actually refusing to let us cross it. In this way Moo-Bee freed himself from the responsibility of taking any action whatever, while at the same time gratifying his well-developed sense of self-importance. However, by the time we found out all this, so many other things had happened that we could look back on Moo-Bee's odd behaviour as more laughable than exasperating.

Chapter 5

But God led the people round by the way of
the wilderness toward the Red Sea.
EXODUS 13 : 18

The Lisu's impelling motive was to find a steady food
supply, and the attraction of Hidden Valley was increased
by a persistent rumour. At one time during our negotiations
with Moo-Bee he had mentioned that it might be possible
for us to buy some needed items of food on the Indian side
of the border. Familiar with his ambiguities, we had merely
noted his remark and filed it for possible future reference.
But some of the Lisu who heard it accepted it as a settled
fact. We did not realize at the time how widespread the
rumour had become that it would be possible to buy all
our needs once Hidden Valley was reached and everyone
was closer to the border.

Acceptance of the rumour was not too surprising, actually.
There had been reports of large shipments of wheat and
rice to India by the United States, and the Lisu thought
that because we were Americans and they were with us,
surely they would be entitled to share some of that food.

Accepting rumours at face value is almost inevitable
among these people. In the more civilized areas of China
and Burma the Lisu are known as 'the wild people'. This
appellation is resented by the Lisu, but they are very
proud of their own name, which I can only inadequately
translate as something like 'loud-custom people'. What this
name, *Lisu*, tries to describe is a people who are very
gregarious, expressive and energetic. Indeed, it may be
partly because of these attributes that the Lisu have found
Christianity so attractive and satisfying. They love the
large gatherings, such as the Easter, Thanksgiving and

Christmas conventions, where there is much preaching and hymn-singing. In any event, wherever the Lisu gather together, the thing they like to do most is talk. Since they are without newspapers, radio, television and the other means of communication so common in more developed societies, talk is their way of passing on news and entertaining themselves. Their talk is spiced with gossip, and the person with the most inventive tongue is likely to be the most popular at any social gathering. As a story passes from ear to ear and camp-fire to camp-fire, it is more often than not embellished and enlarged upon, until the original story may be nearly unrecognizable.

Whatever may have been the reasons for acceptance of the rumour, the result was that many people moved on to Binuzu who might not have gone had they realized that their hopes were without foundation. Some of them became rather bitter when, instead of a ready source of supplies, they found hardship and hunger, just as Robert and I had tried to warn them they might.

The westward movement was not long in beginning; for some families it started within a day or two of the big meeting of the elders at Green Water Flat. It was a touching sight to see babies strapped to the backs of their parents and young adults carrying feeble grandparents piggyback. We only hoped that they would all be able to survive the rigours of the days ahead.

There was nothing for us to do but join the march, however difficult it might prove to be. Still hopeful about Moo-Bee, we noted that, on the map at least, Hidden Valley appeared to be an even better place to cross over into India than the Chaukan Pass near Green Water Flat. Then, too, in going to the uninhabited Hidden Valley we would be entering what was marked on the maps as 'unadministered territory', which meant, in effect, that we would be leaving Burma, or at least that area which was under Burmese government administration and authority.

As before, we Morses had to go in stages because all our loads could not possibly be carried in one march. Drema

Esther and Jesse were among the first to leave, going ahead to set up a base camp for our party in Empty Valley, just beyond the first of the two high ridges we had to cross. There they would store and tranship the loads we were sending from Green Water Flat to Binuzu. My parents moved out next, followed in a few days by my family. Robert stayed on with his family for another week or so, hoping to get some favourable word about entering India.

Travelling along with our family group were several Lisu boys who had stayed with us while attending school in Putao, and two or three girls who helped with the household chores and with the children. They had chosen to come along with us to help us get safely to the border but thought they might stay in Hidden Valley if others did. Two of them were orphans and had more or less 'adopted' us, but all had been with us for some time and were almost like family. Travelling with them was a mutually beneficial arrangement; we shared our food and supplies with them, and they shared their young strength, carrying loads and helping us along the trail in various ways. For instance, because they could travel faster than we could, they would go ahead and pitch camp before we arrived. It was always a great comfort and blessing to find a tent erected, a fire going and a pot of tea waiting at the end of a hard day on the trail.

On our first day out of Green Water Flat, we moved along the half-dry bed of a tributary of the Kamko River. Though the going was relatively easy, that day left us with no illusions about the rest of the trip. Following the easiest path took us back and forth across the stream, wading through icy water that was sometimes ankle-deep, sometimes more than knee-deep. Ahead of us loomed the towering, dark, and somewhat forbidding mountains that we had to cross the next day. That night we camped on the sandy 'beach' beside the river. We had difficulty getting a fire going because a shower came along and effectively dampened our firewood.

Because of the limited amount and variety of foods we could carry, eating was just something we did to keep up our stamina. But years later we would still remember the delicacy that came our way that night. One of the admirable Lisu customs is that they share their food, and when one family came along with some mustard greens, they generously gave us a small bundle of them. Though they had been picked days before and were pitifully wilted and yellow, we accepted them eagerly and gratefully. Something so precious as fresh vegetables could not be squandered, so we used only half the small bundle in our soup that night and saved the remainder for our meal the next morning.

Early the next morning we awoke to a dark, threatening sky, and as we set out on what was to be one of our most difficult days, a light drizzle was falling. Travelling upstream, we passed huge boulders, each as big as a Lisu house. We followed along the stream into a narrower canyon. At one point the high ridges seemed actually to come together about three hundred feet over our heads, so that we could see only a patch of sky through a slit at the top. In the eerie half-dark we stumbled forward into this cul-de-sac, relying only on the fact that the people who had gone before us had managed to find a way to get out of it. Finally we reached a waterfall coming in from the small tributary along which we were next to travel.

According to our Lisu guides we would have to ford the stream at the foot of the falls and head towards what looked like an unscalable wall of rock on the other side. The Lisu had solved the problem of getting up this rock by erecting what for them was a perfectly satisfactory ladder. It consisted of a log about six or eight inches in diameter and twenty feet long, braced against a huge boulder, at the top of which the trail resumed along the rocky face of the cliff. Because a slip could cause a climber to fall into the tumbling rapids below, the Lisu had cut small notches in the log to provide toeholds for their feet. For us, unaccustomed to such travel and wearing awkwardly large rubber-soled shoes, it was a far more hair-raising passage. I led off and the children followed. Helen, watching us, confessed later that she very nearly lost her nerve. It was only the sight of eight-year-old Margaret, the youngest of our children to walk (the other two girls were still being carried by obliging Lisu), scrambling up that log that finally gave her the courage she needed. In view of the unknown dangers that lay ahead, a mother, she thought, simply could not betray fear to her children.

Unfortunately, the log was only the beginning of trouble for us clumsy-footed Americans. At the top of it, we had to go on along the face of exposed bedrock that sloped alarmingly towards the stream and falls below. It had been turned smooth and slippery by the spray from the falls, and losing one's footing here would be even more certain to cause injury than a fall from the log. All of us needed the helpful hands of our Lisu friends to get across this stretch. Helen, who used a stick when she walked, poked it out in front of her to make sure it struck firm ground before she would move a foot. We couldn't help but wonder how my mother and father had negotiated this treacherous part of the trail.

At the head of the waterfall, the valley widened out a bit where there was a confluence of several small streams. For the moment we had easier going, but evidence of great landslides on the hills around us served as awesome warnings of nature's power and violence. We were following up the stream, and as we rounded a bend, before us was a sheer cliff from the top of which, falling free for some five hundred feet, poured a spectacular waterfall. It was such a breathtaking sight that each of us, in turn, rounded the bend and stopped to stare in awed amazement.

A little further on we turned away from the stream and started to climb almost straight up the flank of the ridge that had been shouldering out the sky to the west of us. The trail was an old elephant track that zigzagged across the mountain face but moved relentlessly upward. Each step forward was a straining step upward. Then too, each step was often followed by a backward slide, for the continuing rain made the road muddy. Once more we had to use our hands as well as our feet to make forward progress, and we were frequently forced to stop to rest. There was, of course, no place to sit down, so we could only stand and catch our breath before moving onward and upward.

The climb began in the midst of heavy tropical foliage – trees towering hundreds of feet above our heads and festooned with great ropes of wild vines. As we moved upward, the vegetation began to change to rhododendron trees interspersed with the bamboo brush of the higher altitudes. This thin-stemmed bamboo grows in clusters so dense that it has the appearance of tall, ragged grass reaching sometimes up to fifteen or twenty feet. Up and up we climbed, laboriously, for five hours. Finally we emerged into the sparse vegetation near the timber-line – pines blasted and sculptured by the winds. We climbed a total of four thousand feet, while it grew steadily colder and we noticed pockets of snow in the shady spots.

At the top of the ridge, which must have been at least nine thousand feet high, we paused to look around us. Off to our right, range upon range of sparkling snow-capped mountains rose higher and higher until they reached a jagged horizon in the Tibetan highlands. Even at our high altitude we were in what might be considered a pass, for the peaks around us soared to thirteen thousand feet or more. The valleys on each side dropped away so sheerly that we seemed to be walking on the edge of a knife. Everywhere there was evidence of the tremendous land-slides and wash-outs that resulted from the great earthquake of 1950, which had reshaped this whole area with its violence.

It was here, balanced on this ridge, that I first sensed that we were free at last. We seemed to be at the top of creation, with open land spreading in every direction as far as the eye could see. How could anyone but God keep us from taming this land to our needs? It is difficult now, back in civilization, to evoke the sense of freedom that comes upon a man when he stands on a mountaintop and looks out over tens of thousands of acres of fertile and unexplored land in the valleys below. It is only then that a man knows that, given the wit and will to survive, he need not bow his head to any government, to any ideology, to any small-minded men who feel that they control the essentials of his existence. I understood more fully than ever before why the Lisu had apparently given so little thought to abandoning their fields and their oxen and their other evidences of wealth in the Putao plains to move on into the jungles. Freedom is a far more heady emotion than a sense of security.

Following the ridge, we descended for an hour or so until, about dusk, we came upon a great encampment of hundreds of Lisu. They were spread out across an open knoll and on down the ridge, where the most important element of camping – water – was available. All over this little knoll there were camp-fires, one for each family. As the darkness deepened, these fires created a cheering circle of light within the shadows of the tall trees that surrounded us. Something happened there that, to this day, cannot quite be explained. It was a joyous coming together, like Easter, like Christmas, with the 'noisy' Lisu bringing out their hymn books and singing until long past their usual bedtime. Exhausted as we were, we joined in, and when we finally fell asleep, we did so with that comfortable feeling that, come what may, we were among friends.

The next morning we began the downward trek that would take us to the floor of Empty Valley. About noon we stopped to rest and eat some popcorn powder mixed with honey. Popcorn pounded in a rice pounder until it is a fine powder and stored in airtight containers will keep for several weeks and makes an excellent snack when travelling. From here we had a good view out over Empty Valley and could see it had been well named. At this season the river was low and comparatively small, but the valley floor was fairly wide, covered with sand, rocks and boulders, and completely bare of vegetation.

We could see on the mountainsides evidence of numerous

landslides caused by heavy rains, earthquakes, or a combination of the two. The light exposed areas of the landslides streaked the dark face of the mountains like tinsel on a Christmas tree. In some places, where huge masses of the mountainside had shaken loose and slid towards the river, extensive areas of bedrock were exposed, and a number of great, flat terraces had been formed, most of them even now sporting no cover but a timid growth of new, slender saplings. As we continued downward, we found ourselves following one of the many mountain streams that race over rapids and tumble over a series of waterfalls in their rush to the valley floor. Fed by springs and melted snow, the stream was so beautifully clear that in the occasional level stretches where deep pools formed, the water was scarcely visible. Only the fish darting quickly back and forth and the underwater vegetation moving gently in the current made one realize that it was, after all, water, and part of a stream.

When we finally reached the valley floor we found ourselves among huge rocks again. We spoke of what a tremendous upheaval there must have been at the time all this area was formed. As we moved through this desolate stretch, we thought again how appropriately the valley had been named. Despite the numerous salt-licks that attracted animals, there was no land suitable for cultivation by human beings.

Early that afternoon, a Saturday, we arrived at the camp that Drema Esther and Jesse had established on one of the terraces just above the river. We found everything in good order, all the loads we had sent ahead stored away under a great tarpaulin. We set up our own tent and began to prepare for the weekend. The rearranging of our supplies could be finished on Monday morning, and we planned to leave by noon that day. Lisu families were camped all around the Yangmis and, further down, on other terraces and flat places clear to the river. Many of them were even in the flat, rock-strewn area that would again become the river-bed during the rainy season. There were hundreds of them, and on the next day, Sunday, they all gathered together for worship.

We preached and sang hymns and preached again. We had an important message to deliver. The rumour of help from India had not yet died down, despite our efforts. All these people were moving as rapidly as possible towards Hidden Valley as if it were some kind of promised land. Though we ourselves hoped it might prove a promised land in the true biblical sense, we were very doubtful whether there would be any easy access to food and other supplies. So my sermons exhorted everyone again to trust in God and to be prepared to wrest their living from the land by the sweat of their brows. Once more I warned them that we knew of no help from any source but God, although I assured them that he would keep faith with them if they kept faith with him. And that faith, I stressed, meant cutting and burning and planting fields, meant searching the jungles for game and edible plants, meant trying the rivers for fish.

On Monday morning, instead of being able to rearrange our loads and then start off, as we had planned, we were forced to stay in our tents because of a sudden storm. The wind blew, the lightning flashed, the thunder crashed, and the hail on the plastic sheeting over our heads sounded like miniature machine-gun fire. The storm was so fierce while it lasted that the younger children clung to us in fright and the rest of us prayed for its abatement. In less than an hour the storm's fury had been spent, and gradually the skies cleared. By afternoon the sun came out and we were able to work on our loads.

On Tuesday morning, we were ready once again to join the march towards Hidden Valley. The Yangmis agreed to stay on in Empty Valley to receive the loads being forwarded by Robert and his family and to send along to us those loads we had to leave behind. We didn't know then that it would be months before we'd see those loads again. In any case, we felt that our job was to push on and find out what had happened to our parents, not to mention the thousands of Lisu who were streaming along the trail and over the next ridge like a column of ants.

The day dawned beautifully bright, and only the fluffiest of fair-weather clouds drifted through the deep blue sky, to break along the peaks above us. As we walked along the valley and moved up into the head-waters of the river we felt a sharp sense of the freshness of all the land about us. We were entering into a clean, pure country of God, uncontaminated by mankind. This land was now ours, and we knew that it could support us and give us the joy known only by those who have wrested their living from a virgin land.

When we reached the foot of the range that separated us from Hidden Valley, we decided to make camp. In an effort to travel faster and further while the road was comparatively easy, we had gone beyond the likeliest camping place for this stage of the journey, a cavelike area formed by a huge overhanging rock formation. The place where we finally stopped wasn't an ideal camping ground, and we had to hack our own site out of the thick surrounding jungle, as the Lisu had so often done before us. For the first time we were not close to fresh running water, but, fortunately, we found some small springs not too far away. Later, when Robert's family camped near here, they were not so fortunate. The only water they found was in a few stagnant pools where water had gathered in deep elephant footprints. When the leaves and accumulated scum were brushed off, they were able to scoop up the water and boil it with some tea-leaves. While such water is not to be recommended for taste, it does quench thirst and support life, which is the most important consideration in a situation where survival itself is often in doubt.

That night, although it was only late February, the early spring rains struck. Not as severe as the monsoon rains of summer, these rains pass over in quick, drenching sheets. They pour enough water on the land, however, to make already difficult trails almost impassable and to drench anybody so improvident as to be out in the open. If our camp had been in a better location, we might have waited out the next day, but as it was, we decided to push on.

All day it rained and rained, as we climbed and climbed, trying to reach the top of the pass. The trail, just a footpath that had been cleared of some of the overhanging growth by the machetes of the thousands of Lisu who had gone before us, was a slough of ankle-deep mud and, in some places, almost a running stream. As we worked through the thick growths of bamboo brush up to the heights near the timber-line, it turned bitterly cold. Though it wasn't actually freezing or snowing, we all grew numb with the cold, particularly around our soaking wet feet. Young Margaret thought it would be easier to get a grip on the slippery trail with her bare feet when we started down the other side, so she removed her shoes. It was a mistake. Sinking in the mud, she would stub and cut her toes on hidden rocks. Soon she was whimpering with pain and cold and almost unable to walk. While Helen sat with her beside the trail and tried to comfort her, a passing Lisu youth promised to come back for her once he reached a camping spot. And he did: in what seemed only minutes, he dumped his load and returned to carry Margaret on his back to our own camp.

The encampment this night was not far from a small stream in the head-waters of the Tarung River which runs down through Binuzu valley. In the last mile or so before we reached our own tent site we passed camp after camp. In the process, we witnessed another touching scene of Lisu generosity – and a serious sign that food would soon be our major problem. The passage of so many people had, for the most part, scared game far from the trail, but one of the earlier travellers had managed to shoot a deer. He had made camp early to cut up his meat, and, as hundreds upon hundreds of people passed, he felt obliged by Lisu custom to give each family a small portion for making soup that night. By the time we came along, the poor man had little but the bones left for himself.

That night was one of the most miserable in our memory.

Our tent was on an awkward pitch, and water ran down through it. Making a fire took hours, it seemed, while we shivered in anticipation, and there was no way to wash off the mud with which all of us were caked. But somehow we managed to get enough to eat and enough sleep to arm us for the next day.

Going down along the bed of the Tarung River was almost a repeat performance of the trip into Empty Valley, with one important exception. Though we had to work our way around the same great boulders, though we had to wade across the stream innumerable times simply to find a shelf wide enough for walking, we were conscious that the steep hillsides around us were thick with foliage. This meant, of course, fertile land and unlimited possibilities of game. As the hunters who had gone before us reported, this valley could support life, perhaps for an indefinite time.

Our camp that night was beside the Tarung River, beneath huge jungle giants. There were many wild banana trees in this area, and all the travellers were happy, since this meant plenty of easily obtained roofing material for their shelters. We decided these leaves would be good to place under us, also, because the ground was still quite soft and muddy from the recent rains. Our bright idea back-fired, however, because the banana leaves proved to be full of leeches, which are not the kind of creatures one enjoys as bedfellows. So the 'floor' had to be hastily removed and carried out away from our camp-site. Any amount of mud was preferable to having to pull off leeches all night!

The next day we finally reached Rice Field Camp, the clearing near Binuzu village where our parents and the Lisu had gathered in a temporary settlement. We found that some families were becoming discouraged. The clearing itself was the legacy of a few Lisu families – hunters and adventurers – who had moved into the valley several years before. They had cleared the area of underbrush for planting rice, but it was still dotted with great stumps of trees they had felled. These stumps remained even after the area had been burned off. In and around these stumps thousands of Lisu had set up their little lean-tos or tents and were simply waiting there for something to happen. They had made contact with the few Lisu families remaining in the area and had learned that, officially, the Indian border was now completely sealed. While an advetnurous hunter could slip across the border in the darkness, all the known trails were being closely watched by armed patrols from the Indian outpost just across the relatively low mountain pass to our north. Any hope of getting help from either the Indian government or the established Lisu community on the Indian side of the border was dimming. Moreover, the time was rapidly running out when it would be feasible to cut and burn and plant fields on the wild hillsides around Binuzu. It was easy to see that something needed to be done, and done quickly, to help the people find sources of jungle food. This was not going to be easy, because most of them had lived so long on the plains of Putao that they were not well prepared for the kind of life they must now endure.

A true sense of the wild environment in which we all found ourselves was brought home to us on one of the first nights we spent at Rice Field Camp. The camp-fires had died down to embers and the Lisu had crawled into their shelters for the night. We were enjoying one of our few indulgences – listening to BBC London, which used up precious power from the batteries. Gradually a sound from the jungle began intruding on the broadcast. When we turned down the radio and listened more intently we could soon identify it – the screamlike trumpeting and the thrashing and crashing of a herd of wild elephants. A stampede through the camp would scatter fires, crush lean-tos, and doubtless kill anyone unfortunate enough to get underfoot. We were discussing some way to drive the elephants off without sending them into panic when one of our boys piped up, 'Why not just turn the radio up loud?' It struck us as a good idea, and so the familiar, soothing voice of Alistair Cooke reading his weekly 'Letter from America' echoed through the Burmese jungles.

Evidently it reached the great, floppy ears of the elephants and must have soothed them, because they disappeared into the night.

Within days of our arrival, a few of the more adventurous families began to move even further west. Although they were going into completely unexplored territory, their move would bring them closer to the permanent Lisu community on the Indian side. These settled Lisu had prospered over the years, and they had been gathered by the Indians into one large village. Naturally, the refugee Lisu hoped that, despite the official closing of the border, there would be some way to get help from their relatives in India. They also hoped to find more game and better farming conditions than prevailed around Binuzu, which was rapidly becoming overpopulated as the migration from Green Water Flat continued.

It was about this time that the new order of leadership we had noticed developing among the Lisu really began to emerge. In the settled conditions of Putao, the steadier men – the successful farmers, the pastors, the teachers – had been the dominant figures in their villages. Here in the jungle, however, the hunters, the men with knowledge of the wilds, were suddenly very much in demand. My old friend Khisu, for example, once scorned for his fierce looks and crude mannerisms, could virtually take his pick of offers from family groups. Another new leader – and one of the first to move out towards the west – was the handsome and charming Sukin, who had been an affable trader in Putao. There he used to regale customers with tales of his more adventurous youth, when he had been a stalker of musk-deer in the mountains of Yunnan. Now he was putting these long-dormant talents to good use.

Far too few of the families – perhaps a hundred or so – moved on in those early weeks. The rest remained in the relative comfort of Rice Field Camp, and it soon became apparent that we might have a serious food problem. While some of the more energetic families began clearing fields in the vicinity of Rice Field Camp, many simply took to eating their seed rice and even to killing off the few chickens and pigs that they had brought with them. Obviously we were going to have to depend upon the bounty of the surrounding jungles for survival. It was while we were eagerly awaiting reports from the hunters who had fanned out into the hills that Robert and his family arrived.

The Yangmi family had arrived a few days earlier, and this should have been a joyous family reunion, but I am afraid that I was spreading gloom. 'These people are going to starve', I said. 'With the small number of fields under way at present, there won't be more than a handful of corn or rice for any of them by summer. They still seem to be hoping for help from India, and I am sure that it will not come.'

'Well, why can't we just live off the jungle?' Robert asked. 'I guess you didn't have time to take as good a look at this place as we did. It's really the biblical land of milk and honey. Why, you should have been with us in camp last night. You remember that old fox, Timotsu? Well, he found that all the cliffs around here are simply swarming with bees, and last night we all sat around drinking the most marvellous cliff-bee honey.'

'That's fine,' I said, 'but we can't live on honey. Where's the milk?'

'All around us', Robert said. 'These woods are full of sago and *atu*. And this river here is literally alive with fish. You must have passed that island in the middle of the Tarung a couple of days' march from here. Well, we camped there a few days and joined the Lisu in setting a trap for fish, and the catch was remarkable.'

Robert's boys broke in here to tell their cousins how the inventive Lisu built the trap. They began by felling two large trees so that their trunks dropped across the thirty feet of water running along the left bank of the island, one at the upstream end and the other at the downstream end. Then they filled in the space between each log and the stream bed under it with stones, brush, foliage and mud to create a kind of beaver dam. Fish were caught between these two dams. To get at them, the crafty Lisu opened a small drainage hole in the downstream dam and let the water run out until the fish were isolated in shallow pools. They stayed perfectly fresh until dinner, when they could be lifted out with improvised nets or even scooped up by hand.

Robert's discoveries of natural wealth in the valley were encouraging. But so were reports from an area two to three days' travel westwards, where many of the people had already gone. In fact, some of the reports from there sounded really exciting, for they told of vast areas of land suitable for cultivation, as well as rivers full of big fish, jungles abounding in game, and easily accessible areas where atu, a large, edible fern, was plentiful. So, just a few days after Robert's arrival at Rice Field Camp, he and I decided to go and have a look for ourselves. We were away for a little over two weeks and discovered that, although it didn't quite measure up to the most glowing reports we had heard, it definitely was a good area for settlement. Both of us felt that if we could not get through to India, then this new area would be a good place for us to go with our families, since so many of the Lisu people had already moved or were planning to move there.

It was about a week or so after our return from this exploratory expedition that some new arrivals from Empty Valley came to us with disturbing news they had heard from people who had just come from Green Water Flat. The information had arrived by way of the jungle grapevine, which seems to work as rapidly as though its tangled rattan creepers were a fully electrified telephone system. The news was that a detachment of Burmese troops – and in the Lisu manner of exaggeration, estimates of its size ran from a company to a battalion – had been sent out in search of us.

Chapter 6

And the Lord hardened the heart of Pharaoh
king of Egypt and he pursued the people
of Israel.
EXODUS 14 : 8

The story of the pursuing Burmese forces spread like
quicksilver around the camp-fires of Rice Field Camp.
After patiently cross-questioning later arrivals from Green
Water Flat, Robert and I were able to piece together an
account of what had happened. A company-size force of a
hundred to a hundred and twenty men and officers had
indeed been dispatched westwards from Putao. They had
little difficulty finding and following the trail over which
we and the multitude of Lisu with us had moved. Although
one purpose of their exercise was obviously to seek us out
and perhaps return us to Putao, another was to hold what
in the old British colonial days used to be called a flag
march. A flag march simply served to show that the
Burmese government still held sovereignty over the area
between Putao and the Indian border, despite the existence
of the KIA.

Why the KIA chose to let this flag march pass through
Green Water Flat and on up to the border without an
ambush we do not know. There was a lively battle at the
flat when the Burmese returned from the border. Half a
dozen government soldiers were wounded, and two or
three were killed; similar casualties were reportedly
inflicted on the KIA. Meanwhile, we and the Lisu were
nowhere to be seen, and inasmuch as the territory west of
Green Water Flat was still designated 'unadministered', the
government troops struck their tents after the battle and
marched back toward Putao.

The sudden disappearance from Putao of almost a

quarter of the populace clearly had a strong impact on the local authorities. Was the mass exodus the start of a new wave of insurgency on a much larger scale than any that had preceded it? Were we in league with the KIA insurgents and responsible for the whole affair? Or were we, as my brother Robert's farewell letter had stated, simply trying to obey the expulsion order as best we could? The most obvious way to answer such questions was to send a detachment of troops after us. The commandant must have satisfied himself that we and the Lisu had gone over the Chaukan Pass into India. So he marched back to Putao, probably thankful that the KIA had not caught him in an even more deadly trap.

Of course, at the time we first heard the rumours we had no way of knowing that these were the facts of the case. Around the fires at Rice Field Camp, news of the fighting was so exaggerated by lively Lisu tongues that there was something like panic. Many of these people had been through the hard days in China, when they had seen friends and relatives killed or imprisoned by Communist troops. Now they were certain that the long arm of the Burmese government would reach across the ridges between us and Green Water Flat and seize them. This, on top of the mounting evidence that cultivation of crops would be difficult, made it seem that the ancient curse still pervaded Hidden Valley.

The original curse, it was said, had been laid on the valley by the Mishmi, a large tribe to the north, and the Naga tribe to the south. Though their hunters would venture into the area from time to time in search of musk, both tribes exerted all their witchcraft to keep the valley an empty buffer zone between them. Throughout the whole Himalayan region demonology is, to this day, a powerful force. We had, of course, been preaching and working against this force all of our lives. Especially when we began moving into Hidden Valley, we repeatedly assured our Lisu companions that their Christian faith was ample armour against whatever demons there might be.

Though most of them believed us, still it was hard for them to shake off entirely their animist heritage.

There were many stories that kept belief in demons alive, particularly the account of the fifty Lisu hunters who stumbled into Hidden Valley some fifteen or twenty years before. The two survivors of that tragic venture were not Christians, but they were believable witnesses to their Christian friends back in Putao. Their story was that they had had a very successful hunting trip in the snowy mountains to the north, collecting musk, killing takin and deer, and living comfortably off the jungle. They were coming back rich when they decided to sweep south into Hidden Valley for a look. All of a sudden things began to go wrong. Demons seemed to be everywhere around them. Someone would fire off a flintlock, or maybe just shout too loudly on a clear day, and a heavy hailstorm would come up. There would be unaccountable accidents while they were chopping trees. The whole jungle seemed hostile – some men got lost, others died of unknown disease. In the end, only two of them made it back to the Putao plain, empty-handed and convinced that Hidden Valley was evilly haunted.

The few families who had tried to settle near Binuzu in the eastern end of Hidden Valley had never been able to succeed at farming. They explained that while they were still in India they had watched the weather patterns and had decided that the weather came from the direction of Hidden Valley. So they moved on over when they were sure it would be dry enough to cut and plant. But immediately, the weather changed – unseasonable rains or droughts left them with harvests large enough to supply only seed grain. They had taken to living off the jungle and stayed on only because they were able to realize some profit from musk. Needless to say, their story did not encourage the hopes of our five thousand people, most of whom were in poor condition for survival because of years of easy living in the plains around Putao.

With rumours of the flag march echoing in the background, we held repeated conferences at Rice Field Camp. Meanwhile, we shared out all the seed rice, hoping most of it would be planted. But now people had little heart for cutting fields, and they began eating this rice. Some decided to use it for food while they headed back home, hoping that they would arrive before their absence in Putao was detected. Little by little, family by family, they began drifting east. Eventually, some four thousand of the Lisu returned to Putao. Many of them were the old and the weak, and there were many tragic partings of parents and children, brothers and sisters.

Through all this, at the conferences, the hunters, who were now the acknowledged leaders, were urging us to flee to the hills. We listened with great interest to their reports. The hunter we trusted most was Jyeba, a man who had made his fame back in Putao by capturing a live takin, or snow buffalo, which was sent to New York's Bronx Zoo. He argued hotly that, even without the threat from pursuing troops, we ought to get out of the two-thousand-foot elevation around Rice Field Camp and move up.

'Break it up, break it up', Jyeba would say. 'Move up to three thousand feet, five thousand feet. That's where you'll find the food and game. Not too many of you in one place either. Ten families would be enough in any one group. The jungle won't stand more.'

All the Morses and about fifty other families decided to take his advice. For us, the choice of direction wasn't difficult – the closer we were to India, we felt, the more likely it was that we could keep our options open. We still hadn't given up all hope of being permitted to cross into India or being given some basic food supplies by the Indian government. Moreover, if Burmese troops should penetrate Hidden Valley, we would at least have a choice between surrendering to them or to the Indians. So, on 26 April, we set off up a ridge leading to the north-east and headed for Monkey Tree Hill, which was only about an hour's travel from the border.

The first night out added one more to our growing list of miserable camping experiences on the trail. Just about the time we reached an area that looked suitable for camping, a storm came up. The winds blew, sighing and rattling their way through the tops of the great hundred-foot trees around us. Here and there a branch would give way with a crash and a snap that sounded like firework. We worked feverishly to cut saplings and set up our plastic-roofed tents, troubled because we knew that spring storms like this could produce lethal hailstones as big as eggs, against which the plastic sheeting would be inadequate protection. Pushed by the winds, clouds rolled up over the jungle top, and lightning began forking down around us into the trees.

Probably still thinking about the talk of demons in the valley, Robert's son Joni said, 'I know what's causing this storm. Satan is testing us. I wish Gabriel would knock his teeth in.'

Just then there came a blinding flash and a terrific, bone-jarring crash. Robert, who was standing outside his tent, sank to his knees in terror and awe. The bolt of lightning had struck a great tree near him, stripping it naked of bark clear to the ground. Thunder, erupting almost simultaneously, shook the ground. When the reverberations from the thunder died away, Joni's voice broke the tension. 'Thank you, Gabriel', he said.

This storm convinced us that we would need more permanent shelter – and quickly, before the real monsoon began in June. As we moved up on Monkey Tree Hill, Robert's family and the Yangmis found suitable sites for building houses. My parents and our family weren't so fortunate, and by early May we moved down the ridge again, about an hour's travel from Robert's family and the Yangmis, to a place called A-deh-di, just above Binuzu. Here we found a good location beside a stream, with building materials available nearby, and built a small Lisu-style house for ourselves and another for my parents. Most of the Lisu moved down off the ridge, too, leaving only about ten families strung out along Monkey Tree Hill.

Finding the proper site for a jungle home is not an easy matter. First, there has to be a small area of relatively level land, which Robert found on a kind of saddle along the ridge. Next, you need water, and there was a stream about a hundred feet away from the place where Robert and his family settled down. Finally, you have to be close enough to available building material, the most important of which is roofing. A good roof is most easily fashioned from a kind of tangled, creeping bamboo called *diji*. There was a large clump of it just below Robert's site.

Diji is one of the most intriguing of jungle growths. Unlike most bamboo, it is vinelike, covering and smothering everything in its path. Though it rises to a crest at fifteen or twenty feet, nothing thrives under diji; it conquers the jungle. Diji can climb over the tops of hundred-foot trees and bring them down. The tangled stalks of this bamboo are impenetrable, and they are under so much tension that if you try to cut them with a machete, they will spring up and gore you. But each stem sprouts a fan of leaves so dense that you can walk on top of a patch of diji if you are careful. Once Robert's sons Bobby and Stevie were traversing a diji thicket when Stevie disappeared. Bobby, turning back to look for his brother, found Stevie's gun 'floating' eerily on top of the foliage. Then he heard a 'Whoo! Whoo!' Peering down through the tangled growth, he saw Stevie fifteen feet below on the jungle floor. Somehow Stevie managed to claw his way up and out, both boys worrying all the time about the deadly vipers that inhabit the diji groves. But, of course, leaves like this, fanning out six to ten to a stalk, make marvellous shingling for the roof of a house.

Before a house, or even a camp, can be built in the jungle, the first problem is digging a toilet. The next job is to clear the site right down to bare earth to eliminate the hazard of leeches and ticks. Once this has been done, building can begin. The two essentials of a house in a tropical rain-forest are a roof to keep off the water and a floor to insulate the inhabitants from the more harmful creepy-crawly jungle pests. While the diji leaves provided roofing, it wasn't until many weeks after Robert had settled into his site that he found a grove of straight-stemmed bamboo that, when cut into ten- or twelve-foot lengths and flattened into planking, could make a floor. Walls were another matter. In the humid, tropical summer they were needed not for warmth but to keep out the driving rains. Also, they provided a kind of protection against wandering beasts and a comforting psychological sense of enclosure. In winter, these flimsy walls of woven bamboo, even with their many cracks, would provide at least partial protection against the icy winds sweeping down from the snow-covered peaks above.

So Robert and the boys worked hard, and finally, long after the bamboo-leaf roof and the split-bamboo floor were finished, they managed to erect walls of woven bamboo. Walls never reach the roof line in any Lisu-style house because ventilation is needed for the fireplace, which is just an earth-filled box set flush with the floor in the middle of the room. Robert's house followed this pattern, so the smoke would drift up and out, while the mountain mists of the rainy season would drift in, dampening everything in the house. When finished, the house was just a one-room, twelve-by-fourteen-foot enclosure with bunks around the walls. The one redeeming feature of this crude structure was that it afforded a view that was simply marvellous. To look across a valley, up the lower slopes clad in rich green jungle growth, and appearing deceptively smooth, on up to the jagged, ten- to twelve-thousand-foot peaks on the other side of the river – two days' travel away, but seemingly much nearer – was a visual feast.

In some ways, Robert and his family were better equipped than the rest of us to handle jungle living. His three boys, Joni, Stevie and Bobby, had been honing their jungle skills ever since we left Putao. Indeed, Robert had sent them off on a week-long expedition from Green Water

Flat with Jyeba to learn how to find and process one of the most important jungle staples, sago. As Bobby recalls, 'We were really greenhorns. We had to learn to humble ourselves and to take embarrassment. Take a little thing like cutting a tree. All you have to do is get an axe and chop away, right? Not at all. I was cutting away for a whole hour on small hardwood tree – a chinquapin about six inches in diameter – cutting away on all sides like a beaver would gnaw on a tree. This Lisu guy – he was a stranger at the time – comes up and laughs. Then he teaches me that first you cut on one side, in the direction you want the tree to fall, and then you cut from the other side, and it will fall where you want it to. And then he teaches me how you give one whack a little below and one whack on top to make a whole chunk fall out. The angle of the notch determines the speed of your progress. The steeper, the faster. An angle between forty-five and sixty degrees is best. Well, that's how we learned to cut trees, and I think the people were impressed that we were willing to listen and to admit what we didn't know.'

A lot of tree cutting is involved in processing sago, a sort of jungle palm that yields a coarse, starchy fibre that can substitute for grain in a jungle diet. The pith of small saplings can be eaten raw, and often on sago hunts we would subsist on it while chopping up the larger trees to prepare food to take back home. Especially in the tender saplings, the sago heart has the soft, crunchy consistency of a bamboo shoot and a naturally salty flavour. Sago is processed by cutting the tree into sections, stripping the bark, and pulverizing the fibre by pounding it with wooden mallets. Then the starch is washed out in a series of banana-leaf troughs.

On Monkey Tree Hill, atu, a kind of fern, was more available. Not only is it less palatable, but, unlike sago, which can be eaten right away, atu requires several weeks of preparation. The palmlike fern is large, usually ten to twelve feet tall and eight to twelve inches in diameter, and has a very hard outer bark. Once this bark is removed, the inner portion of the stem or trunk is chopped and beaten into a pulp. A raised area, from six to twelve inches off the ground, is prepared. It may be an actual platform made of bamboo, or it may be the unusable portions of the atu stalks piled up to form a sort of cushioned area. This raised area is covered with banana leaves, in which holes are made with a pointed stick. The atu pulp is then placed on the leaves and left to be washed by the monsoon rains. The washing process removes the sap, which is harmful to humans, and all the liquid drains off through the perforated banana leaves. The combination of constant moisture and summer heat results in a rotting or fermenting of the pulp. After about three weeks, it has aged sufficiently to be edible. By this time it looks and smells – and, I'm sorry to say, also tastes – rather like some form of garden compost. But pressed into flat cakes and pan-roasted, or cooked in the hot ashes, it becomes more palatable. We had prayed, 'God, when we don't have the food to suit our taste, then please give us a taste to suit our food.' And our prayer was answered, because we were able to eat the atu and even to enjoy it. Certainly we could not have survived without it, and knowing this, we were thankful for it.

Within a short time of settling on Monkey Tree Hill, Robert's sons, along with their cousin Sammy, the Yangmis' adopted son, became some of the best young hunters on the ridge. Though they had never gone out without Lisu guides before, they soon learned, like all the rest of us, that jungle survival demands independence and courage. Despite their tender ages – Joni was sixteen, Stevie thirteen, Bobby twelve and Sammy eleven – they rapidly picked up the jungle lore they needed for both their success and their safety. For one thing, they had absorbed the lesson of the buddy system: you never go into the jungle alone. For another, they had learned that many of the best beasts for eating – especially deer and boar – could be summoned within shooting range by a simple call that was executed by putting two leaves to the lips and inhaling. Indeed, Joni once whistled so expertly that a small barking deer ran right under his legs before he could raise his gun to get a shot. The boys also learned that the same call might attract tigers in search of a meal, so they must always be on the alert. The point of their expeditions was never sport, but bringing back the most game with the least possible expenditure of ammunition.

Though the boys enjoyed the chase, killing was never easy for them. To this day, Bobby, the youngest, has not forgotten the shattering emotional experience of shooting his first buck. 'He looked right at me when he was dying,' he explained to us later, 'and he seemed to be asking me, "Why? Why?" I wanted to give him some answer – but I had none to give.'

The answer was, of course, that we were at the most primitive level of subsistence. It was a question of kill or die, because our bodies demanded the protein that only game could provide. I think one thing that helped the boys with their moral problem was to see how well whatever they brought back was put to use. In Lisu fashion, their family would share the meat with all the other families along the ridge, including ours. Parts like entrails, head, liver and lungs would go into a large cauldron and be boiled into a nourishing soup. Anyone could come by with his bamboo cup and dip into the cauldron. This was truly a godsend to people living mostly on leaves and other jungle foods.

The Morse boys, both Robert's and ours, made use of our small assortment of .12-gauge shotguns and .22 rifles, but they also learned to use the traditional Lisu crossbow, especially for smaller game such as birds and squirrels and the ubiquitous rats that came around the houses. This weapon is usually constructed of a hardwood stock on which is mounted a strong wooden bow designed to shoot eight-inch split-bamboo arrows about a foot in length. When not in use, this light bow is slung over the arm in such a way that it can be whipped into shooting position as fast as a holstered Colt revolver. The slender bamboo arrows are grooved in a spiral pattern for about an inch to an inch and a half from the tip. Poison is lodged in these grooves, and because the arrow is so thin after being grooved, it breaks off in the animal and the poison is released. When possible, the arrows are tipped with metal to aid in penetration of the game. A dozen or two of the dartlike arrows, usually fletched with carefully folded slivers of bamboo rather than feathers, are carried in a shoulder-strap quiver. Attached to the quiver is a small bamboo vial of poison into which the tip of the arrow is dipped before shooting. The preferred poison is aconite, usually in the form of a sticky black, brown or whitish paste, made from a certain root. The poison is so effective that sometimes small animals like monkeys or flying squirrels drop dead in mid-air when pierced by an arrow; yet it doesn't impair the nutritional value or flavour of the flesh. The meat directly around the arrow is cut out, and the remainder of the animal is safe to eat.

In the area of Monkey Tree Hill, the boys concentrated on the kind of game that was most appropriate to their rather light armament and most easily available to provide daily rations of protein. This included monkeys, known as tree pork, deer, and even rats. The rats in the mountain jungles should not be confused with the loathsome rats of urban civilizations all over the world. Clean and attractive little creatures who live on acorns and other forest delicacies instead of human refuse, the jungle rats rather resemble the grey squirrels of the United States. Their tender flesh tastes a good deal like suckling pig, and their soft little pelts can be stitched together to make warm and attractive quilts or bedspreads. In later years, the boys were to have some harrowing contacts with snakes, elephants and tigers, but by that time they had gained not only respect for, but a certain valuable familiarity with, the habits of these beasts through daily contact.

During that first season in Hidden Valley, Robert's house was a veritable zoo. Betty, an enthusiastic herpetologist, had a penchant for collecting the jungle's most deadly snakes. While in Putao, she had kept cobras, banded kraits, and even Russell vipers, whose bite will kill in ten minutes, in box cages in their house. In the jungle, less deadly but more troublesome 'pets' than the snakes were three tiger cubs that a Lisu hunter had presented to Robert's family. Named Tiger Mike, Tiger Helen and Tiger Betty, they were as playful as kittens, but because they were so much larger than kittens, their playfulness often made life in a one-room house almost intolerable. As susceptible to the miseries of rain as their human owners, the tiger cubs would crawl into the children's beds. On one notable occasion Tiger Mike wormed his way out of the covers and, finding Joni sound asleep with his mouth wide open, proceeded to use it as a convenient toilet. Joni's horrible awakening was followed by the tiger's being thrown screaming into the wet jungle, but he managed to crawl penitently back into the covers an hour or so later. Such pranks, and the fact that the little tigers grew into animals capable of biting or clawing seriously even in play, caused Robert to send them off with a Lisu who promised to deliver them to the Rangoon zoo. Unfortunately, they never arrived.

But living with the tiger cubs taught Robert and his family some valuable lessons. One of them was a piece of tiger language – a guttural sound, rather like a human clearing his throat, most often used by Tiger Mike, the biggest and most obstreperous of the cubs. This odd noise, more like a grunt than a growl, meant roughly 'Cut it out' in a positive sense. It signified that Tiger Mike was definitely tired of whatever game was going on and was preparing, if need be, to prove it by extending his retractable claws. All three cubs understood the sound perfectly, and reacted accordingly, whether the noise was uttered by one of them or one of the people in the house. Later, using the same sound in the wilds proved an effective way of keeping a stalking tiger away.

During the long months of rain, distractions like snakes and tigers in the house were valuable diversions. We were as effectively housebound as New Englanders in a giant snowstorm. Drenching rains alternated with short periods of hot sunlight that turned the whole jungle into a kind of dripping steam bath. What trails there were became mud slides slippery as ice, and every leaf bred the most dreaded of jungle pests – the leech. It is difficult to describe how horrible these leeches can be. Only the people who had to hunt for food or those on urgent missions of mercy dared attempt a passage through the jungle in the face of this threat.

There is no really effective weapon against the leech. Instead of keeping them away, wrapping up well often tends to hide leeches from your sight. During the rains we learned that even wearing shoes can be a hazard, because leeches hiding in a shoe can turn your foot into a bloody mess before you feel their bite. Leeches dread fire and ashes, and many American and British soldiers virtually chain-smoked their way through the Burma campaign of World War II in an effort to keep them at bay. But we learned the Lisu technique of scraping them off with a sharp machete, a process that had to be repeated every few minutes to keep them from sucking blood. On one occasion my brother Robert helped his wife scrape 102 leeches off just one of her legs after she had been walking only five minutes. The mobility of these wormlike creatures is incredible. You can look at what seems to be a totally quiet area of jungle foliage, wave your hand, and suddenly find leeches crawling out from under every leaf, where they have been hiding from the rain. They almost seem to jump the last half-inch or so to reach any available piece of warm flesh. If a man opens his fly to relieve himself along a jungle trail, later he will very likely find that at least two or three leeches have managed to make their way to his groin.

Once a leech has attached itself to you, it injects an anticoagulant into the surrounding area of flesh. It drinks until it swells up like a miniature sausage and then falls off. But because of the anticoagulant, you continue to bleed, and anybody who gets a number of leech bites is likely to suffer seriously from loss of blood. Nobody who has lived in the jungle during the rainy season underestimates the danger of leeches or ignores the importance of seeing to it that everything, from houses to toilets and other buildings, is made as leechproof as possible. Basically, this involves clearing and burning an area before constructing any building and keeping it clear of undergrowth.

Although our movements were somewhat restricted, our days during the rainy season were surprisingly full. Unless they have experienced it, few people realize how much time it takes simply to support life under primitive conditions. A typical day for us began at first light, when we would be awakened by the insistent hooting of a mountain owl, called butaloo because of his cry – *boo-too-loo*. This was followed by the chatter of squirrels and then the whooping cries and shrill muttering of the gibbons. Their talk usually provided a fair indication of the sort of weather to be expected later on: a lively uproar meant a fair day, while less agitated conversation foretold clouds or rain.

In our house, the first act in the morning routine was to build up the fire. This meant uncovering the embers remaining from the previous night's fire, blowing them to a blaze, and adding more firewood. We always tried to bank the fire at night, to avoid having to use up our precious matches. Then we would take turns washing, after which it was time for our morning devotions – some ten minutes of prayer and Bible-reading – followed by breakfast. This meal almost always consisted of tea and atu, our regular staple diet. The atu was prepared by forcing the doughy substance through a sieve or colander; this removed the larger remnants of cellulose fibres and squashed into more edible form the worms and bugs that had accumulated during the three-week processing period. The bugs added protein to the concoction without impairing its already far from appetizing flavour. It was then ready to cook. We would either form it into lumps or balls and roast it by burying it in the hot ashes, pan-roast it like a pancake (without oil), or drop it by spoonfuls into some kind of soup, rather like dumplings. When it was available, we also used sago. The sago was either mixed with water into a sort of pudding, sweetened with cliff-bee honey, if we had any on hand, or else mixed with a little water and made into something resembling pancakes. These could be flavoured with jam or jelly made from jungle fruit or berries.

Despite its uninspiring taste, breakfast was a hearty meal that kept us all going until four or five in the afternoon, when we usually ate the second, and last, meal of the day. This would include more tea and atu, accompanied by meat, eggs or fish, depending on the success of our boys in their activities in field or stream. Between dinner and the fall of darkness, our time was fully occupied in repairing tools or readying weapons for the next day, listening to radio news reports on our small, battery-powered portable set, or, less frequently, reading. We were ready for evening prayers by candle-light and then bed not long after the sun went down.

During the day, none of us had much leisure time. The men and boys shared the heavier work so necessary in this primitive type of life. This work included the original construction of the house and then all the maintenance needed to keep it waterproof; finding and splitting firewood; hunting and fishing; and going out to prepare or carry home atu or sago. The women were also kept busy, even though they had some help from Lisu girls. It was up to them to keep track of the meagre food supplies, to see that they were stretched as far as possible while providing as much daily nourishment as possible. They also had to see that the family's clothes were kept clean and mended. Then there was the matter of trying to teach the younger children at least the three R's, using the few books we had with us. And, of course, it was the women who had to care for any of the family who might get sick or hurt. We Morses had no rice-fields that first year, because, even in the midst of the struggle for survival, we were continuing to teach and preach at every opportunity. Besides, we knew that when the Lisu Christians had a rice harvest they would give their tithes to the church, and we would receive a share, along with the Lisu preachers who were in the area, for this was the way all the preachers were supported.

So the days slipped by, through May and June into July. It was then that a small miracle occurred. Some corn, which had been planted in fields cleared before the flag march, ripened. The news came to Robert's family, isolated up on Monkey Tree Hill, far more dramatically than to the rest of us who were living down near the fields. Robert had walked down to visit our parents, and they gave him one and a half ears of corn to take home as proof that something could grow in the valley.

Towards dusk, Robert started to make the two-hour walk back up to his home. As night fell, he got some dried bamboo and split the ends to make a torch for protection against tigers. As Bobby recalls the scene: 'We saw Dad coming with the torch, and we all thought he had some kind of news. But it was a total surprise to see the corn. It sounds ridiculous now, but just that little bit of corn brought us all a sense of security and hope. We roasted the corn on the ear, and we tore off the outer leaves for my sister Deedee, who wanted them as a memento. Then we ate the kernels, one at a time, as a sort of special dessert. It worked out to fewer than twenty kernels each, but that was one of the greatest times I can remember. Then we said a special grace, read the Bible, prayed, and thanked God. We wanted to, you know. As Dad said, "Finally the jungle has yielded up some fruit for our efforts, a symbol that the land is good and will support us." '

Chapter 7

Would that we had died by the hand of the
Lord in the land of Egypt, when we sat by the
fleshpots and ate bread to the full; for you
have brought us out into this wilderness
to kill this whole assembly with hunger.
EXODUS 16 : 3

The celebration of the corn harvest turned out to be somewhat premature, to say the least. There was enough corn for almost every family to have some every day. Even the old folks, who couldn't eat it right off the cob because their teeth, if they still had any, were in bad condition, could cut it off and cook it into a sort of gruel, or else grind it between stones into a pasty consistency and make corn bread. But there was still a period of some four months until the main rice harvest, and everyone knew that this harvest would be very limited. It was expected to provide only enough for seed the following year, and food for perhaps three to four months. This meant that we would be eating atu through the next summer also. Many people had abandoned their newly cleared fields at the time of the flag march, and the amount of grain we could count on would therefore be much less than we had estimated in the spring. So the prospects for the following year, while not hopeless, still held no promise of ease and plenty.

Ventures across the border into India to seek help from relatives in the Lisu village there were risky. Moreover, at best these forays produced only an occasional few measures of grain or a little salt or tea. A determined mountain man moving by night could get through the jungle and across the border, but he always faced the possibility of running into trouble. Anything that looked like an established trail was patrolled regularly, and any Lisu caught crossing the undefined border was jailed.

All of us learned what it meant to be constantly hungry, as we never had enough to feel satisfied. But after the first six months we knew we could survive. The young people who had travelled with us continued to help our family and my parents, especially with the preparation of atu. My parents, being older and less able to do things for themselves, were taken care of by us and our Lisu brethren. When people came to ask my father for medicine, they often brought a small basket of atu or some jungle greens or mushrooms, and later on, corn and cucumbers and squash. Even in the most difficult days, my father did his best to try to treat those who came to him for medical care. And all of us adults did all we could in continuing to help in the spiritual development of the people who had stayed in the Binuzu area.

Yes, in those first months in Binuzu we learned that hunger can be an almost overwhelming force that drives away any squeamishness with regard to food, and sometimes, unfortunately, even caution. Once Joni came back from a hunting trip so famished that, even though he should have known better, he picked up a likely-looking root from a table where various jungle roots and greens were lying and started to eat it raw. One swallow was enough to let him know that he had made a ghastly mistake. Immediately he was seized in the throat with what the Lisu called *ga-dah*, or poking pain. 'It was just like needles in my throat,' Joni said, 'needles jabbing in all directions.' There was no antidote available to help him, and all anyone could do was pray. Fortunately Joni had swallowed so little of the root that he suffered no long-lasting effect.

Even such an incident did not curtail our efforts to experiment with anything that might conceivably be edible. When they were out hunting, Joni and his brothers brought back whatever they could find. One time, for example, Joni was stalking a deer when he noticed that its droppings seemed to contain some unusual, round, hard objects. Stopping to investigate, he found that they were *a-leh-si*, the seeds of a jungle vine, which the deer had apparently swallowed without chewing and passed with their shells intact. Joni put the nuts in his knapsack and when, further along the trail, he came on more of the same, salvaged these as well. Darkness fell before he could catch up with the deer, but he brought back at least a pint measure of excreted nuts. After washing them off in the stream near the house, Joni passed the nuts around that night as an after-dinner delicacy; nobody declined to eat them. Later, we found that civet cats – small, wild, catlike animals with a strong scent – could be counted on to collect the same kind of nuts and package them for us in the same informal style.

In view of the difficulties we faced in those first few months, we were not surprised, when the monsoon rains were about over, to find that many of the Lisu who had not panicked earlier were beginning to drift back towards Putao. Life in the jungle was inexorably separating the more resourceful from the less able. Take the case of a leader like Fu-cheh-duh, a steady, middle-aged man, a wonderful diplomat and politician in Putao, where he had been responsible for much of the valley's development. Fu-cheh-duh led a group of families out of Rice Field Camp to what seemed like a beautiful location for a village. They began building and clearing fields, but within weeks they found that they had chosen the wrong spot. There wasn't enough water, there were no roofing materials, and they were three days' journey from any source of jungle food. The people began, of necessity, to drift off, and Fu-cheh-duh himself finally gave up and returned to Putao.

In the end, we found that survival in the jungle was as much a matter of mental attitude as of experience. In the first place, you needed a kind of pride, a feeling that nothing could defeat you. In many people, this pride was often coupled with a dream, a goal, a drive for a new life free of the fears and repressions they had suffered in Putao. But even this sense of pride and motivation was not enough without still something more: an openness to new experience, a willingness to improvise, a capacity to trust in providence.

'The way it is in the jungle', as my brother Robert put it, 'is that if one thing doesn't work, another will. You need that you-just-can't-lose frame of mind. The people who had a relaxed expectation that things would work out got through, and the people who had a negative outlook gave up. We all knew that the jungle would keep producing. Cut it down, and it'll grow back; pick a whole mess of bamboo shoots one day, and a few days later there will be another mess of them. Knowing that, feeling that, it was always possible to sustain hope, even in the worst of times.'

While the jungle defeated many people, it was the making of many more. One such was Timotsu, a small man, quick and wiry, with a perpetual smile and merry eyes that were so sharp he never missed the smallest movement in the forest around him. It was he who had found the cliff-bee honey that had so lifted the hearts of Robert and his family when they first came over into Hidden Valley. Gathering around him other adventurous Lisu, Timotsu turned honey-hunting into his speciality and thereby became one of the most valuable men in the whole exodus. Because we had no source of sugar, we all had to rely on honey, not only for sweetening but for quick energy. Bee grubs, too, could supply a useful adjunct to a diet that was dangerously lacking in certain nutrients.

Sago and atu can sustain life, but, as was found after months of subsisting almost entirely on these staples, they produce a change in body chemistry. A sudden big meal full of protein, such as we might indulge in after a successful hunt, can produce a kind of protein poisoning. The victim tends to be sick for several days, like any person who eats too much after he has been rescued from starving. After a long period of subsisting on atu, sago and jungle greens, even a meal of such ordinary things as corn or rice is likely to result in body swelling, indigestion and violent cramps. In view of all this, the bit of sweetness we could extract from the hives was well worth all the courage and effort it took to get it.

Cliff bees, as their name implies, build their hives on the rocky valley walls. Their huge combs, from three to four feet wide and some six to ten feet long, hang beneath the overhangs of what always seemed to be the sheerest, most inaccessible cliffs in the area. Perhaps these areas were chosen to gain protection from bears and other natural predators. Though Hidden Valley abounded in these cliffs, they were usually two or three days' tough walk from any river valley, trail or logical settling area. So Timotsu, as well as men in other villages who were equally fearless, would lead parties of men into the hills twice a year – usually in May and September – after the bees had made their honey, to bring back as large a supply as possible.

None of the hives was in what could be called by any stretch of the imagination an accessible location. The hunters would be called upon to employ every bit of ingenuity they had, not only to reach the hives, but to evade attacks from these vicious bees, which are more than an inch long and as round as your little finger. If it was at all possible to reach the hives from below, the honey-hunters lashed together ladders from bamboo and rattan; otherwise, a man was let down from above on a rattan sling. Fortunately, these materials are always at hand in the jungle. Rattan ropes, as big around as your thumb and as much as two or three hundred feet long, snake along the ground and up and down the trees. They are as strong as nylon line, and all a bee-hunter had to do to get a rope was cut the right length with his machete, split some into strips so he could tie a sling for himself, and then have a couple of companions belay the vine around a convenient tree to ease him down to the hive. Meanwhile, others in the party continually tended fires directly below the hive hoping the smoke would drive off the bees.

The men who actually went up to remove the honey were

usually selected because they were known to be unaffected by heights and somewhat immune to the bee stings. Since light-coloured clothing seemed to attract the attention of the bees, hunters usually wore black or other dark-coloured clothes, and they covered as much as possible of their head and neck and face with a towel or some piece of clothing. But, in spite of the precautions of smoke and protective clothing, they were almost sure to be stung. There was no way to escape the barbs, because the hunter needed his hands and even his feet for this work.

Dangling from a rattan rope two to three hundred feet above the ground, the bee-hunter swung back and forth like a pendulum, trying to get as close as possible to the back of the cliff and to drive several wooden spikes into crevices at various points in the cliff face. Next he tied rattan strands to the spikes, and by either holding these or standing on them, he steadied himself and manoeuvred into the most convenient position for working. Then, firmly anchored, the hunter signalled for the men on the cliff above to let down a container. This might be a large, round-bottomed cooking pot or one of the large bamboo tubes that served as buckets. Lacking anything else, the Lisu sometimes used one of their ordinary closely woven carrying baskets lined with banana leaves. If the bees were not attacking very much, the hunter removed the hive in sections – first the lower portion containing the bee grubs, then the top section containing the honey. But if the bees were causing a lot of trouble, the hunter removed the hive as close to the top as possible, and the separation of sections was done on the ground.

While the man above was doing his work, the men on the ground were also busy, not only keeping the smoky fires tended, but also spreading out plastic sheets. If sheets were unavailable, then the plentiful and versatile banana leaves were used. The purpose, of course, was to try to conserve as much as possible of the honey that dripped down from above while the hive was being removed.

The honey, very different from that of the small honeybee, is a sticky, watery substance. Much of it is unavoidably lost in the removal of the comb from the cliff, and also the unfortunate hunter is usually covered from head to toe with the sweet liquid. But most hunters usually persist until the hive is removed as completely as possible. The honey must be boiled to a thick consistency before it can be eaten. Although a few people can tolerate the raw honey, most people become extremely nauseated and dizzy as a result of eating it.

Going after honey is a very uncertain undertaking, so far as gain is concerned. A poor hive may yield a gallon or so of honey, but a rich hive might give as much as fifteen gallons or even a little more. Besides the honey, there is the royal jelly, of which there may be as little as a quart, or as much as a gallon, depending on the size of the hive. This is always separated from the honey, because it has a very distinctive flavour, and some people prize it as a delicacy. But the bee grubs are considered a delicacy by all, and a good hive may have several pounds of them.

An added inducement for making one of these dangerous expeditions is the fact that from these cliff-bee hives it is possible to obtain a good amount of beeswax, which is very much prized for lighting purposes. After the bee grubs are removed, the empty combs are placed in a big kettle of boiling water and allowed to cool. Any impurities that may remain in the wax settle to the bottom of the water in the kettle, while the wax rises to the top. After the wax cools and becomes solid, it is removed from the kettle. Sometimes this process is repeated as many as three times in order to remove all impurities. This produces a very good quality wax, which can be sold for as much as seventy-five cents per pound or traded to neighbours under the local barter system. At Binuzu, we used the beeswax for making candles.

Though most bee-hunters looked upon stings as a kind of routine occupational hazard, they did try to be especially careful to prevent stings around the neck. For some reason, the toxin would work rapidly from a sting in the neck area and begin to restrict breathing. Men have been known to die from only two or three such stings.

The worst bee accident we had in the valley happened to a friend of Jesse's named Aki. He was trying to reach a hive from a ladder that was too short when the whole hive seemed to open up and pour a rain of bees down on him. Before he could descend the ladder, his whole body began to swell, and Jesse and his other companions had to carry him into camp. There they rubbed Aki from head to toe with tiger fat, which we used in the jungle for treating cuts and abrasions much as the American pioneers used bear grease, and he recovered within three days. (This natural tiger fat should not be confused with the 'Tiger Balm' sold throughout the Orient by the late renowned Au Boon Haw of Hong Kong and touted as a remedy for all sort of ailments from burns to tennis elbow.)

Another insect, more deadly than the cliff bee but equally worth the hazards of the hunt in terms of enriching our diet, was the ground hornet. Early in our stay in the valley, Timotsu's quick eye spotted a hornet going down to earth. It was on the side of a steep hill at an elevation of about four thousand feet. Immediately, he marked the hole by blazing a tree and then planting a sapling so that it pointed right at the opening. Then, knowing that this type of hornets' nest always had three exits, he went round until he found the two other holes. He marked these, too, and came back looking for help.

Dropping in on Robert's family, he told them about the nest. 'This is a nest of *jeh-tu*, and they're fine eating', he said. 'They're very good for older people, too, just like vitamins!'

Timotsu explained that he needed at least eight people to watch all three holes. Conveniently, Robert and his boys would make up half that number if they were interested. 'Aren't they dangerous?' Robert asked.

'Oh, yes, the worst bees in the jungle,' Timotsu said, and then laughed, 'but when they see greenhorn white boys, they won't know what to make of them. They will probably die of fright.'

It was more than Robert or his sons could do to turn down this cheerful little man. When they agreed to go along, he told them more seriously of the plans and precautions for the hunt. It was necessary to go soon, in the full of the moon, when the larvae had developed enough to be edible but not enough to be too hard. The full moon would help, too, as a kind of protection, Timotsu promised, because its reflection on the jungle leaves would attract any hornet that might escape the attack. Hornets are so attracted to light that Timotsu told the boys to build paddles to swat them with, about six inches wide and a foot long, and to make them white enough to reflect the moonlight. The only other equipment they needed were large loads of torches made of lengths of bamboo with the ends spread, shredded and dried.

When, in the full of the moon, the party found the hornets' nest, their first job was to build a big fire from which to light their torches. Timotsu assigned small groups – the three Morse boys in one – to each hole. The attack had to be perfectly timed, and they all waited, wrapped in blankets and with flaming torches in hand, until Timotsu cried, 'Let's go.' Then they stuffed the torches right into the holes. The object was to smother the bees, then go in and dig them out. But the 'greenhorn white boys' were a little slow, and several angry hornets came through the wall of fire after them. They began swinging their paddles wildly. One hornet lighted on Stevie's back. Joni saw it and swung so hard he nearly sent his brother sprawling.

'Cut it out! What do you think you're doing?' Stevie snarled.

'Look, look there on the ground', Joni said.

When he saw the dead hornet, an evil-looking thing a good inch and a half long, Stevie calmed down. 'Hey, thanks', he said.

It took nearly three hours of shoving torches in the

holes before Timotsu calculated that it was safe to go after the prey. Even then, most of the hornets were not dead, but only stunned – and a stunned hornet can still sting. Taking big bamboo 'tweezers', which Timotsu had fashioned for the purpose, they began collecting the hornets and putting them into basketlike bamboo traps (in the style of fly-traps) from which they could not escape. The combs containing the larvae, and some hornets as well, were removed from the hive, placed in baskets, and carried over to beside the fire, where they were then dropped into waiting pans of boiling water. After a few moments they were removed, with any remaining hornets safely dead and the larvae cooked and ready for eating. The larvae are greyish-white and when cooked tasted something like cottage cheese. And, as Timotsu had told us, they do seem to be a source of quick energy – probably because of some sort of trace element or enzyme.

Exciting as such a hornet-hunt could be, it did not even compare on the scale of jungle excitement to an encounter with a tiger. Stevie was the first of the boys to have this frightening experience. Though the mighty Bengal tiger will soon be extinct unless firm restrictions are applied to hunting it for sport, there were few signs of this approaching doom in our Hidden Valley. There the Lisu saying that between sunset and sunrise the jungle belongs to the tiger was still very much in force. Its validity was brought home to us every time we noticed tiger tracks on the jungle trails. Several times we found these pug-marks within a few feet of our house, and though it is generally recognized that tigers are not inclined to attack humans unless provoked, no one has any desire to test this rule for fear of being the exception to it. But tigers are as curious as house cats and quite bold about satisfying their curiosity, as evidenced by their frequent visits to village pigsties.

The most dramatic display of a tiger's curiosity that any of us experienced was an episode involving Stevie and Sammy that took place during the course of our second winter season in the valley. The two boys had been hunting over new territory since daybreak and, in the late afternoon, found themselves still far from home on a ridge some miles to the south. Just as the sun was setting they came to a tree which, from the droppings beneath it, they recognized at once as the home base of a tribe of monkeys prized as tree pork. The two boys decided to make camp beside a little stream a short distance downwind from the monkey tree. If the monkeys returned to their roost during the night, the boys might well be able to bag a couple of them the next morning.

After a sparse supper of boiled rice, dried meat and tea, they were getting ready to crawl under their blankets, when Stevie heard the sudden snap of a bamboo branch on the other side of the stream. From the nature of the sound he knew that the broken branch was a good-sized one. This suggested that it had been snapped by a sizeable animal, perhaps one of the larger species of deer such as a sambar, coming down for a drink. Stevie reached for his .22 rifle, listening intently for what would come next. A few moments later, another bamboo stalk snapped, this time closer at hand. Stevie called softly to Sammy, who was getting crossbow arrows ready for use at first light the next morning. Now both boys listened for several minutes without moving or speaking.

Suddenly, a third stalk broke, this time on the near side of the brook; and this sound was followed by that of a large animal crashing through the underbrush, accompanied by the snapping of many twigs and branches. When the startling uproar ended, the animal was evidently not more than a dozen feet away, though still entirely invisible in the dense foliage. The question of what was making the noise now became one of much more imperative interest. Both boys moved quickly from beside the coals of their fire to a high rock ledge that bordered their camp-site on two sides. They waited. They could hear nothing at all. But whatever it was must still be there. Its next move would tell them what they had now begun to suspect. Soon they heard the unmistakable sound of soft footfalls in the dry underbrush, making a slow and careful circuit of their camp. This could mean only one thing, but a sort of deep dread prevented either of the boys from giving it a name.

Like all jungle animals, tigers fear fire. When camping in territory known to be frequented by tigers, prudent hunters usually lay out several camp-fires in a square and sleep within this perimenter. Another ruse often used under such circumstances, when there are two hunters present, is for both to sleep under the same blanket, with a head sticking out at each end. The theory is that the perplexed tiger, not knowing which head to pounce on first, will wind up by not pouncing on either. Stevie and Sammy realized that the most essential thing for them to do was to keep their fire burning brightly and make some sort of noise, as much to sustain their own courage as to try to scare their visitor away. They kept up a stream of conversation, dealing with the events of the past day and their plans for the morrow. The footsteps around the camp continued for about an hour. From time to time they stopped to listen, but when finally no further sounds were audible, they concluded that the tiger had either crept quietly away or gone to sleep. Each boy had with him a dagger as well as his .22 single-shot rifle – hardly the ideal weapons for the occasion, but at least better than none. Each kept both weapons at hand for the rest of the night. Exhausted by their long day's hunt, they dozed fitfully, taking turns in replenishing the fire from a dead tree within easy reach.

When they awoke the next morning, they found fresh pug-marks of a tiger only about twenty feet from where they slept. The boys were content to leave the monkey tree to him and headed straight for home as rapidly as possible.

Among the thoroughly mixed bag of books we had brought with us from Putao, a well-thumbed volume was the *Memoirs of James Corbett*, the story of the famous Anglo-Indian tiger-hunter. Stevie in particular was almost as familiar with this as with the Bible, and perhaps learned as much from Corbett as from his Lisu colleagues in our own community. The Lisu differed most from Corbett in that they were usually equipped, not with high-powered, big-game rifles designed to kill a tiger or elephant with a single shot, but with native crossbows or firearms intended for wild fowl, squirrels or rabbits. Instead of seeking encounters with the great cats, the Lisu avoided them as far as possible. What sometimes made this difficult was that tigers, at least in our valley, where human beings were still something of a novelty, would often follow a person through the jungle on a parallel path. Sometimes a tiger would even come out of the foliage and walk along in plain view, beside or behind a jungle wayfarer, apparently motivated more by mere curiosity than by hunger or any desire to kill. On one such occasion, when being followed along an elephant trail by a tiger who remained concealed in the underbrush, my brother Robert tried using the grunting noise he had learned from Tiger Mike. It worked, for the tiger slunk off into the underbrush without coming any closer.

Another time when the paths of tiger and human were likely to cross in our neighbourhood was when both were hunting the same quarry. One day Tommy was out hunting meat for the evening meal of the party of bee-hunters he was with. He came upon the trail of a barking deer, followed it, and at last spotted it. He was able to move to a point about thirty or forty feet away, from which he brought the deer down with a single shot through the heart. He saw the deer drop and started running towards it, when something made him stop and listen. Hearing nothing, he started to move towards the deer again, but at a walk. Then he heard a rustling in the underbrush off to the side. As he looked that way, he found himself staring into what he described as the biggest eyes he'd ever seen, and they belonged to a tiger!

'I was really scared,' he later recalled, 'as I realized I was only about fifteen feet from the tiger. I knew that he could be on me in about two leaps. My first instinct was to turn around and run, but I knew that if I turned my back to the tiger, I was done for, for sure. I remembered having read and heard that if you can hold the gaze of a wild animal, it has something like a hypnotic effect on it and it won't attack. So I kept staring that tiger in the eye and started slowly – very slowly – backing away in the direction from which I had come. I knew there was a big tree back there that I could climb, if I could just get to it. It seemed like hours that I was holding that tiger's gaze, but it probably wasn't more than a minute or so. As I got further away I moved a little more quickly, and when I knew I was near that big tree, I turned around and jumped behind it, ready to go up if the tiger came after me. The tiger gave one leap, then walked to the point where I had been standing and just stood there, looking around as if puzzled over the whole affair. I had my .22 rifle ready to fire over his head if he started in my direction, because I figured that would frighten and confuse him sufficiently to give me time to get up the tree. But he seemed to lose interest after a moment and turned around and went back to where the deer was lying. I decided I wasn't going to dispute his claim to the deer – maybe he'd been following it longer than I had anyway. I was plenty glad enough to just get out of there in a hurry and look elsewhere for our supper.'

The jungle was obviously a place of excitement at times, and even of terror. It was also a place of tedium and the kind of weariness that comes from low vitality. But there were compensations. For all of us, but perhaps at different times and in different degrees, there was a feeling of living within God's natural world that we had never known before. In a sense unknown to people who live within the sounds of civilization, there was a profound silence in those high mountains, the kind of silence that lends emphasis to every sound, whether it be the moaning of wind in the trees, the chatter of a rock-strewn brook, the crackle of a falling branch, or the mating call of a bird. By learning to listen to the jungle, you could read the state of the world around you as surely as any American gazing at his colour television set.

At night, for example, when the jungle was full of sound

– all the chirpings and burpings of cicadas, frogs, and the like – you knew that all was well. Indeed, there was an owl, called the *kampta* by the Lisu, whose cry – a kind of double *doo-doo* – would go all through a peaceful night at three- to five-minute intervals, like the 'all's well' call of a night watchman in a medieval town. And for weather-forecasting there was the rain-bird, which started singing thirty minutes before every downpour. Time and again we doubted his message and got wet – until we started timing it.

Quite apart from the animal sounds, there was a voice to the jungle that imparted a continual impression of ongoing life. Moving under a canopy of trees a hundred to a hundred and fifty feet high, you could hear the wind above you keeping the leaves dancing and rattling. Pine forests were the noisiest, with the breezes turning their singing boughs into a kind of natural orchestra. Leaves, branches, nuts and fruits were always dropping, tinkling and crashing from level to level through the tall trees with a kind of *che-che-che* sound. Often it was almost unnerving to experience such a state of continual motion around you in what was supposed to be the placid heart of nature. But in the end it became a reassuring evidence of the ongoing cycle of life.

Though the deep jungle could be a tangled, almost claustrophobic labyrinth, the hilly terrain was certain to provide a wide open vista around the next bend or the one after. This sensation of openness was reinforced by the way loud sounds like thunderclaps would echo for minutes from hill to hill, for miles. In an area where walking a straight mile could mean actually walking two miles down and two miles up, the Lisu had learned to use the echoing hills as a means of communication. By converting their tonal language into a kind of yodel, they could converse from one hillside to another. It was comically striking to hear two women chatting in clear falsetto yodels across a chasm of the wildest and most beautiful countryside in the world, saying such mundane things as: 'Come over here, there's a lot of firewood to be gathered.' 'No, you come over here, there's a lot of vegetables to be carried home.'

The freedom we had all sought in leaving Putao was certainly there around us in these lush jungles and open mountains. Even with the daily struggle for food, and the larger uncertainty of what the future might bring, none of us in the Morse family ever thought of turning back. But, as favourable reports began to filter back from those pioneering families who had gone into the wilder western section of Hidden Valley, we did begin to think of going forward. The hope of passage through India, which had led us to move up towards the border from Binuzu, faded as month after month went by with no more word than we had received at Green Water Flat. The problem now was finding a place where food could be grown, where we really could settle for as long as the Lord willed it.

In October 1966 everyone was looking forward to the first harvest, small though it might be. Plans were made in Binuzu for a Thanksgiving Service – the usual convention-type gathering, beginning on Friday evening and continuing through into Sunday. We were quite pleased to hear that a similar gathering was being planned in the western part of the area, at Chinquapin Hill, and to receive a request for some of us to attend. We had been wanting to go there anyway, to see how the people were getting along and find out what developments there had been in the area since Robert and I had visited it in April.

So in mid-October David and I, along with several Lisu companions, made the two-day journey to Chinquapin Hill to attend the convention. We found about a hundred and fifty people gathered for the services. In accordance with custom, they served one meal a day to all those present; it consisted of one small leaf-wrapped package of rice and one of meat. But they had difficulty in finding enough meat, since no one had pigs or chickens that could be used for the occasion, and they were dependent on what wild game they could find. But they had enough for a small package – a couple of tablespoonfuls – for each person.

While we were eating, David said, 'Hey, Dad, look at this.' I saw that he was holding a piece of bone, which I didn't consider strange, since he was eating meat. Then he said, 'You know what? I was just thinking as I ate that they had done a real good job of cooking this meat, and it tasted real good. Then, as I was gnawing on this bone, I suddenly thought that it was rather a funny shape for a chicken bone, and I looked more closely. Guess what! I've been chewing on a rat's nose! I was going to throw away the rest, then decided that since I liked it before I knew what it was, I could eat it just the same, knowing what it is. But next time, I think I'll ask!'

We found that the settlement at Chinquapin Hill was doing very well under the capable leadership of Sukin. They were making plans for gathering into one or two regular villages instead of being scattered about. But they wanted some of the missionaries to come and live in that area, so they could continue to have short-term Bible-training schools. I couldn't give them an answer, but I promised to talk it over with our families. They promised to build a house for whoever would come.

Meanwhile, I had also been talking to some of the people who had come to the convention from an area another day's travel to the west beyond Chinquapin Hill. They wanted me to come and look over their area and see if it would be suitable for our family to move to that location. David and I went, and both of us were even more favourably impressed with this valley, called Mu-pah (Big Valley), than with Chinquapin Hill. They said there were enough people in the area, not only to help us build a house, but to clear and help us plant a field to take care of our grain the following year, if only we would come and live there. In my own mind, I think, I was pretty sure even then that this was where our family would eventually settle, although I didn't know just when. I had to go back and discuss it with the rest of the family, and also with the elders and leaders in both Chinquapin Hill and Binuzu. As we were getting ready to leave Chinquapin Hill to return to Binuzu, a couple of the elders said, 'Don't forget that we will be having a Christmas convention. Some of you had better plan to come for that, too.'

As it turned out, it was Robert who went to the Christmas services at Chinquapin Hill. He had been there in April and had liked the area then. Now, seeing the new developments, he liked it even more; so it wasn't hard for the elders there to convince him that this was the place for his family to settle. Meanwhile, it had been decided, after much discussion, that I should make another trip to Big Valley to make the final arrangements for our family to move there, along with Drema Esther and Jesse. My parents felt they were needed in A-deh-di, although they wondered whether they could stay there alone if the rest of us moved. It seemed that the question of where to settle for the next year was gradually being answered for each family.

Chapter 8

... behold, tomorrow I will bring locusts into
your country, and they shall cover the face
of the land, so that no one can see the land;
and they shall eat what is left to you after the
hail, and they shall eat every tree of yours
which grows in the field.
EXODUS 10 : 4–5

Robert and his family were the first to move from A-deh-di into the area to the west. They started out early in January 1967, in the middle of the winter dry season, when travel is easiest. Betty had been suffering from severe arthritis for several years, even in Putao, but it became worse after they entered the valley. It was their hope to find a higher, possibly drier, climate that might ease her pains. Robert's boys looked forward to the move; the whole area within a few days' walk of Monkey Tree Hill had been thoroughly explored, and they were eager for new places to investigate. Betty was pregnant when they set out, and we promised that we would follow them in time for Helen to help at the time of delivery.

Our parents weren't very eager to move away from A-deh-di because they were nicely settled into a routine of useful work there. Furthermore, the villagers begged them to stay. 'Don't you folks go, too,' they told my parents, 'or there won't be anyone here to help us when we get sick or to teach us more.'

But we were committed to the move, and when I returned from another visit to Big Valley, it was to get my family. All the arrangements had been made; the house was under construction – in fact, it was about half finished – and the field area had been cleared. But two problems remained unsolved. We still worried about leaving my parents alone, lest they got sick or had an accident and were unable to cope with the situation. And we didn't have enough porters to carry all the things we would need ın our new location. Oddly enough, the solution to the two problems came in one package, although we didn't realize it at first. Because of Betty's approaching confinement, we decided to go ahead, taking just the things we had porters for, knowing that we would need to send for our other loads. So when we started westward on 16 February, it was with the expectation that the boys and the loads would catch up with us in two or three weeks at the most. Helen said afterwards that if she had known how long it would take them, she would never have left the boys, because it was to be ten and a half months before our family was all together again.

By the time we arrived, Robert and Betty's new house was beginning to take shape. The framework and roof were completed, and one big room in the centre, where the fireplace was, had flooring, and walls on two sides. Tarpaulins were put up on the remaining two sides, both as a windbreak and to afford privacy. The big room was the kitchen, dining room and living room for the moment, as well as the place where helpers and children slept. Robert and Betty were camping in the small building that had been erected to serve temporarily as a church. We had planned to camp out, but after getting caught in a downpour the very first night, stayed in the other half of the little church, while our children slept with Robert's children in the new house. Our porters stayed with friends or relatives in the village, and many of them returned to their homes the next day. The spring rains set in the day after we arrived and continued for about ten days. At that altitude, it was quite cold, with the temperature dipping to about forty degrees at night. We knew the rains would last for only a few days, so there was no point in trying to arrange more permanent quarters. It was also obvious that Betty's baby was due shortly.

About 4.00 a.m. on Monday, 27 February 1967, Robert came to call Helen. Going outside, she saw that Robert had rigged up an outdoor delivery room similar to the one Jesse had erected for Drema Esther. In a small clearing, Robert had built a fire and had strung blankets between the trees to provide some privacy. He had also fixed a bed for Betty by putting tarpaulins on the ground and then fixing bedding on top of that. Helen found Betty on this bed, near the warmth and light of the fire.

'I found her having a pretty hard time', Helen recalls. 'She had gone into labour about midnight, so by the time they called me at four o'clock her labour was well advanced. I thought the baby would be born almost right away, but her labour dragged on until about 6.00 a.m. I realized what the trouble was: it was a breech birth, buttocks first. This realization gave me butterflies in my stomach for a time, because I had helped with this type of delivery only once, years before, when working in a hospital, with a doctor attending. We prayed for Betty, and for the child, and when I saw the baby was about to be born, I felt I should tell Betty, so she could co-operate fully – and that she did. She was a very good patient.

'The baby, a little girl, was born about 7.00 a.m., with no complications. She was a very small baby, less than six pounds, I would guess. She gave us a few anxious moments at first, but soon was crying lustily. We prayed again after the baby was born, and thanked God that both Betty and the baby were all right.'

All the little girls – sisters and cousins – were thrilled upon hearing that the baby had actually been born. And for two days, there was a great deal of rivalry and jealousy over who was next in line to hold the baby or carry her on their back, Lisu-style.

The baby was named Genevieve after her maternal grandmother. Her birth rounded out the curious family pattern of the second generation of Morses; like us, Robert and Betty now had three sons and three daughters. Two days later, assured that Genevieve was thriving and Betty doing well, our family moved on west into Mu-pah and Zi-yu-di Village.

From the ridge that overlooked this part of Hidden Valley, it was immediately apparent why Mu-pah held promise of being able to support a larger number of people than the area around Binuzu. A sort of shallow bowl some ten miles in diameter, Mu-pah provided land far more suitable for clearing and planting fields than the steep hillsides to the east. As we viewed it from our lookout point, we had a strong feeling that this was the land to which the Lord had been leading us, the place where he wanted us to live. Before we headed down into the valley, we stopped for prayer – not only a prayer of thanks but a prayer for protection. We asked God then and there to help us overcome the evil spirits that had held undisputed claim to Hidden Valley for so long, and to bless the hard work of this adventurous people.

From the lookout point we had been able to see the smoke rising from the houses in Zi-yu-di, and it looked quite close. Actually, we still had about two hours of travel, for to reach the settlement we had to descend to the river, wade across it, climb up a slippery shale embankment, and continue on up the steep hillside. Our route lay through an area that had been cut for a field but not yet burned, which meant rough going. The path was blocked by fallen trees, and we had to make our way over or along the trunks of these fallen jungle giants. Progress was slow because we had to clamber over limbs that had not yet been removed and pushed our way through leafy branches. But we eventually reached the top of the hill and emerged suddenly on to a flat area. We passed several houses, stopping to shake hands with the people who had come out to welcome us 'home'.

On the far side of the village, we finally came to the clearing that was to be our field. Our new neighbours had prepared a big field, about four or five acres, at one side of which was the partially finished house that was to be our home for the next three years. The framework and floor were finished, and the roof about two-thirds complete. There were no walls, but tarpaulins had been fastened around the sides to keep out the cold wind and rain. Waiting to greet us were Drema Esther, Jesse and their children, who had arrived two weeks earlier, and were to be staying with us until the completion of their own house on the other side of a small stream. It was good to get a place we could once again call home. Our one regret was that David and Tommy were not there, so we could enjoy our new house together. It was such a vast improvement over the tent and then the small, crowded house, where all eight of us shared one bedroom, that had been our quarters during the past year. By comparison, this new house – the largest in the village – seemed really spacious, a veritable mansion, and we thanked God for it.

As teachers and preachers, we never tried to farm the mountain jungle ourselves, except for clearing one small plot when we first arrived in Zi-yu-di. This effort only increased our admiration for the Lisu planters, not only for the amount of labour they were willing to perform, but for their technical skills. The slash-and-burn form of agriculture that the Lisu have practised since the dawn of their history may seem crude to farmers elsewhere, but it requires considerable knowledge and expertise. First the area to be burned off must be judiciously chosen for quality of soil, exposure to sunlight, water-supply and accessibility. Then the existing jungle growth has to be carefully appraised and the burning procedure skilfully executed.

In clearing jungle terrain, the first step is to cut down all the undergrowth, leaving only the trees standing. The trees are then felled, so that the wood in their crests can be used as the primary tinder for the flames that must also consume the dense jungle underbrush, converting it all into wood-ash fertilizer as evenly distributed as possible. The trunks are usually too big to be consumed by the flames, and remain on the ground to serve as paths through the eventual crop area. The only tools available to the Lisu besides the fire itself are machetes and primitive axes. Hence the number, the size and the position of the trees that need to be felled must be accurately taken into account. For a field about an acre in size, four or five trees between one and two feet in diameter are ideal. Trees too big or too numerous take too much time to cut down and trees too small or too few will not provide enough of the right sort of fuel for the purpose at hand.

To fell the trees so that their trunks serve as pathways and their limbs provide proper fuel is a task that calls for a high degree of woodcraft and manual dexterity. Incisions in the trunks must be placed only after shrewd calculation of the angle of growth and weight distribution of each tree. Sometimes, in the case of trees with especially thick trunks, cutting platforms are built so that the incision can be made ten, twenty or even thirty feet above ground, where their diameter will be smaller.

The first thing most Westerners ask about regarding this slash-and-burn technique is the danger of forest fire. In reality, this presents no problem at all. The main concern is how to coax the foliage to catch fire in the first place, and then how to keep it burning. Both feats can be performed in the rain-forest jungle only towards the end of the six-month dry season. Felling the trees so that they fall into a favourable pattern and then setting the flames to work under advantageous wind conditions are both critically important – and, of course, a heavy shower at any point in the procedure can be a serious setback or even a catastrophe. Even after the flames have consumed most of the foliage, the farmer will always be faced with much work in clearing away the remnants of vines, shrubs and weed cover with his axe and machete.

Once the foliage has been burned and the ashes smoothed out evenly across the cleared areas, the seed rice, carried in a basket, is planted with a sharp stick. The farmer uses the stick to make a hole about two to three inches deep and drops in a few seeds. Corn and other fast-growing grains are usually planted along with the rice seed, so that their stalks will shelter the slower and more delicate rice shoots from both heavy rains and the fierce heat of the tropical sun. Even in the monsoon season of torrential showers, the sun is likely to shine during many hours of each week. In addition to its value as a fertilizer, the blanket of wood ash that covers the seeded area has another, more specialized function – to rid the area of leeches that could make working the fields an intolerable torture.

There are two seasons of crops for which the grower must prepare. The early crops, which ripen in late June or early July, include such things as millet, corn, squash and cucumbers. These provide the main items of diet until the earliest rice is harvested, in late September or early October. The main rice crop follows in late November and early December. The summer diet may also be enriched with several varieties of mushrooms that are found in the jungle, as well as with various leaves and roots.

When we reached Zi-yu-di – which in Lisu means 'Zion', or 'the heavenly city' – all the news was good. Though the people were still living mostly off the jungle, their first crops had yielded enough seed grain to make adequate fields during the 1967 spring planting season. Thus there was real hope that the coming harvest would yield more than enough food to sustain life and allow the people time to turn their hands to other productive work. All together, some hundred and fifty families, or about seven hundred and fifty people, had by that time scattered themselves around into small villages in Mu-pah Valley, and they included some of the most enterprising and independent of the people who had left Putao with us. Of course, they owed much to their exceptional leaders.

One of these, a man named Boyenu, was literally outstanding. Five feet eleven inches tall, he towered a good four inches over the average Lisu. He was a typical hunter-turned-leader. Back in the Putao days, he was always off in the jungle and had earned an undying reputation for strength and courage by surviving a barehanded fight with an elephant. The incident occurred when Boyenu, trying to shoot one elephant, realized that another elephant was charging him. He tried to run away, but stumbled over a log, and the elephant came right down on top of him, trying to pin him against the log with its trunk and crush him to death.

A muscular, agile man, Boyenu began to kick the elephant's trunk. He succeeded in kicking the trunk into the elephant's mouth, and, apparently confused, the great beast kneeled on top of Boyenu, pinning him against the log with its chest. Somehow Boyenu clung to the elephant's chest, and when it reared up in another effort to crush him, slid out between the elephant's hind legs. The elephant went on over the log, and Boyenu ran for his life. The only injury he sustained in the battle was a broken rib, but he developed a lifelong respect for the speed and power of an angry elephant.

Boyenu's clan, the Lah-puh, were generally big and strong, and they had a spirit of co-operation that made things easier for their leader. Still the superb hunter, Boyenu kept the whole village of about a hundred people supplied with meat. In return, he asked for a kind of obedience. 'You, you, and you,' he'd say, 'go out and find some mountain ferns. You, you, and you, come hunting with me. You, you, and you, start clearing fields.' The people jumped to follow his orders because they had found quite early that he had the canny knowledge of the jungle and the inventive turn of mind that would assure their survival.

Boyenu's astuteness first became evident in his selection of a site for the village. It was on a ridge called Gu-to, meaning Wintergreen Knoll, which everyone else had passed by because of its great wintergreen trees rising to heights of two hundred and fifty feet or more. Although these trees exude the sweet fragrance of wintergreen, from bark and leaf alike, they represented formidable obstacles to the average Lisu farmer. Their trunks were some twelve feet around, and it would take a hard-working man two days to cut down just one tree. But Boyenu reasoned that soil that could produce such jungle giants would be equally productive for rice and other crops. The problem was how to fell enough trees in the time allowed by the short dry season, and the solution Boyenu proposed was ingenious.

Knowing he had a group of followers who were willing to work together, Boyenu instructed them to build bamboo platforms around each tree until they reached a height where the trunk was slender enough to make for easy cutting. Tree after tree was attacked this way, from platforms ranging up to thirty feet in height. By the time we had a look at the Gu-to fields, they were unlike anything you could imagine in an agricultural area. Great stumps stood about them like the massive pillars of some prehistoric forum. But Boyenu had been right about the soil. Around the stumps, corn and rice grew profusely.

Another successful leader in the western end of Hidden Valley was the charismatic trader, Sukin. Unlike Boyenu, who was basically a clan leader, Sukin had gathered around him a polyglot group of people who knew and trusted him as a result of his dealings back in Putao. If Boyenu's tight, co-operative operations were somewhat communal in nature, Sukin's were pure free enterprise. To begin with, Sukin established his leadership by relieving his followers from their debts to him in return for a certain amount of manual labour. As a result he was able to push them into clearing fields that were at least three times the size of those at Gu-to. When the harvest came in, Sukin distributed it much as a stock company might give out dividends to shareholders – to each according to his contribution. Many of Sukin's followers, therefore, had more rice or seed than they could use and were able to begin trading for other necessities.

Whatever the social system – indeed, both groups respected each other's methods and had established a sort of friendly rivalry as to results – the people in Mu-pah were far more successful than their discouraged friends and relatives in the Binuzu area. Given any kind of luck, they would soon be needing our services in such longer-range projects as religious instruction, teaching and building schools and churches. So we decided to devote our efforts to getting a roof over our heads before the rains came again.

Obtaining food had been very nearly an obsession with us for more than a year now, and we were intrigued, and very encouraged, when some villagers came round a few days after we reached Zi-yu-di and told us there was a lot of meat a few hours' walk away. The only member of the family we could spare to go with them was young Ronnie, who was thirteen at the time. He recorded the experience in his diary:

'It was sort of mysterious at first. They wouldn't say what kind of meat it was, but after a while it became clear that a lot of other people were going too, and we asked if it was elephant. They said yes, it was. They thought that it would be good to share it with everybody, as it was so humid and hot that the meat would spoil immediately. On the way up they told me the story.

'The Lisu don't like to kill elephants, because they are such good trail-makers. But for food, in time of necessity, they thought it was worth a try. They really didn't have the weapons for killing elephants, so they tried different methods of loading spears in a muzzle-loader. They made a kind of spear with a sago-palm shaft, rounded and smoothed and tipped with a little peg with gunpowder inside. The shaft would penetrate the elephant's skin like a harpoon and then explode. Sometimes they put poison on the tip, too.

'So they brought this elephant down, and he had fallen in a little clearing on his knees with his back feet stretched out. They opened its side with an axe, cutting through the ribs and spreading them like opening doors. When I got there, some fifteen people were working around the elephant, and there were these huge racks about two feet off the ground with fires underneath where the cut meat was drying. The skin of the elephant was so tough that the men would sharpen their knives on it before going in after chunks of meat. They had pulled the insides out, and they were piled alongside the carcass like huge bags. It was unbelievable that even an elephant could carry so much around inside him.

' "Well," someone said to me, "help yourself." So I got out my knife and started to cut, sort of sawing away in a wall of meat. I just cut out this great chunk – and suddenly the smell hit me! It was awful. And when I put my hand inside, the meat was hot to the touch. I don't know whether it was from rotting or not. People were cutting meat as fast as they could and just throwing it on the ground, and the flies and maggots were already crawling around. It just gave me the creeps to see all those maggots and swarms of flies laying eggs as fast as they could! I could hardly wait to get away. I cut about three chunks of meat and ran a stick through them so I could carry them back and left.'

Meat was protein, and we ate the elephant, as we ate everything else that came our way during those days. Through the rains, we prayed for a bountiful harvest, and when the fields began to ripen, it looked as if our prayers had been answered. We were particularly excited because, true to their word, the villagers had planted fields for us. It was our first experience of being 'farmers' in this way, and we were eagerly looking for results. Then one day the headman of Zi-yu-di, Heh-ah-tsah, reported seeing some caterpillars in his fields. What happened next was recorded by our son Ronnie in his diary.

'They didn't seem to be a danger at the beginning, as they were only the size of a pencil lead, and a quarter-inch long. Some were black, others were striped, some were ringed, and the colours, too, differed in a few ways: green, black, orange, speckled, and so on. They would begin in one spot and eat outwards in all directions on the tender rice seedlings. The rice was in the prime of growth, ten, fifteen, eighteen inches high. And the bugs grew rapidly. In a week, they had tripled in size, and where the rice had been so thick there now remained only the tough parts of the stalks, stubble only three or four inches high.

'The headman wasn't worried at first, thinking they would soon go away. But they didn't go away, no, they spread out and grew (and their appetites with them!) till the whole field was reduced to stubble. With half his field gone, on which he depended for all next year's food grain, the headman was definitely worried. He pleaded with the others of the village to come and see and also asked everybody to pray for his field, that the Lord would stop the plague.

'At first no one was much concerned, till some folks happened to go down and saw for themselves what was happening. When they, in turn, began spreading the word, everybody woke up to the danger and began to be concerned too. The field was about two-thirds consumed when we went to have a look. It was at the extreme lower end of the village, and we lived at the extreme upper (north) end, so it was not too simple to just look in. But one day we did go with a couple of others. There's no way to describe what I saw; it petrified me, stunned me, and chilled my blood. Ever creeping, ever eating away like mad, ten to twenty bugs were racing up and down a single clump of rice plant, steadily reducing the plant, the field, to waste. Here, before my eyes, was happening what I had only read in books or heard told.

'I tell you, I sure felt a surge of pity for the headman's family, and what can one say to a person in such a predicament? "Never mind, it will soon pass", or "It will grow back again", or such like? Would it? Even the old folks, who were learned in such things, couldn't say what was the cause of it or from where the bugs came. Neither did anyone remember anything like it in the past. They were nonplussed, to say the least. There was no remedy either. The only thing left to do was to pray. Though nobody said it, everybody knew what could be the result if this plague wasn't stopped. At first, everybody was asked to remember the matter and pray about it, and at every church service, prayers were offered.

'Yet the plague, for that's what it was, continued to spread – like wildfire, I'd say – till almost every field was full of the things. Unable to just stand around watching all their work going up in smoke, as it were, most folks tried out ways to save their fields, or at least part of them. They would take their chickens and let them loose in the fields. The chickens ate the caterpillars, but they soon were filled up, and hardly a dent was noticeable in the caterpillar population. They just marched forward, in a mad frenzy to eat all they could and grow.

'Some people, one family in particular, went out in their field with baskets, men, women and children, from early dawn till late at night, picking up the caterpillars and putting them in their baskets. When one basket (about a bushel size) was full, they dug a hole and buried them! In just one day one family gathered three bushelfuls, from only one field. Yet the caterpillars were never scarce. In fact, they seemed to multiply. They weren't hairy or fuzzy like other caterpillars, neither did they sting. But they did bite. They were wicked-looking things – their faces, I mean. Oh yes, they had faces, all right.

'One day we found that they had arrived in our field, too. Then word came that people in every village were experiencing the same trouble, in some places more than others. This was very bad news. Everywhere reports came in of how their fields were being consumed steadily, right before their eyes, and they were powerless to stop them. Different ways were tried, but they all ended the same way: failure to halt the pests. We were no exception. We, too, tried on our own, but failed like everyone else. What to do? came the despairing cry from everywhere.

'Pray. We had done what we (as humans) could. We had prayed, but not as intensely as we should have. I wouldn't say all the prayers offered were unanswered. Some were delivered. But mostly, no one had heard any word of anyone being delivered by the Lord – not yet. Also, who knew how much worse, or faster, the pests might have devoured the field, were it not for all the prayers? As it turned out, most folks' fields were about one-half gone when the village folks – preachers, teachers, elders, deacons, song-leaders and congregation members – came to meet together to decide on a course of action.

'It was decided that evening that one person from each

family, if not more, would meet, and they would go from field to field, stopping in each field to sing and pray for those fields. In a single day we went to every field and sang and prayed in earnest for the deliverance of the crops from the caterpillar pests. We all knew that only God could save the crops now. I truly believe that people don't pray in real earnest ordinarily, until something really hopeless comes along – then they throw themselves upon the Lord in utter dependence and reliance. This may not always be the case, but it is true in a lot of cases. It certainly was true in ours. We *knew* how helpless we were and how futile were our efforts to find a way of deliverance (we had no sprays, no insecticides, nothing). I think the Lord wanted us to see how futile our efforts were, to really see for ourselves how helpless man is without God's sustaining and preserving care. Otherwise, why didn't he answer our prayer at the first? He could have, but he didn't. Not because he didn't want to, or couldn't, but because we didn't turn to him in utter dependence as we should have. So he waited till we did – just in time.

'After we did the touring, we waited for God to show his hand. There, too, our faith was put to a test. That the Lord would save the crops we were certain, but how, or when, we knew not. One day passed, then two days, and that evening some folks testified that there didn't seem to be quite so many caterpillars. Another man said he saw a lot of birds flying into his field, and it looked like they were pecking at the caterpillars. Still another said he noticed that the caterpillars seemed to all be crawling down into the base of the rice plants. These were only observations, no solid testimony of complete deliverance yet, as we had prayed and asked for. Yet it strengthened our faith, everybody's faith, so we prayed even more earnestly that night, for a *complete deliverance*.

'The next day, the third day, I went out early into our fields to have a look. I didn't dare look. Slowly, I began to search the plants for the caterpillars. There was one! I looked closer. It turned out to be an eaten-out section instead. I searched the plants more carefully. No sign of any activity anywhere. I looked in the roots, and there I found some, stock-still. Only the shattered ruins remained to testify that there had been a very destructive force here. All that day we kept an eye on the field, hardly daring to believe what our eyes saw. Yet we rejoiced, for, once the Lord starts to work, it isn't in a slipshod manner. It's in a cool, decisive, clean-sweep job. And that is what happened. Everywhere, people were waking up to find that the pests were entirely gone, plumb disappeared, or else very nearly so. What rejoicing and praising there was then! Our faith in God was very much increased by this experience, or strengthened rather. We had seen God in action, and we felt the power of his word.'

To add to our assurance that the Lord had truly answered our prayers, we heard on the radio broadcast from Rangoon that the same or a similar type of plague was destroying thousands of acres of crops in lower Burma, and none of the insecticides seemed to be effective against it.

When the caterpillar plague had passed and it was evident that there would be some harvest, enough at least to guarantee seeds for the following year, the people of Mu-pah began to plan for a great Christmas convention such as we had not enjoyed since our days back in Putao.

The convention was held at Lahwazado, or Tiger Feast Hill, the largest village in the whole western area. The reason for choosing Lahwazado became apparent the minute we rounded a corner in the narrow jungle trail and came upon the church house the village people had erected for the occasion. To us the sight was as inspiring as the vista of a great medieval cathedral rising out of the European plains. Although it was, in fact, only some forty feet by sixty in size, it stood in a wide clearing and dominated the surrounding space in the same way that Notre-Dame and Chartres dominate the urban landscape around them. Even more impressive, perhaps, than its size was the fact that it was built of wooden planks split from jungle trees, rather than bamboo. With its four solid walls and its ridge-pole some twenty-five feet above the ground, it represented a spectacular accomplishment for people who had moved into virgin jungle only eighteen months before.

Some four hundred people gathered for the event – a remarkable turn-out, considering that each delegate had to leave several members of his family at home to care for the children and livestock. Much too numerous to crowd in under the church roof, the group spread out under lean-to coverings that extended the area of the church house by ten or fifteen feet on all sides. Services began in the evening and went on by the light of beeswax candles late into the night. On one of our three nights there, most of those attending gathered around a big camp-fire in the church-yard and stayed on until dawn. They were so happy to be reunited after months of solitary jungle life that they could not bear to break apart until the next day's first light showed how long they had stayed.

With their penchant for making joyful noises, the Lisu indulged in a great deal of hymn-singing, as well as preaching and praising God. There was much to rejoice about. A good part of the 1967 harvest had, indeed, survived, and with seed to spare and growing knowledge of the area, there was every reason to hope that the following year would be even better. The people of Hidden Valley were putting down roots now. This once wild and lonely pocket in the high Himalayas was becoming home.

But there was another kind of prayer, too. Evidence abounded, at least as far as the Lisu were concerned, that the demonic spirit of Hidden Valley had not yet been fully laid to rest. Not only was the caterpillar plague fresh in everyone's memory, but there was particularly distressing news from the ten or so families who had pushed west beyond Mu-pah into another gentle depression called Bamboo Flats. There was something almost oppressive in the air, they reported, and every one of them had suffered from frightening nightmares almost every night. Weird accidents occurred, occasionally bringing death. For example, a child was killed when he fell out of a tree he was climbing.

We decided as a congregation to ask that God's power be exercised against these unseen forces of evil. Though Robert and I were practical men, trained in Western theology, we had experienced enough of what an actual, or even a supposed, curse can do to take these matters quite seriously. We do not believe that evil spirits can be overcome by dramatically flashing a symbol such as a cross or a Bible in the place where they are thought to be. But we do believe in the power of God to arm the believer inwardly, so that he can overcome whatever malevolent forces may be at work, either in the environment around him or within his own mind.

So we all prayed together to overcome the influence of these evil forces in the entire area, and the prayer was dramatically answered – at least from Bamboo Flats. A letter came from there one day not long after the gathering, reporting that one of the people had dreamed of a horrible monsterlike beast that was being trussed up and burned in a big bonfire. The beast was utterly destroyed in the flames, according to the dreamer. Was it just a dream? Perhaps so, but these simple people believe that God is able to send them dreams, and that they have meanings. At any rate, from that time on, the people stopped having nightmares in Bamboo Flats, and there were no more inexplicable accidents. Remarkable? We no longer thought so. It was just another instance of God's unseen hand at work. Without such evidence that faith can work miracles, we – not only the Morses but our Lisu friends – would long ago have flung ourselves on the mercy of the nearest authorities. With such faith, we held the future to be full of wonders.

Chapter 9

If you will diligently hearken to the voice of the
Lord your God, and do that which is right in
his eyes, and give heed to his commandments
and keep all his statutes, I will put none of
the diseases upon you which I put upon the
Egyptians . . .
EXODUS 15 : 26

Even though Robert and I thought it was best to settle in
the western part of Hidden Valley, my parents were
reluctant to leave the little village of A-deh-di, near
Binuzu, where they had once more begun to put down
roots. In the course of a long life, they had moved often,
each time taking up their work of teaching, healing and
planting. But we could understand how, at the age of
seventy, weakened by their limited diet of jungle food, another four or five days' move seemed almost too much for
them. As somebody pointed out to us, 'Even Moses led only
one exodus.'

In any case, we were all aware that the work they were
getting under way would later prove of value to all of us,
wherever we were in the valley. At A-deh-di, as in Putao,
my father's first priority was his limited practice of medicine,
for this was the field in which he had specialized during his
more than forty years in the mission field. When he was a
high-school student in Tulsa, his dream had been to
become a doctor, but the dream could not be realized
because he lacked the money to study medicine. However,
he took courses in practical medicine while he was in
seminary and pursued his medical studies further in 1929,
during his furlough. In addition, he had obtained and
studied a number of good medical books, and his studies,
together with his practical experience and opportunities for
observation, had given him a wide knowledge of semi-
tropical diseases and their treatment.

The beginning point for medical treatment among the

people with whom we worked was the introduction of rudimentary Western concepts of hygiene and sanitation. We all tried to help in this 'public health' phase of our work by teaching and emphasizing these concepts wherever we went, to whoever would listen. And after a number of years in the Putao area, not only were pigs kept penned, not only did each family have its toilet, but these things were an accepted way of life, not just some peculiar idea of the white teachers. It was the missionaries who first introduced a spray campaign in the Putao plains – using gammexane, and treating each house in a village – in an effort to reduce the incidence of malaria, a scourge in that area. Later the spray campaign was taken up by the government, on a much larger scale than we were able to afford, and malaria was very nearly eliminated from the plains.

However, it was not in this broad and rather impersonal field of public health that my father gained his reputation, but in the careful diagnosis and treatment of individual patients. For instance, his efforts helped reduce the high rate of infant mortality. When we arrived in Putao, four out of five babies born to the tribespeople died before reaching the age of seven. Those who were not Christian, and even some of the new Christians, attributed the death of small children to evil spirits. They would often give their children dreadful names like Pig-turd or Cross-eye, believing that the spirits would not bother to attack a person so obviously worthless. As a result of my father's treatment of their children's illnesses – medicine administered along with prayer – and of their own increased knowledge of the basic rules of hygiene and sanitation, the death-rate had dropped to about one in ten by the time we left Putao.

Of course, no one knew better than my father the extent of his own limitations, and there were many times when, puzzled and not knowing what treatment to administer, he prayed for – and received – the wisdom he needed. I think that is why, even in Putao, where there was a hospital with a qualified doctor, people came to my father from far and wide, often travelling several days. They had confidence in the white teacher who prayed for them and treated them with loving concern as well as medicine. Because of the limited facilities and primitive conditions amid which he worked most of the time, my father acquired a philosophy that was perhaps best articulated by the late Dr Tom Dooley, who observed that under such conditions, 'the perfect becomes the enemy of the good'. He always tried to do what he could for everyone who came, even if he wasn't able to do all that was needed.

My father and mother quickly established the routine that had become so familiar to them during their nearly fifty years of missionary life. In the morning, with my mother often helping too, my father conducted a free clinic, dispensing medicines, treatment and advice to all comers. His dispensary – actually the living room and kitchen of the two-room house – was about twelve feet square, with a Lisu-style fireplace in the centre.

His working day usually started early, about dawn, when people began the day's activities. Someone might be getting an attack of malaria, perhaps, or had a headache or otherwise felt bad, but he still had to work and needed medicine to keep him up and going. Sometimes it was a hunter, carrying his crossbow; or it might be someone on the way to his field, with his basket of seed; or it might be someone on his way to the jungle area where the atu grew, and where he would be staying a couple of weeks or more, who wanted some aspirin or malaria medicine to take with him in case he got sick while away from home. Later, after the morning chores were finished, came those who were too sick to go out to their work – sometimes an expectant mother or a mother with small children; frequently a grandmother who was either sick herself or brought a sick grandchild for whom she was caring while the parents went out to the fields. These patients would come in and sit on the floor beside the fire. As the crowd grew, some of the people had to sit at the back, against the wall, and sometimes there was an overflow that had to move to the porch. Babies cried and were fed, and people exchanged titbits of news and gossip while they waited their turn. Meanwhile, my father interviewed and treated the patients. All this often took until midday or later, but during the afternoons my father usually managed to get away from his 'office'. Back in Putao he had spent a lot of time working in his orchard, or making house calls. But here he had no orchard as yet, and many of the homes were too far away to visit, so he worked in the yard and visited those nearby homes where he was needed.

House calls outside a radius of five miles – within which some eighty families were then living, in three or four villages – would have kept my father away from his consulting room overnight or even longer. Therefore, patients from further away with severe injuries or ailments would be brought by litter to A-deh-di. There was no space for them to stay at my parents' house, so they would have to be billeted in the other five or six houses in the village. With one or more patients quartered in each of them most of the time, the village homes looked rather like miniature hospital wards. The villagers were wonderfully tolerant about this arrangement, probably because most of them had also had the experience of being sick while away from home and had stayed with other people.

My father has a tremendous thirst for knowledge on subjects in which he is interested. He would spend hours pouring over his medical books, trying to learn more about the illnesses he saw every day. In his many years in the Orient he had also developed a respect for the knowledge of the herb doctors – not the quacks who bottled coloured water and sold it as a cure-all, but those who had studied the various plants and really knew their properties and uses. Back in Putao, for example, we had learned the efficacy of a certain leaf that, when crushed and made into a tealike brew, promoted the healing of broken bones. When my mother fell from a horse and broke her shoulder, she was given this medicine. Her arm healed perfectly, even without having been in a cast. Even after arriving in

Hidden Valley, my father had had occasion to witness the effectiveness of other jungle medicines.

One of our faithful Lisu pastors, who was living in A-deh-di, was very skilled in the use of herbal medicines. He had learned a lot from an old Chinese herb doctor he had known when he was growing up, and had subsequently added to his knowledge from a variety of other sources. Herb doctors are usually very close-mouthed about their remedies, but this man shared with my father a few of his jealously guarded secrets. He knew that the knowledge would be used, not for personal gain, but to help other people. Jungle medicine, as developed by the hill tribes over the centuries, is by no means a matter of superstition and folklore. Many of the forest plants of which they have traditionally made medicinal use – for example, oil of wintergreen, quinine, witch-hazel, and, of course, opium – still retain an important place in our Western pharmacopoeia. The tribespeople know about literally hundreds of others that are comparably effective, such as those they use to stop bleeding, or to relieve the discomfort of strained or fatigued muscles. Most of these medicines they distil or press from bark, leaves or petals, but there is an even wider array of ointments and elixirs derived from jungle animals. Indeed, the Lisu love to take medicine almost as much as they love to talk. They will try anything – once. One intrepid man, afflicted with a persistent stomach disorder, decided that gammexane, which had proved so effective in suppressing malarial mosquitoes, might work in destroying the germs causing his sickness. It worked all right: after a swallow or two produced some days of agony worse than anything he had endured up till then, he pronounced himself cured. It was always a wonder to us that more of these self-appointed medical guinea-pigs didn't kill themselves.

Most of my father's practice in Binuzu was conducted on a strictly utilitarian plane. He set bones fractured in accidents, performed minor external surgery, and prescribed remedies from the limited stock of brand-name or trade-marked drugs that we had brought with us. For the first year or two, much of his practice consisted of treating chronic malaria cases, the disease having been carried with them by long-time residents of the Putao plain. Because there were fewer mosquitoes in the higher altitude of our Himalayan valley, most of these cases gradually cleared up. Even some cases of tuberculosis were cured or showed marked improvement. Digestive and other difficulties brought on by the rigours of life on the frontier became the common complaints. Actually, the death-rate from illness among our settlers was astonishingly low – not more than ten or twelve among the entire two thousand people during the six years of our stay.

By far the most frequent acute ailment among the Lisu in Hidden Valley, as it had been in the plains, was simple toothache. For this complaint there were not many effective remedies. The Lisu sometimes use finely powdered elephant tusk, which they pack into a cavity in a tooth, as well as poultices and solutions made from roots or leaves. My father could give them the old stand-by, oil of cloves. But if all these failed to give relief, the only remaining treatment was immediate extraction. My father once estimated that the number of teeth he had pulled in the course of his career totalled well into five figures.

My father's other main interest outside religious instruction and spiritual guidance was horticulture. In emulation of Johnny Appleseed, whose legend had made a deep impression on him during his younger days, my father began planting apple trees in Yunnan. He soon found that the mild and sunny climate there was equally well suited to fruits like peaches, plums, pears and grapes. Moreover, some varieties of citrus were native to Yunnan, and the growing of oranges – which Marco Polo originally brought to Europe from China – was an important adjunct to the agronomy of the whole area. Before we left Yunnan, oranges had become a major crop, along with several varieties of peaches, most notably the J. F. Hale. Meanwhile, my father trained himself to be an expert at grafting procedures. And, best of all, he developed reliable sources of supplies in the United States, which stood him in good stead when we made the move to Putao after World War II.

The great advantage of fruit-growing was that it offered the quickest and least expensive way of improving both the health and the economic status of the whole community. The sole requisites from outside were pruning knives, stones on which to sharpen them, and an adequate supply of scions, the cuttings from fruit trees of proven excellence, that could be grafted on to the stocks of the hardy but less productive indigenous trees. My father got his scions mainly from growers in Florida and California. He had contacted them while in the United States, through members of some of our supporting congregations. The pruning knives and whetstones were sent as a gift by a Boy Scout troop in Oklahoma. This came as a result of his having renewed a lifelong friendship with a former school-mate who was still active in Scouting. The only other ingredient needed was the knowledge of how to do the actual grafting – and in this speciality the Lisu quickly proved themselves apt pupils.

In the hill country above Putao, wild lemon trees – whose fruit was so dry and bitter as to be virtually inedible – had traditionally been used for fences around pasture-land because of their murderously sharp thorns. Offshoot root growth from these wild-lemon fences provided a good base on which to graft some of the finest varieties of oranges and other citrus fruits grown in the United States. In Putao, as in Yunnan, my father found an almost perfect climate for citrus culture. Though we might get a bit of frost on winter nights when the temperature could drop as low as 34 degrees, it was never a killing frost. High temperatures would range in the summer to 90 degrees but never over 100 degrees, and there was moisture to spare, particularly in the heavy monsoon months of July, August and September. Robert kept a rain-gauge in his yard in Putao for two years and recorded an average of sixty inches of rain in July – occasionally four to six inches in twenty-four hours. Though there are brief periods of sun during the monsoon, everything gets wet and stays wet. In our houses, where we kept linens, clothes and books, it was next to impossible to avoid mildew, dry-rot, and all the other discomforts of damp decay. But the citrus trees loved the climate.

Among the different species and subspecies that my father brought to the area were Washington, Valencia, Temple, King and Ruby oranges; Samson tangelos; Dancy tangerines; Marsh seedless grapefruit; kumquats; loquats; Eureka lemons; and several varieties of lime. He also had good success with other fruits that grew in lower Burma – papaya, mango, lychee nuts, avocados, passion-fruit and pineapple. Marketing was a problem at first, but by 1965 fruit exports from Putao to the rest of Burma totalled thousands of pounds a year and were so much appreciated that our oranges and grapefruit were on the breakfast menu at the elite Strand Hotel in Rangoon. Income from fruit crops boosted the level of well-being of the community as a whole. Each year more and more farmers netted at least three hundred dollars from fruit trees tended in their spare time. The total number of fruit trees in and about Putao by 1965 was estimated to be over fifty thousand. In addition to all this, fruit-raising had spread from Putao to other parts of north Burma and had become an important national asset, potentially capable of transforming the economy of the entire area. Shortly before our expulsion, ironically, my father had received from the Department of Agriculture a certificate of merit, citing his outstanding achievements in horticulture and thanking him for his services to the nation. This precious document was lost in the confusion of our sudden and obligatory departure from the scene of his contributions.

The confusion and haste of our departure from Putao had also made it impractical for my father to prepare and bring with him any cuttings from our orchards there. But, after our first monsoon season in the valley, a certain amount of clandestine traffic sprang up between Binuzu and the plains. Before the winter was over, my father had received two small bundles of precious scions from our own citrus trees. He was overjoyed to receive them, but his joy was short-lived. When he unwrapped one of the bundles he found, unfortunately, that all the tender cuttings were brown and dead. To say he was disappointed is a gross understatement. But the remaining bundle was in fairly good shape, and my father sent word by the men who had brought the cuttings that he would like more of the same kinds. Undaunted, he was soon hard at work grafting the good cuttings on to the wild lemon trees that were almost as plentiful around Binuzu and A-deh-di as they had been at home in Putao. I should note that if even half of the scions were still in usable, viable condition, it was probably because A-deh-di was three days closer to Putao than the new settlements to which Robert and I had moved. Probably none of the cuttings would have survived an additional three days' journey.

Given the available stock trees and virtually the same climate as we had in Putao, the outlook for citrus culture in Hidden Valley was good – except for one important element: a more or less permanent settlement. Grafted fruit trees take several seasons to produce; and what came to be known throughout northern Burma as a Morse tree demands a putting down of roots almost unknown to the nomadic mountain tribes. Doubly influenced by their tradition of slash-and-burn agriculture and by a lush environment in which vegetation was something you had to cut back instead of nurture, the Lisu found my father's prescription for growing a successful fruit tree almost incomprehensible. He taught them that before they planted a tree, they had to dig a hole five feet deep and six to eight feet across, put in leaves and grass for mulch, add limestone or crushed egg-shells and pulverized bones from their meats, as well as chicken, pig or cow manure, if available, and throw in some top-soil. Though this amounted to very hard work, the results at Putao had demonstrated to the Lisu that it paid off. Trees they planted in their casual way grew but didn't bear fruit; Morse trees were always productive.

This being the case, my father realized that the creation of orchards in Hidden Valley would have to await the establishment of reasonably permanent homes in favourable locations. Therefore, he developed a threefold plan. First, he had to determine which of the many varieties introduced at Putao would thrive best in the new environment. Next, he planned to start a nursery or seedbed of these. Then, when the settlers had found permanent locations, they could get scions from these trees, or even use some of the small trees themselves, and begin orchards of their own with a minimum of delay.

In the afternoon, whenever the demands of his medical work allowed him to get out of doors for a few hours, he set about creating a new citrus orchard around his sparsely furnished two-room house. Aided by one or two of the local villagers, he would go to the jungle to find groves or thickets of wild lemon or other suitable stock, dig up healthy young trees, each with a good-sized ball of earth around it, and bring them back to be replanted near his house. Grafting the scions imported from Putao was done in his spare moments. This less time-consuming procedure involved cutting off one or more branches of the stock and joining the scion to it with an improvised grafting wax made out of pine resin and cliff-bee wax, boiled down together into a sort of sticky liquid. My father would then wrap the graft carefully with either plastic or cloth soaked in the grafting wax, so as to keep out all moisture during the rainy season and thereby avoid rot.

The orchards that my father developed, both at Binuzu and later at Zi-yu-di, flourished as well as, and perhaps even better than, those he had started at Putao. By the time of our departure, they had provided scions for grafting to scores of trees, to begin new orchards in the dozen or more villages that were by then established in permanent sites throughout the length of the valley. The trees were only just beginning to bear fruit by the time we left, but they gave sure promise of making Hidden Valley just as rich in this respect as the land we had left behind in the plains.

In addition to fruit culture, another development in the Binuzu area was to have a lasting effect on the whole valley, and particularly on our oldest son, David. This was the scavenging of World War II aeroplane wrecks to produce the materials for mechanical innovations. When we left David and his next younger brother, Tommy, with their grandparents, we had no idea how productive David's inventive bent would turn out to be. In so far as jungle living was concerned, David was handicapped by increasingly bad eyesight. He felt useless on the hunt or on the trail. Like any near-sighted person, he found his eyes becoming weaker as his adolescent strength grew. It got so that he could hear the birds but not see them at a distance, or that his keen-sighted cousins would baffle him by pointing out an animal on a limb of a tree when he could see only the tree. So David buried his nose in books, among them a United States Army series on electronics that I had stuffed into our loads when we left Putao.

As he developed an understanding of electrical and mechanical matters from his reading, David began to be intrigued by what the Lisu were doing with the old plane wrecks that their hunters found in the high altitudes of Hidden Valley. As I have said, some two thousand planes went down during the period when the United States was flying materials over the Hump to China. The mountain people had been salvaging material from these wrecks for twenty-five years, but, because of its reputation, Hidden Valley was still almost virgin territory when we reached it. It was also one of the most atmospherically turbulent areas the planes had to cross. We weren't in the valley long before we noticed that the force and direction of the winds varied almost with each hour of the day. At about 1.30 p.m., for example, the wind would be blowing straight up the valley, and farmers learned to burn their fields at that hour. By evening the winds, equally strong, would be blowing in the opposite direction. We concluded that, during the war, unsuspecting pilots of overburdened planes were probably sucked into the high mountains.

Soon after we first settled in Binuzu, several downed aircraft were found within a radius of two or three days' travel from our village. Others were discovered later, higher up in the mountains. The Lisu regarded these chiefly as a source of much-prized aluminium. They would tear the fuselage apart and, at the scene of the wreck, melt down the aluminium into ingots small enough to carry back to our villages. There the tribespeople would remelt the ingots and pour them into moulds made out of sand, clay and ashes in the form of whatever they needed.

The most prized aluminium products were deep bowls or kettles of the type used for boiling large quantities of meat or rice. Certain of the tribespeople became especially adept in fashioning these, and the way in which they did it offered a fascinating spectacle. First came the mould, which was made from a special kind of sticky, claylike sand that could be readily shaped into the desired form. A mound of this sand was placed in an open box. Then the bowl the craftsmen wanted to duplicate was inverted and pressed firmly down on top of the mound. On top of that they pressed another boxful of the prepared sand, to receive an indentation representing the exterior of the bowl. The upper box was then carefully lifted off and the model removed. Both surfaces were then sprinkled with ashes to keep the sand from adhering to the hot metal when it was poured in the mould. Then the top part of the mould was replaced. This procedure left a space between upper and lower moulds in the exact shape of the vessel that had been removed. At this point, two tribesmen, both usually barefoot, carried an open pailful of molten aluminium from their fire to the mould. Through an opening in the top, they poured the molten aluminium down a funnel into the bowl-shaped space. After the metal had cooled for an hour or so, the upper mould was removed, revealing, if all went well, the exact replica intended.

This delicate process – essentially the same one used by the tribespeople from time immemorial in making primitive utensils of all sorts out of other metals, from copper to silver and gold – soon provided enough aluminium pots, pans, bowls and spoons to satisfy the needs of our entire colony. Relatives and visitors who began to arrive from Putao during the fourth and fifth years of our stay in the valley admired out kitchenware as being lighter and easier to handle than the cumbersome iron models that were on sale in the Putao shops. Presently, quite a few of the utensils from our area found their way back to the plains. By the time we left, traders from Putao were coming to our villages with items we needed – cloth, tea, salt, canned foods, seasonings and patent medicines – and bartering them for our aluminium vessels, which they carried back and sold at a handsome profit as rare items much in demand.

David rightly suspected that the wrecks, if properly examined, might yield items far more useful than scrap aluminium. As David recalls, his first real intimation of this came when he talked to a hunter who had just come back from a high-altitude wreck: 'He said he had found a metal tube and it was real heavy, and there was a shaft on it, and "I turned it and it turned, and I spun it and it would spin." And I said, "Good grief, you mean even while it was cold it was doing that?" And he said, "Yep, there wasn't a bit of rust on it." I asked then, "What did you do?" He said, "Oh, I tried to open it, but I couldn't. So I put my axe to it and hit it with another axe, and after about an hour I finally opened it." Well, by then I knew it was a generator and all I could say was, "Aaarrrggghhh!" '

David realized that the Lisu were dismantling and destroying all the engine parts they found, just for the bits of steel and copper wire they would yield for immediate use. So he took to visiting wrecks himself, whenever possible. At one he found a four-engine cargo plane so damaged that he couldn't identify it. Vines were growing all over it, and the engines were stuck into the mountainside. Even so, he and his companions were able to recover such useful items as screws, bearings and valve springs. The Lisu would turn the steel from these springs into such things as punches or replacements for the springs in their flintlocks. Once David made the firing-pin for a shotgun from this metal. But his big find at this one wreck was magnets, which were the key to a hydroelectric scheme still hatching in his mind.

In the months they spent with their grandparents in A-deh-di, my boys had acquired knowledge and skills that promised to be as useful as the jungle craft of Robert's boys. By the time I went down to get them early in December 1967, our home was well established in Zi-yu-di. It was evident by then that we would again be called upon to perform our traditional roles as leaders in building, teaching and planning for a long-range future. The boys would be a help in this, but we needed my parents too. By this time there were more people in need of medical assistance in the western end of the valley than around Binuzu and A-deh-di. Realizing the greater need for their services in this new area, my parents promised to join us as soon as a place could be prepared for them to live. But, in response to the many requests from the Binuzu-area residents, they agreed to hold one final Bible-training school, during the first two weeks in January 1968, before they left for Zi-yu-di. The year 1968 started with the delightful promise that all the Morses would once again be living and working within a few hours' walking distance of each other.

Chapter 10

Then the Lord said to Moses, 'Pharaoh will not
listen to you; that my wonders may be
multiplied in the land of Egypt.'
EXODUS 11 : 9

The year 1968 remains in our minds as the year of settling
in. By the end of January my parents had arrived in
Zi-yu-di to join our family and Drema Esther and Jesse.
Their house, only about ninety feet from ours, had been
built without pay by people from several villages who came
to help as an expression of their appreciation of what my
parents had been doing for all of them for so many years.
All our houses were built in the same style as those of our
Lisu brethren, and anyone entering the village could not
have identified our residences on the basis of external
differences. All had bamboo floors, and walls of either
woven bamboo or hand-split rough boards. Each roof was
thatched with bamboo leaves. Our 'stove' was the same as
in any Lisu house – an iron tripod set in the fireplace in the
centre of the room. Only inside our homes could one find
evidence of the presence of Westerners, in that we had a
little more furniture. When we were camping in tents or
living in crowded quarters in Binuzu, we had made no
attempt to have any furniture. But once we arrived in
Zi-yu-di and felt more of a sense of permanence, we began
to make a few things. We started with tables and simple
benches, then progressed to beds, tables of a slightly better
style and more comfortable benches. These houses were not
as comfortable as those in Putao, perhaps, but they were
adequate; and because we were willing to live in this
manner, we grew closer than ever to the people around us;
we really felt accepted as family.

But even in the comparative security of our homes we

were constantly reminded that we were, after all, in the jungle, still at the mercy of nature and the elements. Each year the spring rains often cause flooding of all the streams because they help melt the snow in the mountains. But 1968 was different. Instead of melting the snows, the spring rains deposited more on the mountains around us, so much more that the snowline extended further down than it had all winter. This unseasonable snowfall drove musk-deer, takin, and other mountain animals down to the lowest levels Lisu hunters could recall. It also forced the hunters to come back down the mountains into the villages to take refuge from the bitter cold.

One of these hunters, accompanied by his father, an elderly tribesman we had known for years, dropped by Robert's house one evening shortly after the storm. The younger man, prompted by his father, told us of encountering one of the most elusive beasts in the world, the yeti, or abominable snowman. We had heard, of course, during our many years in the Himalayan region, of this strange creature; indeed, around 1955 my brother LaVerne once came across its strangely human tracks while on a preaching tour in the mountains east of Putao. From all reports, we had concluded that the yeti does exist, but in small numbers and in regions so inhospitable that human beings are seldom, if ever, on hand to glimpse him. On the other hand, we had become convinced that most writers on the subject exaggerated the yeti's human qualities. We felt sure that it had to be a type of monkey, rather like a large gibbon, and our hunter friend confirmed this assumption.

'It happened about a week ago, and not ten miles from where we are sitting', he told us. 'I started tracking a musk-deer through this snow when I noticed running across its tracks some footprints of a kind I had never seen before – something like those of a big monkey or maybe a new kind of bear. They were twelve or fourteen inches long, shaped like a man's foot, only narrower. I gave up the musk-deer and followed the new trail. About four or five miles further along it brought me to a wide clearing where, when I looked ahead, I suddenly saw this strange animal standing directly in front of me, not more than forty or fifty feet away. It had apparently heard and seen me before I saw it, because it had turned away from the direction of the tracks and was looking directly at me. I would say that it was about seven or eight feet tall, but except for the fact that it was standing upright on two legs – as, of course, I knew it would be from the tracks – it did not look in the least bit human. It was covered with reddish-brown fur with a sort of mane of longer fur on its head, which looked like a big monkey's.

'The funny thing was the way it behaved when it saw me. Every time I made a move of any kind the animal copied it exactly, just as a gibbon will do sometimes, though of course it was several times as big as a gibbon. When I raised my hand, it raised its hand. When I brought up my crossbow to take aim, it pretended to raise a bow and do likewise. When I let go my arrow, however – it was, of course, a poisoned one that I had had ready for the musk-deer – this game came to a sudden end. The arrow hit the yeti in the chest, but it must have struck solid bone, for instead of entering the body it dropped to the snow. At that, much surprised, but apparently not much hurt, the yeti turned around again and bounded off into the wilderness. It made no sound at any time.

'I went back to the village to get a friend to help me follow the track, thinking I might need help in carrying the body home. About two hours later we came back to the spot where I had shot at the yeti. From a rattan vine nearby, against which he had been standing when I shot, I rechecked the animal's height – between seven and eight feet. My friend and I then began to follow the tracks.

'I had expected that the poison on the arrow would take effect fairly soon, even though it hadn't penetrated far. Apparently, however, the arrow had either not broken the skin at all or had done so at a point where there were no blood-vessels, because the tracks never showed signs of slowing down or wavering, as they should have done if the animal had been suffering from the effects of the poison. When the sun began to get low in the sky my friend and I gave up the chase and came home.'

Despite this tale, none of us ever really worried about encountering a yeti, but we felt quite differently about tigers. We seldom saw them, but we often found their pug-marks quite close to our houses, especially after we began keeping chickens and pigs and other animals they might consider easy prey. Gradually, we came to have confidence in the theory that a tiger will not attack a human being unless it has been wounded or is desperately hungry. Then, perhaps the exception that proves the rule, the only death from tiger attack after we settled in Hidden Valley was reported by a runner from a nearby village. (Three or four people were killed the first spring (1966), before we were really settled in the area and while we were still searching for village sites.)

A dozen or so villagers had gone into the jungle together to gather bamboo stalks for making water containers. On the way, three of the younger children were loitering on the trail when, suddenly, a tawny shape shot out of the sur-rounding underbrush and made a dash towards them. Two of the children ducked aside, but the tiger pounced on the third, a boy of thirteen, and broke his neck with one crunch of its jaw.

All this happened so quickly that the few villagers in a position to see it hardly knew what had taken place. At first, in fact, one or two of them had mistaken the beast for a running deer. Closest to the tiger and his prey was the victim's older brother, who ran towards the fallen figure, drawing his two-foot machete as he did so. Just as he reached the tiger – now standing over the prostrate body with twitching tail – the older boy slipped and fell, uttering a sharp cry of rage and frustration as he did so. Apparently frightened by the shout and the unexpected attack, the tiger bounded off into the jungle.

The villagers tried to revive the fallen boy, but it soon became clear that he was already dead. Later examination showed that the tiger had broken his neck just below the skull. The villagers carried the corpse back to the village for burial, but they expected that the tiger would return to the scene of his kill and, finding it gone, follow the tracks back to the village. Indeed, the next morning it became obvious from pug-marks around several of the houses, and from the partially eaten body of a pig, that this was exactly what had occurred.

Once a tiger has tasted human blood, he is likely to consider man one of his favourite morsels. Therefore, it is customary to mount a concerted effort to kill the marauder before he does further damage. That same day the villagers carried the carcass of the partially devoured pig to a nearby spot in the jungle. There they built a machan, a raised platform on which several hunters can lie in wait under conditions of comparative safety.

As was anticipated, the tiger showed up to claim his kill at about ten o'clock that evening. Searchlights were beamed at him from the machan, and his eyes flashed back brightly in the reflected light. They would have provided an excellent target, except that the tiger – apparently a female, since it was accompanied by an almost full-grown cub – leapt up on a nearby log, from there to a high rock, and then back into the protective darkness of the jungle. She was so quick that none of the gunners could take aim satisfactorily. One man risked a flank shot, but it failed to prevent the tiger from making good her escape.

The next morning the hunters found enough blood along her trail to indicate that the tiger might well have been severely wounded. A posse of the best huntsmen in the village – including Steve, with his trusted dog, Viking – set off to track down the wounded animal. The hunt lasted all day, but the hunters were unable to catch up with their quarry. A discouraging sign was that, whereas a severely wounded tiger will usually head downhill or hold to a level track, this one went uphill most of the time. Moreover, she moved so rapidly that, even with Viking and the rest of the dog pack, the trail grew colder rather than hotter.

The exhausted hunters returned to the village, where they were greeted by the news that another tiger had been seen there by some of the men who had stayed at home. The hunters thought it could have been the cub separated from its mother, and so they stayed close to the village the next day. Neither of the tigers showed up, however, and Steve and the other huntsmen finally gave up all thought of catching this particular man-eater, who never reappeared in our neighbourhood.

If tigers generally left us alone, we returned the compliment. Even among the Lisu, tiger meat is seldom eaten, because, like the flesh of most carnivores, it has a pungent, unpalatable flavour. But tigers are prized for medicinal purposes. Tiger bone is cooked – a complicated ten-day process requiring constant attention – until it becomes a jelly that eventually solidifies. This jelly is supposed to be good for such diverse ailments as arthritis and lack of appetite, while tiger fat is a balm for healing cuts and abrasions. We weren't properly armed to hunt tigers, but brushes with these beasts and with even more formidable wild elephants were inevitable, inasmuch as we were still constantly out hunting for meat.

Of all the Morse clan, Robert's son Joni was the one who most often seemed to have harrowing experiences with the larger animals. One night he had unexpected encounters with both a tiger and an elephant. Let him tell about it in his own characteristic way:

'A teacher friend, Yuliya, and I were going out to make a tree house over a salt-lick. We knew elephants and deer came there, and we were hoping to bag a deer. We both carried shotguns, that time. His was a pump-action, mine a single-barrel. Mine had a shell in the chamber. So we were walking along, and it was getting dark, but there was a full moon. Just before we got there, there was a stream, and on the other side of the stream we saw wet pug-marks. A tiger was just ahead of us. So we debated whether we should head back. "No," Yuliya said, "he's going his way, and we're going our way."

'A few feet from the river we heard this sound like a bird – *dee-dee-dee-dee-dee* – but it wasn't a bird. Whatever it was ran off about fifty feet, making a lot of noise. We turned our torches on it, and out of the foliage glared the two bright, round, reflector-like eyes of a tiger. Yuliya brought his gun to level, and – click – it wasn't loaded. So I aimed right between its eyes, and – whammo! The tiger just flipped over and tore around for a few minutes and then took off down the hill. We went over there real quick, but there was nothing we could do right then, so we planned to look it up next morning.

'We headed for the salt-lick. As we got there, we heard some splashing in the pool. We crawled down to the pool and turned our torches on. There was a big tusker, right smack in the middle of the pool. Instead of backing up and trying him from our tree machan, Yuliya started firing away. As soon as he shot, I loaded my gun and shot too. So we shot at the elephant and it charged at us. By the time Yuliya had pumped in another shell, it was right on top of us, so I just dropped my gun and turned around and ran up the hill. Just as I was running, Yuliya got off his last shot, and that last shot – I don't know why – made the elephant spin around and tear off the other way. It was probably a mock attack. Shotgun pellets couldn't have done any damage to him. His skin is an inch to an inch and a half thick. Real thick. You can sharpen a knife on that skin.

'So we climbed up in the tree as fast as possible, afraid he might come back. But he didn't. So that night, later on, a deer came, and we shot him. After that, we went every half-moon and full-moon, twice a month, to this salt-lick.'

From our point of view, it was just as well that Joni and his friend Yuliya didn't get the elephant. We shared the Lisu feeling that an elephant was far more valuable alive than dead. Only on a very few occasions during our time in the valley, such as the one just after we arrived in Zi-yu-di, when the people were desperate for food, was any real effort made to kill an elephant.

In the jungles of northern Burma, the elephant's chief value to man is as a kind of natural bulldozer. Underbrush and foliage are so thick in most places that a human being, even when armed with a machete, can hardly hope to cover a mile a day through a trackless area. Thus, the trails on which almost all pedestrian jungle traffic moves are those opened up by the elephants. Their huge bulk and the way they use their tusks and trunk enable them to crash through dense thickets that most creatures, including man, would find completely impenetrable. Elephant herds, which rarely have more than two or three dozen members, usually go through the jungle in single file. But the herds are numerous and continuously on the move, looking for new forage areas, so their constant travel provides the rest of the jungle population with the equivalent of a highway network.

Tribesmen who have studied the behaviour of elephants have told me that the herds often cover as much as thirty or forty miles a day, feeding on the trailside foliage as they move along. They cover so much territory that the visits of any one herd to a particular feeding place or water-hole may be spaced as much as twenty years apart. Their apparent ability to recall forage areas after such a long period accounts, in part, for the legend that these animals have phenomenally good memories.

Elephant trails, especially those going up or down mountains, tend to be so circuitous that the agile and impatient Lisu often try to improvise short-cuts whenever the underbrush, which is usually thinner on the steepest mountainsides, permits it. Still, the Lisu are thoroughly aware of their debt to the elephant for opening up regions of the jungle that would otherwise be impervious to travel of any sort. Indian and Burmese game laws, which prohibit the shooting of elephants, are deeply rooted in ancient tribal law and willingly obeyed by everyone, except under the pressure of the greatest need.

When we did kill an elephant, I must say that the results were astonishing in terms of what they produced. Indian elephants are smaller than the African variety and quite different in conformation, with a forehead that slopes back at about forty-five degrees instead of ascending vertically above the trunk. Unlike the scrawny, run-down specimens usually seen by Westerners in zoos or circuses, wild elephants, especially in the rich rain-forest areas such as our own valley, are bursting with health and well covered with a thick layer of fat. After the kill near Zi-yu-di, the tribespeople in our area took turns carving up the carcass and carrying the meat back in seventy-pound loads. This one animal, according to my rough count, provided over seventy loads of edible meat, or something in the neighbourhood of five thousand pounds. Even more vital from our viewpoint than the lean meat was the fat, which could be boiled down into cooking oil, of which there was a chronic shortage. This one carcass provided an unusually large amount of fat, no less than thirty five-gallon tins, which was enough to supply the needs of all the families in Zi-yu-di and one of the neighbouring villages for several months.

No part of the carcass of an elephant goes to waste, least of all the bones, from which are made all sorts of objects. They are frequently used to make the scales for weighing produce in shops all over India and Burma. The even curvature of the ribs and the ease with which they can be whittled or sandpapered down to perfect symmetry, as well as their durability and strength, make them ideally suited for this purpose. Elephant bone, when heated in boiling water, becomes soft and relatively easy to whittle into all sorts of intricate shapes. Most of the carved combs, pill-boxes and other 'ivory' knick-knacks sold to tourists in Asia are actually made from softened elephant bone, which takes on an ivorylike polish after it has been allowed to cool and harden. Elephant tusks will also soften under heat, which helps in preparing carved tusks of astonishing intricacy. These handicrafts were highly prized in pre-revolutionary China, and a single craftsman might spend several decades working on one. Elephant hide is as tough as sole leather and often more than an inch thick. Although highly prized (and priced!) in the outside world, we could not make much use of this exotic leather because we lacked facilities for tanning and processing it.

Merely to relate the experiences we had with the most awe-inspiring of God's creatures may not convey to the reader the deeper meanings they had for us. We were always aware of both the naked power and the beneficence of nature. And experience also made us aware, as in the case of the caterpillar blight, of our own insignificance in the face of these forces. Like the children of Israel or the pilgrims who first settled the American wilderness, we found ourselves repeatedly turning to God for direct intervention when we were confronted with events beyond our control.

One instance of this was the afternoon my nephew Bobby was shot. I was teaching a Bible class in the little open-sided church in Zi-yu-di when Bobby and his constant Lisu companion, Yuda, walked by on the path outside. Minutes later I heard a gunshot, but thought nothing of it until I saw Bobby staggering back down the path, calling out, 'I've been hit. I've been hit.' When I told them that Bobby had been hurt, the whole class immediately ran outside. Tommy was the first one out, leaping over the low bamboo wall to reach Bobby. Everyone gathered around as I stooped over Bobby, who had collapsed from shock just as Tommy reached him and was now lying on the ground. Someone took off Bobby's jacket, rolled it up, and put it under his head for a pillow. When I opened his bloody shirt, I found that the bullet had made a short trajectory through his body about four inches above the belt line, just below the ribs on the right side.

Hoping it was little more than a flesh wound, and knowing the need to calm everybody down, I kept saying, 'It's not very serious, just passed through the skin.' Besides, if it were serious, I knew that any kind of surgery was beyond our capabilities. Bobby would simply live or die, as God willed. But I sent immediately for Robert, who was working up at the other end of the village, and for Drema

Esther and Helen, both of whom had nursing experience. Perhaps the whole story is best told in Bobby's own words:

'Daddy was down teaching in Zi-yu-di that day, and Yuda and I wanted to go down and see him. But I've got to tell you about Yuda. After we met at the big Christmas convention at Tiger Feast Hill, he became my best friend. You know, we had the buddy system for going hunting, and we would go out together. Three nights a week I used to go to Yuda's house, and the other three nights he would come to my house. So the way it was, where I went, Yuda went.

'This day in August 1968 was a funny day. Only since I've been back in the States and seen the movie *Deliverance* do I understand it. It was one of those days when everything goes wrong, and you don't know why. Mother didn't want us to take a gun down to Zi-yu-di, but we argued her into letting us have one .22 because we might find some valuable game. So we started out, promising Mother we'd be careful.

'Along the way, we picked up some friends, some little Lisu boys. When we got to the river – it was a big river that divided the eastern side of the valley from the western – we said, "Let's take a swim. We're in no rush." But the river was really high, and one little boy about eleven started to drown. I had to jump in to save him, and we were pretty shook up. So we decided to forget swimming and go on to Zi-yu-di.

'When we got to the village, the preacher's wife asked us to come in for lunch. So we ate. And while we were eating, another kid came along and started fooling around with the gun, which we had left outside on the porch. He put a bullet in the chamber, where it shouldn't be, and then leaned the gun against the wall again. Then another guy came along and cocked it and left it off safety. We didn't know all this when we came out, and Yuda picked up the gun and slung it over his shoulder. When we started past the church where Uncle Eugene was teaching up toward my grandfather's house, I was following him.

'Just then the preacher's wife called out to me. I turned to wave, and Yuda, whose finger was on the gun's trigger, slipped a little. The gun went off. Thank goodness I was turning, because if I had been walking straight, it would have hit me right in the belly. As it was, it hit me on the side. The .22 slug tore right through me, and the next day a piece of liver came out through the wound. But at the time all I could feel was like when someone pounds you on the back. The preacher's wife said she heard the shot and then saw me spin around three times. I didn't have any sensation at the time – I guess I was in shock – and so I started running back down toward the church.

'There I fell down, and a puddle of blood started gathering under me. The heat of all the people who rushed out of the church and the smell – I thought it had hit my intestines – got to me. I was really scared then, though my uncle kept saying, "It's not too bad, it's not too bad." The people started praying right there – all preachers and elders – murmuring, each praying individually but out loud. Then Aunt Drema arrived, and she said, too, "Don't get excited; it's not too bad." They took a door from a house nearby, untying the rattan hinges, and used that for a stretcher to take me up to my grandfather's house.

'When I got there, Daddy came along, and I looked up at him and said to myself, "Oh, oh, it must be really bad." I doubted everyone who said it wasn't bad, because everyone was trembling. Aunt Helen and Aunt Drema got some Mercurochrome and stuffed some cotton in the wound. The people there say that if you drink cold water after a gunshot wound you will go into shock. So my friends kept saying, "No, no! Don't drink water!" So I was scared to drink any water, even when I was extremely thirsty. After about four hours, I began having a sore, throbbing sensation. But there wasn't much they could give me. Four APC tablets, two sleeping pills, one penicillin shot – that was it. That and a lot of prayer.

'From when I was shot until three nights later, there was twenty-four-hour prayer. I was repenting and confessing and making promises to myself like I was going out right then. A large crowd gathered outside grandfather's house and sang all through the night. Joni had written a few songs just the day before, and they were singing them too. It was then I realized how much concern all these Christians had for one another.

'But the prayer didn't stop the pain, and on the third night it was so bad I was screaming. But I had a piece of wood – Yuda's mirror, the handle of it – in my mouth and I would bite down on it and keep from screaming. Finally, though, it got to where I couldn't stand it, and I screamed, "Take me to India. Do something!"

'That's when my father took over. The constant praying outside had stopped, but he sat by me and prayed. The thing that was hurting was a broken rib pressing into my lung. My father put his hands gently on me and asked God to heal me. When he said, "In Jesus' name", I could hear the bone go right back into place and the pain was completely gone. The next day I was ready to walk home. There's no other way to describe this than a cure wrought completely by prayer.'

I can only agree with Bobby. Healing by prayer and the laying on of hands has become so acceptable now, even in some of the most conservative denominations of the West, that I have no doubt others will agree too. Certainly the Lisu Christians found nothing unusual about it. Particularly in the years since we left Putao, they had seen God answer prayer after prayer, and no miracle would have astounded them. We encouraged the Lisu in this attitude, though we were careful to point out the corollary to this reliance on prayer – 'God helps him who helps himself.' They had seen this too. They were fully aware that no tree bore fruit unless its roots were planted deep, that no field flowered unless it had been properly cut and burned, that no game fell to the hunter who was noisy and careless. To all of us in Hidden Valley, the fundamental laws of creation seemed so obvious that there was no place for theological hairsplitting.

In view of this, it is not surprising that we were called upon on several occasions to help cast out demons from someone who was being troubled. Perhaps the most interesting case of this kind was one Robert encountered. It began in characteristic Lisu fashion. Robert was sitting at his desk, working on his translation of the New Testament, when a Lisu man came in and sat quietly by the fire. The man was obviously worn from a long journey, and in due time Robert asked him, 'You must be somebody from a long distance – what did you come for?'

'Oh, I just came for nothing.'

'Where did you come from today?'

'Over at Binuzu.'

'But that's three days' journey. Why did you come so fast? Is everybody all right?'

'Oh, yes.'

'And has anything happened?'

'Anyi-Yomajeu had her baby.'

'Oh. Boy or girl?'

'A girl.'

'And is the baby all right?'

'Oh, yes.'

'And is Anyi-Yomajeu all right?'

'Well, she has bled a lot and is out of her mind. That's why I came.'

Immediately Robert moved into action. We all knew Anyi-Yomajeu, a small, beautiful girl of about twenty-three. She lived in a three-family hamlet on a ridge just above Binuzu. We had heard gossip to the effect that she and her husband were not getting along well. He would desert her, particularly when she was pregnant, taking to the hills on the pretext of hunting. Nevertheless, she remained sweet and even-tempered, according to the messenger, until the time came for her delivery. Because of her small frame, it was a hard delivery, and, being alone except for her mother, she was frightened. Although the baby survived, Anyi-Yomajeu underwent a complete change of personality. She would sulk, curse her mother,

153

swear at her husband. From all Robert could gather, it appeared to be a classic case of demon possession, at least in the way the Lisu defined this ailment.

Knowing it would take him three days to get to Anyi-Yomajeu, Robert went up to our father's house and got medicines to send back with the runner – vitamin K and coagulants to stop the bleeding, sulpha and antibiotics for puerperal fever. When, at last, he climbed the hill from Binuzu, fending off the fierce dogs that came out to attack him, Robert went first to the elder's home. 'We don't know what's wrong with her', the elder said. 'But it looks like evil spirits. The medicine stopped the haemorrhaging, but her mind is still unsettled.'

With the elder accompanying him, Robert climbed warily up the ladder leading to Anyi-Yomajeu's house. He couldn't have been more surprised by her demeanour. Normally a demure young woman, she was positively flirtatious. Though a Lisu woman is usually shy in front of visitors, she came right up to Robert, shook his hand, and told him that she had been longing to meet him. Then she led him over to a mat and gestured for him to sit down beside her. In view of Lisu morality, Robert was glad that the elder was there and that Anyi-Yomajeu's mother, cradling the baby, was looking on too.

When Robert offered to pray, she said, 'Oh, I don't need prayer.'

Robert was surprised, but merely said, 'I see you have a nice baby.'

'Oh, I don't want that baby', Anyi-Yomajeu said.

At this her mother broke in, 'See how she is. She refused to take her medicine. I have to fight to get her to take medicine.'

'Well, I'll help you take your medicine,' Robert told Anyi-Yomajeu, 'then I'll pray.'

At this, Anyi-Yomajeu collapsed. She fell to the floor, moaning, complaining that she didn't feel well. She resisted all efforts to get her to take her medicine, pretending she had fainted or was asleep. But Robert turned back her

·eyelids and found her awake. Though they finally got the medicine into her, she would not respond in any way, would not even sit up when Robert did begin praying.

It took three days and nights of prayer before Anyi-Yomajeu was finally delivered of whatever dark spirit possessed her. Robert was joined by two other preachers, who had been notified of the difficulty. Together and separately they prayed for the young mother and her child, and each time in closing they followed the scriptural example of addressing the evil spirit: 'In Jesus' mighty name we rebuke you and command you to leave.' Finally, the young woman returned to her senses. Her husband happened to come back during Robert's stay, and there was a joyful reunion. No one can tell that family, or six or eight others in the valley who had similar difficulties, that God does not 'work in mysterious ways his wonders to perform'.

Chapter 11

... and I will be with your mouth and with
his mouth, and will teach you what you
shall do.
EXODUS 4 : 15

I anticipated that our boys would be a help in the con-
structive phase of our work in Zi-yu-di, but I have to
confess that I underestimated their ingenuity and ability,
as well as their willingness to work. The boys' total involve-
ment in mission work began in typically Lisu fashion.
Late in January 1968, we had a visit from Heh-ah-tsah, the
elderly Lisu who was headman of the thriving community
of Zi-yu-di. His exceptionally luxuriant white beard and
deliberate manner of speech provided an engaging contrast
with his viewpoint on life, which was notable for its down-
to-earth practicality and generous seasoning of sly hum-
our.

'Do you realize', he said, 'what is happening to our
children here in this place where we have so much to be
thankful for?'

'No', I replied. 'It seems to me that most of them are
thriving.'

'Indeed, they are thriving so far as their health is concerned, but is that the only thing we have to think about?
The children of the monkeys who live in the jungle are also
in the best of health, so far as I can tell, but do we want
our children to grow up like little monkeys?'

Now I began to see what he was driving at: something
that had concerned much of our own family for some time.
We had now been away from Putao for just over two years,
and during that time not one of the children in the community had experienced a single day of schooling. If they
were not to grow up as ignorant as monkeys to whom

Heh-ah-tsah had aptly compared them, it was high time to do something about it.

'Children are supposed to be a blessing from God', the old headman continued. 'Surely we should show our gratitude by seeing that our children learn a little more than the monkeys do. In short, we must have a school here, and we want you to help us start one.'

Heh-ah-tsah's visit to me was not the first step he had taken in his programme of education for the children of Zi-yu-di. He had, it seemed, already approached Jesse Yangmi about the need. Jesse's studies in the mission and government schools in Putao had given him a good command of English, which he improved by practice in speaking with us and by listening to the radio. Heh-ah-tsah had enlisted Jesse's wholehearted co-operation in getting the project going. Several village families with children of school age agreed to co-operate in providing Jesse and Drema Esther with rice and other available food if, in turn, they would set up a curriculum. The plan was to begin the school year that coming March, when the rains would make outdoor work impossible. They could use the church for a schoolhouse until we could build something better. All this, I found, had already been agreed upon, and where my assistance would chiefly be needed was in the actual construction of the proposed schoolhouse.

Naturally, I agreed at once to do all that I could to advance the project. Work on the new school building began about two weeks later, with most of the able-bodied villagers helping out whenever they could. The first problem that arose concerned the number of pupils there would be. What Heh-ah-tsah probably had in mind, and Jesse certainly did, was a modest little one-room institution for ten or a dozen pupils whom Jesse would instruct in English and Drema Esther in Bible studies. However, it appeared that there was much greater interest than had been anticipated, and the list of applicants had grown rapidly to about forty-five pupils. Most were from Zi-yu-di, but a few were from the other villages nearby. Some of them proposed to walk as much as four miles a day, mostly through jungle, to get to the school. Others would be able to board during the week with relatives or friends who were willing to give them food and lodging in exchange for a reasonable quota of work in the house or field.

To accommodate this unexpected influx would clearly present a serious problem for Jesse and Drema Esther, who were accustomed to teaching the children on Sunday but not to a workload of these proportions. Nonetheless, there seemed to be nothing we could do except expand the schoolhouse considerably from the size of our original plans.

School began in March, as had been planned, but the schoolhouse was still in the early stages of construction. The church building was not equipped for classroom use, nor was it really large enough to accommodate all the students. But these were not the only problems. When the enrolment figures soared, we thought we would divide the students into two or three classes, for ease in teaching. But we found that there was such a wide range in both age and experience that it was almost impossible properly to categorize the students. In age they ranged all the way from little six- and seven-year-olds to young adults nineteen to twenty-one years of age. There was just as much disparity in their background. Some had never seen the inside of a school before and were illiterate, while others were able to read and write their own language. A few had been to school before and knew some Burmese and Kachin, and even a little English. Because of these inequalities, the kindergarten included some fifteen- to sixteen-year-olds, and the advanced group included children who were only ten or eleven, but who had studied as much as three years in Putao.

Another problem was the teaching staff. Besides Drema Esther and Jesse, a young man with some teaching experience in Putao had agreed to help. But, just as school was beginning, he came down with an attack of chronic illness (which my father later diagnosed and treated as an allergy), and this, of course, placed the entire burden of instruction on the Yangmis.

With only two teachers, things were arranged so that while Jesse taught English to one class and Drema Esther taught the Bible to another, the third class was either combined with the others or dismissed to play in the yard outside. But the uproar from the children playing in the yard distracted the attention of the students inside. Obviously, something had to be done about getting another teacher.

Heh-ah-tsah made this his main concern and set about it in his characteristic style. One evening he dropped in again at our house and asked to see my son David. After the customary preliminaries, he came to the point, which David had foreseen from the outset – would David be willing to fill in for the ailing teacher by taking over the youngest class in the school?

David, then seventeen, gave a typically modest reply: 'I wish I could do it, but the truth is that I should really still be in school myself. I just don't know enough about teaching even to attempt the job. I hope you will understand how I feel and find someone who is better qualified.'

Heh-ah-tsah accepted David's excuse for the time being, but the next evening Jesse himself dropped in and made much the same proposal.

'I know what you said to Heh-ah-tsah', he said. 'Still, it would be awfully nice if you would come and help us for a little bit, at least until my other teacher gets over his illness.'

David had a twinge of conscience, but stuck to his position. 'You know as well as I do that I'm just not up to it, Jesse', he explained. 'As you know, I need to be studying myself. To be a teacher – well, I just wouldn't have the nerve!'

Two nights later, Heh-ah-tsah was at our house to see David again.

'Tell me,' he said, this time a bit more sternly, 'you say

that you spend most of your time in studying. What is the subject that interests you so much?'

'Well, mostly these days I study electricity and electronics.'

'Tell me: To do that, don't you need to know a little something about arithmetic?'

'Well, yes, a little bit.'

'And do you still remember your ABC?'

'Oh, yes, if I didn't remember that I couldn't even look up a subject in the index!'

'I see', said Heh-ah-tsah. 'Well, now let me tell you something. Most of the pupils in our school don't know their ABC in Lisu, let alone in English. Instead of knowing arithmetic, they can't even count "one, two, three, four". If you know arithmetic and if you know your ABC, you already know plenty to be a teacher in our school!'

The upshot of it all was that David started his pedagogical career the following Monday.

Even with the problem of teachers solved, there were still difficulties to be overcome. Consider, for instance, that we had no blackboards or chalk; no textbooks, exercise books or writing-paper of any kind; and no pens, pencils or other writing utensils.

Meanwhile, work was going ahead on the school building. First we had to find and clear a level space big enough for both the school building and a play area for games at break-time. We set up an A-frame structure, with the roof coming down low enough to provide shelter from the rain in the monsoon season. Actual construction presented no particular difficulties, once the materials had been obtained from the jungle – posts and timbers for the framework, bamboo for the walls, ties for the roof, and leaves for the roofing. The side walls were raised only halfway up to the eaves line, while the end walls extended all the way. We anticipated having only three grades, and so partitioned the interior into three rooms, each about fourteen feet by sixteen feet.

Following the style common in schools throughout

northern Burma, we installed rows of benches, each intended to seat two or three children, varied in height to accommodate the different age-groups and mounted with dowel-pins on stout posts driven into the ground. A similarly supported writing-shelf, consisting of a single board about ten inches wide, ran along in front of each bench. At the front of each room we built a desk for the teacher – a large board, about two feet long and eighteen inches wide, supported in the same manner as the students' benches and tables.

The schoolhouse was completed in early April, and we invited all the villagers to the dedication of the new building. There was a lot of speech-making, which the Lisu love, and a prayer service asking God's blessing on the new building and those who would be using it. To complete the occasion, there was a meal, with leaf-wrapped packages of rice and meat. That afternoon none of us could foresee that, four years later, the school would be enlarged to six rooms and an office, with a staff of six teachers and an enrolment of nearly eighty students.

The operations of the school were all transferred from the church to the new building. Although the teacher who had been ill was now able to teach, David was asked to stay on in the job. He taught English and arithmetic to the two lower classes and science to the upper class. The teachers had to prepare their own teaching material, so David's presence gave all of them more time for this. Drema Esther continued teaching Bible lessons to all three classes until she and her family left, after which the classes were taught by Ronnie. Jesse and the other teacher, Yuliya, taught classes in Burmese and Kachin that included reading and writing in those languages, as well as history and geography. The three men teachers took turns in teaching music. The school day began at 8.30 a.m. and ran until 3.30 in the afternoon, with an hour out for noon break. In Burma the classes follow the British system, where they run from kindergarten to the tenth standard, which is the equivalent of the American high school. Eventually, our school went up to the fifth standard, which is about the equivalent of the American seventh or eighth grade. However, our pass mark was 60 per cent, as opposed to 40 per cent in the state-run schools elsewhere in Burma.

In the new school building, the need for blackboards, chalk and other writing materials became more pressing than ever. It was frustrating to realize that while some schools in the United States were installing teaching machines and computerized questioning devices, we lacked even such old-fashioned items as pencils, paper and chalk. We had to find some materials, and a purposeful search along the river revealed a place where there was slate that could be polished smooth with rocks and sand. Small pieces of slate could be used as pencils. The students had been using foot-square sections of banana leaves in lieu of paper, writing on them with pieces of charcoal. A little later, deposits of light grey chalky clay were found. After a lengthy refining process worked out by Jesse, the clay was rolled into round strips and put in the sun to dry. This baked clay proved to be very satisfactory chalk. Blackboards for the teachers were made of hand-hewn chinquapin boards cut to the right size and painted with a mixture of egg white and the powdered carbon black from used-up torch batteries. The egg whites were furnished by the pupils. On the day when a blackboard was to be refinished, each child in a designated class brought an egg to school. The whites went into the paint pot, but the yolks usually provided a meal for the teachers, although eggs without the whites were not much of a treat.

As classes progressed, the need for textbooks became increasingly evident. While we did not have enough paper to provide exercise-books, or even scratch-pads for homework, we did have a small stock that could be used for textbooks. We also had stencils and a ninety-five-pound Gestetner duplicator, which had been the most formidable single item in the three hundred loads of baggage we had brought with us from Putao. However, someone had to write the textbooks.

Here Helen, who had specialized in English at college, got into the act. Her contribution was a series of graded English readers that included a vocabulary of simple words referring to things and actions familiar to the pupils, along with sentences in which the words were used, and simple grammar lessons. Later, as higher grades were added to the school, new books were added to the series, until there were six. The readers for the lower grades eventually went through several editions of fifty copies each and were used not only in our school in Zi-yu-di but in Gu-to and Binuzu as well. The books proved to be an invaluable help. Their preparation took a great deal of Helen's time, because she not only wrote and revised the material, but also typed the stencils for me to run off. The pages were then gathered into books and stapled.

In addition, Yuliya, the fourth teacher in our school, assembled material for a small reader in Kachin. This, too, was stencilled and made up into a booklet.

For other classes, each teacher prepared his material and put it on the blackboard for the students to copy. Later, after the students had become more proficient in writing, the teachers dictated their material to save time. But in either case, each student had his or her 'textbook' in hand.

Later on, in teaching English to the higher grades, David tried to insist that no other language be spoken during the one-hour class, aside from a few necessary explanations. He was pleased and often surprised at the rapidity with which his students picked up new words and mixed them into their Lisu conversation, much to the mystification of their parents and other uninitiated listeners. This was particularly true in the case of words learned in David's science class. There anatomy was studied, and the names of the bones were learned in English. One day a child who had been kicked in the shin during recess came in complaining, '*Ma-pa, Ah-pu ni ngw* tibia *ma kwa* kick *la sih a la* crack *ye cheo*', which meant, 'Teacher, Ah-pu kicked my tibia and almost cracked it.' Another boy, who had a history of malaria, appeared in class one morning suffering from what he described as 'a pain in my cervical vertebrae' – that is, a stiff neck.

As a teacher, David was a great believer in practical demonstrations to illustrate his lessons. Partly to show his science students how electricity worked, and partly for our own convenience, he decided to go ahead with the construction of a hydro-electric system at our new house. It was based, of course, on the knowledge he had gained while studying his electronics books, and he planned to use some materials readily available locally, as well as some of the parts he had been able to get from downed aeroplanes.

His scheme was simple but ingenious. After studying his meticulous drawings, I encouraged him to go ahead and promised to help with any carpentry work and in any other way needed. The heart of the project was a multipole magnet in relatively good condition and some copper wire from an old transformer. It had taken nearly a year of sending out word through the jungle grapevine before he collected enough material to construct a magneto of sorts. By the time he joined us in Zi-yu-di, he had this essential part of his generator in working order.

There was a steeply inclined, swift-flowing mountain stream near our house, and we had already built a hollowed-out split-log sluiceway to divert some of its flow into a water-powered rice-pounder. David's initial plan called for adding another section of log to the sluiceway, in a sort of Y formation, so that he could activate a water-wheel by switching the flow on to it when the rice-pounder wasn't in use. The wheel was made out of half-inch wooden flanges mortised into a hardwood hub and mounted on iron axles driven into each side of the hub. Lubricated with a piece of bacon rind, it was able to turn at about sixty revolutions a minute.

Because he needed a much higher speed at the generator, the next step was to make a simple reduction gear. David made pulleys by setting dowel-pins at regular intervals around a wooden disc, drilling holes in the dowels, and interthreading the outer tips with rattan in zigzag fashion to form a kind of cage wheel. The large pulley was four feet in diameter, and the small pulley that drove the magneto in the generator was only an inch and a half in diameter. After many experiments, David discovered that the belt that would work best was a ninety-pound nylon fishing line rubbed with yellow beeswax to keep it from slipping. Once in operation, this rig resulted in two thousand revolutions a minute at the generator.

The purpose of the generator was to send enough current into our house to light some small bulbs David had saved from our torches when their batteries gave out. Naturally, it had taken quite some time for David to put this rig together, and the curious Lisu followed his progress with great interest. Some forty of them were on hand when at last he was ready to give it a try. As the wheel began to turn, the bulbs began to glow, somewhat dimly, to be sure, since the sun was still high in the afternoon sky, but brightly enough to evoke a kind of gasping chorus of 'Ah-neh! Ah-neh!' – meaning, roughly, 'Look at that!' – from the surprised onlookers. By nightfall, when it became apparent that we would have enough light to eat by, they were even more amazed. 'No more candles to blow in the wind!' they said. 'No more ways for fire to start when a candle falls on the floor! No more dripping wax! Ah-neh!'

As successful as his hydro-electric system appeared to be, it was far from satisfactory to David. With the water-wheel turning at only sixty revolutions a minute, he could get only six to twelve volts out of the generator. Moreover, it produced a truly alternating current, with the result that the illumination from our lighting fixtures tended to wax and wane in a very disconcerting fashion. So David reasoned that if he could bring more water-power to bear and have a faster turning wheel, he would then be able to produce direct current at a higher and more uniform voltage.

The solution David thought up was to construct an aqueduct that would carry water from a pool some eight hundred feet upstream and deliver it to the wheel with considerably more impact than that of the water delivered by the sluiceway designed to activate the rice-pounder. The river dropped at least seventy-five feet in its course from the pool to the wheel. David figured that it would be entirely feasible to dig a ditch parallel to the course of the river but much less steep, providing for a concentrated vertical drop of thirty feet or more at the point of contact with the wheel. But the difficulty with this scheme was that, with our limited supplies of tools and labour, such an excavating job seemed roughly comparable to digging the Panama Canal.

With his devoted disciples and assistants, Ronnie and Tommy, David spent several months making drawings to scale and still more time surveying a route the aqueduct could follow, roughly parallel to the river, but with a much less precipitous fall. When David was completely convinced that the job was feasible, the three boys laid out the course for the aqueduct, using two carpenter's levels to ensure a steady downgrade. They could only afford to spare an hour or two a day from their other chores, and the only tools they had were a single shovel and a heavy-duty hoe, so they made slow progress, averaging perhaps eight or ten feet a day.

Their path was blocked by a tangle of jungle and out-croppings of enormous rock. The worst of the jungle was rattan, growing in clumps of twenty or thirty shoots, many of them two hundred feet long, with very sharp thorns at the base root. These all had to be hacked off and dug up before any trenching could be done. In addition, the boys had to cut through fallen trees. As for the rocks, they were forced to call on friendly Lisu in the neighbourhood to help them pry these obstacles out of the way with improvised crowbars. They had little trouble in getting such assistance, because the Lisu were fascinated with the project. Some, having faith in David's demonstrated mechanical ability, were sure it would work. Others, dubiously eyeing the contrast between the gentle gradient of the aqueduct and the steep pitch of the river, were sure it wouldn't. 'Anyone can see your ditch tilts the wrong way', these sceptics observed. 'Water won't run uphill. It'll never run. You wait and see.'

David and Ronnie consulted their surveying tools anew and toiled on, inching their way up towards the source pool, while suspense in the village mounted. Finally, the great day arrived when the last ten-foot segment of earth between the water-wheel at the lower end and the source pool at the upper end was about to be removed. As David and Ronnie lifted out the last few shovelfuls of earth and laid in place the section of wooden trough that would direct the flow and, at the same time, prevent erosion, some fifty villagers and students were on hand for the moment of decision. When the water from the pool began to trickle into the ditch, the onlookers began to move along beside it. Many were still sure the flow would stop and the water spill over the sides when it reached what appeared to be an uphill stretch of the ditch – no matter what the 'bubble eye' of the carpenter's level said. Others were equally convinced that it would run on as it was meant to do in order to reach its final destination. The argument continued as they ran or trotted along beside the advancing trickle, which soon became a steady and increasingly rapid stream.

'See, see, it is surely going to reach all the way!' shouted the believers. 'The bubble eye tells the truth!'

'No, no, wait a few minutes, you'll soon find out. The stream won't ever reach the wheel!' shouted the sceptics.

Tripping over each other as they scrambled along the embankment beside the ditch, the spectators kept up a constant babble of controversy for the whole twenty minutes or more that it took for the water to reach the wheel. At the lower end, David and Ronnie had constructed a steep sluiceway about forty feet long, made out of two twenty-foot sections of a huge log cut in half and hollowed out to accommodate the stream of water, and angled downwards about forty-five degrees. At the bottom of this sluiceway stood the motionless ten-inch water-wheel, a fragile-looking object whose six thin wooden blades looked as though they would break off as soon as the water struck them. Actually, the blades were solidly mortised into a hardwood hub, mounted on ball-bearings from a downed aeroplane, surrounding a steel hub well anointed with bacon grease.

When the stream finally encountered the blades of the wheel, they began to move just as they were intended to do, slowly at first, but rapidly accelerating to what David later estimated to be some 340 revolutions a minute, which, in turn, meant over 2500 revolutions at the generator. This was much faster than he had foreseen in his most optimistic calculations. The new rig provided not only enough current – some twenty volts – to light up our house, but enough extra to run our cassette-players and even the precious radio on which, using the power of our now almost exhausted stock of batteries, we had been able to follow the nightly news programmes from Australia and the BBC.

Unlike its predecessor, the new system had no tendency to surge or vary, nor was it susceptible, like the first one, to intermittent breakdowns. Controlled by a rattan pull-switch on our porch, which diverted the flow of water from the sluiceway directly back to the river when no current was needed, it proved to be a dependable household helper through the remainder of our stay in the valley. When we left, in 1972, it was still in top-notch working order, and by this time David had taught several of the tribesmen enough about maintenance to keep it running almost indefinitely.

David's inventiveness was not limited to electronics. Though he couldn't hunt successfully himself, he contributed to this very necessary aspect of our survival by modifying weapons. Among other things, he created a series of specially shaped arrowheads designed to penetrate different portions of a quarry's anatomy. And he developed an explosive shotgun slug. This he made by hollowing out the slug and inserting behind the head a charge of home-made gunpowder that would explode on impact.

Making the gunpowder was a delicate and dangerous

undertaking. Only three ingredients were required: charcoal, saltpetre and sulphur. There were two methods of combining them. One involved mixing the ingredients after they had been pulverized by pounding them in a large wooden mortar. The quality of the finished product depended a great deal on the skill with which the ingredients were pounded. The test of quality was to take a small – a very small – amount, place it on a piece of paper, and then hold a red-hot coal from the fire close to it until it ignited. If it went up in a sudden, bluish-white puff, creating no smoke and leaving no residue, then the powder was pronounced excellent.

A second method was to combine the ingredients in a cast-iron pan, add the proper measure of water, and heat the mixture until the water evaporated. As the water disappeared, the amount of heat was reduced, and a close watch kept on the contents of the pan. When the moisture was all gone, the powder was put into the wooden mortar and the procedure outlined above was followed. This method was considered very dangerous, and there were several accidents in which people were severely burned when the mixture ignited unexpectedly.

David wasn't the only member of the family involved in the school. When the Yangmi family left, my youngest son, Ron, took over the teaching of Bible classes, as well as some English classes in the lower grades. In addition to our school at Zi-yu-di, one was started a few weeks later at Binuzu. About the same time a third school was opened at Gu-to, in which Joni was one of the teachers. The following year it was moved to Sour Fruit Hill (Si-chuh-do) and Steve was added to the staff. After Robert's wife, Betty, and some of the children (including Joni) left, Steve continued to teach in the school at Sour Fruit Hill until it combined with the one at Zi-yu-di in 1970.

My three daughters and Robert's oldest daughter, Deedee, attended the schools as students, and all of them did well. My oldest daughter, Margaret, and Deedee had both started school in Putao, and when they resumed their education after a two-year hiatus, they picked up where they had left off without difficulty. For Margaret, the only drawback in attending school was that it separated her for several hours every day from her pet bird, Ko-kee-la-cah, which she had found as a nestling and raised by hand, feeding it kernels of green corn and giving it water with an eye-dropper. For a time Ko-kee-la-cah followed her to school every morning as faithfully as Mary's little lamb. It would then fly home, stopping *en route* to beg for titbits in the houses of certain favourite neighbours, and then rest by perching on Helen's typewriter while she worked. Finally, when Ko-kee-la-cah was fully grown, the call of another member of its species caused it to desert its nest in our house for one in the nearby trees.

We could not be sure how well the school had done its job until we got back to the United States, where our daughters entered school in Terre Haute, Indiana. It took all three of them a few months to catch on to the new language of instruction, but once they had done so, we were quite pleased with their performance, especially with Margaret's. Going straight from the fourth standard at Zi-yu-di into the ninth grade at Terre Haute, Margaret had caught up with her class by her second term there. Robert's girls also entered American schools and were able to keep pace with their classmates.

The play areas we levelled off adjacent to the schools became places where the students and other children could come to play when school was not in session. Play equipment was as scarce as anything else in our valley, and my second son, Tommy, with some of his brother's mechanical bent but a greater interest in sports, went to work on the problem. He tanned deer hides, and, using a paper pattern that he and David worked out, cut them to the official specifications for a volley ball. He then stitched them by hand, using the locally made homespun thread. He also turned out badminton rackets strung with nylon fishing line and shuttlecocks of balsa-like wood, fletched with chick feathers. Besides Tommy's products, other improvised playthings included skipping-ropes made from rattan vines and spinning-tops whittled out of chinquapin roots, with metal pegs made out of bits of steel wire or an occasional nail or screw.

Then there were the universal children's games that needed no equipment. One of these was hide-and-seek; another was known in our valley as 'leddy' – the Lisu corruption of the English word 'Ready?' which is called out by whoever is 'it' in the game. In selecting an 'it', incidentally, I was fascinated to find that the Lisu children would chant an equivalent of 'eenie, meenie, minie, mo'. Nothing made us so certain that Hidden Valley was truly a kind of Shangri-la as the sound of children's voices singsonging their games in the quiet dusk.

Chapter 12

Then the Lord said to Moses, 'Behold, I will
rain bread from heaven for you . . .'
EXODUS 16 : 4

In 1968, having won the struggle for survival in the jungle,
with good houses built and schools established, the people
of Hidden Valley began to branch out into other activities
that were destined to turn this once isolated stretch of
jungle into one of the richest communities in northern
Burma. World events played a curious part in this development. That summer, India and China were engaged in an
undeclared shooting war along most of their long mutual
border from Kashmir to Tibet. One result of this conflict
was to bring some two thousand troops into the tongue of
Indian territory adjacent to our valley. Ironically (in view
of Indian intransigence in 1965), the need to feed these
troops caused the army commissariat to close its eyes to the
fact that the border was supposedly sealed and seek whatever food the Lisu of Hidden Valley could spare.

Grain was still in short supply in our valley, but one item
most Lisu families had brought from Putao had thrived
beyond all expectations in the jungle – the lowly chicken.
This may not be too surprising, in view of the fact that some
historians claim the common barnyard chicken was once
an Indian jungle fowl that the soldiers of Alexander the
Great domesticated and imported to Europe. In fact,
there are still wild chickens in the jungles of north Burma.
Our chickens, at any rate, deprived of any sort of grain,
let alone commercial chicken-feed, proliferated on a diet
of grubs and insects to the extent that nearly every family
had a flock of twenty to fifty fowl by 1968. So there were
eggs to sell to the troops, as well as live chickens for roasting

or stewing, along with pork, venison, fish, and any other jungle meats our hunters could supply. In return, rupees began flowing into Hidden Valley and became an accepted medium of exchange.

Obviously, we had not for many years had any real need of a money economy. What exchange took place in the valley in the early days took the form of either Lisu-style sharing or barter. Many of the Lisu had brought with them a store of small change, which was used mainly for offerings in church on Sunday or at the conventions, in accordance with the usual practice of taking a collection at these services. The collections, even at the conventions, always included offerings of eggs, chickens, little pigs, scraps of cloth, smoked meats and the like, as well as some cash. It was considered neither strange nor improper to lead a little pig to the front of the church and tie it to the leg of the table, or to carry a chicken in a basketlike cage and deposit it in front of the table. These, too, were offerings to God. The Lisu had learned from experience that those who tithed not only their cash income, but their animals and produce as well, were blessed in many ways. So tithing was a usual practice, but it was always done voluntarily, because the people felt it was the right thing for them to do.

Despite the shortage of cash, most Lisu managed to keep on hand a small supply of negotiable gold and jewels. There is gold to be panned along almost all the streams in northern Burma. In winter the people go down to the stream bed and look for gold in the sand exposed by the receding waters, using methods similar to those used in the American West in the days of the gold rush. The gold dust they find is packaged in little bamboo tubes. Then it is weighed on small scales made especially for that purpose. Like anything else from nature, gold often seemed to us to come as a direct gift of God. Once in Putao, for example, a starving widow went down to the stream bed one afternoon, dipped her rice bowl into the sand, and began idly panning it. All the while she was praying to God for some way to get rice for her children. Suddenly she found a gold nugget in her bowl, a nugget large enough to buy forty five-gallon tins of rice.

Burma is famous, of course, for its rubies, jade and sapphires, some of which come from mines just to the south of Hidden Valley. Being so common throughout northern Burma, these precious stones, particularly rubies, were handed about rather freely among the Lisu. Many people wore them for adornments in rings and necklaces and the like, except when swimming in the mountain streams. The reason for this taboo was one of the strangest and deadliest of all the creatures we ever encountered – the *bu-rin*, a giant water-snake.

Some sceptics claim that the bu-rin is a sort of Asian Loch Ness monster, but our experience would give it far more substance than that. True, these snakes are rare, and their existence, especially among the loquacious Lisu, is more a matter of fearsome fancy than fact. But they are so firmly a part of the lore of the area that they must be the original model for the Naga, or serpent-god, that figures so conspicuously in the superstitions and the art of both Burma and India.

The full-grown bu-rin is apparently about the same size as the land-based python or boa constrictor – up to forty or fifty feet in length, and as much as eight or ten inches in diameter at its thickest point. The resemblance ends there. The python, rather like the creature portrayed in Kipling's *Jungle Book*, tends to be a somewhat torpid and even benevolent serpent, and its presence is not merely tolerated but welcomed by many villagers throughout the whole of South-East Asia. Capable of crushing a deer or even a tiger to death and then swallowing it whole, the python is usually content to live on much smaller creatures, like rats or mice, and is for this reason often considered a definite asset to any small community or large household. The bu-rin, on the other hand, is not only shy of mankind but hostile to all invaders of its watery habitat. As a result, there are numerous well-authenticated stories of its attacking swimmers in forest pools or of its upsetting rafts and small boats, whose occupants are then more or less at its mercy.

There is one incident involving a bu-rin that I can authenticate. An outdoor Bible class was being held by one of our Lisu pastors beside a river near Putao. When the class broke up, its members went swimming in a nearby pool. One of the group, noted for his ability as a swimmer, ventured further out in the pool than the others. When he shouted for help and then suddenly submerged, his companions at first supposed that he was joking. It was only when he reappeared some distance further down the stream and again shouted for help that the other members of the party saw that he was actually being dragged under by a gigantic snake, which had coiled around his arms and pinned them to his sides. They rushed along the bank to the point at which he had surfaced, but by this time he had been dragged under again. Neither he nor the bu-rin ever reappeared.

Numerous other reports of similar happenings, all from reliable eye-witnesses, have convinced me that the bu-rin is indeed a creature whose existence should be acknowledged by all travellers in the hill country of southern Asia. The snake apparently looks a good deal like the python, except that the head of the male is surmounted by a central ridge or crest, somewhat in the manner of a cock's comb. Bodies of bu-rin victims that have later been recovered have also shown numerous punctures, indicating that, unlike the python, which depends wholly on its constricting powers, the bu-rin also uses fangs, poisonous or otherwise.

The only time members of our family saw what they took to be a bu-rin was when Robert's three sons were on a hunting trip. They had camped near a river, and Bobby was left to tend the fire while his two older brothers and some Lisu companions went out in search of game. Coming back to camp, the hunters noticed a great gash in the sand bank, as if something had been dragged up from the river. They supposed Bobby had found a heavy piece of driftwood to use in the fire. When Bobby said he had nothing to do with the strange marking, the talk turned to the possibility of there being a bu-rin in the river. Some of the Lisu were planning to go upstream to cast a fishing net; they decided to go anyway, because one of the tales about the bu-rin was that metal like silver or lead will drive it away. The net had lead sinkers.

'So they went fishing,' Stevie later told us, 'and about the time they had thrown the first net into the water, we heard this big splash. Joni and I just sat there, but Bobby stood up, wanting to see how big a fish it was. It sounded like a terrific big fish. But he cried out, "A snake! A snake!" We stood up and could see from the ripples that some very long thing had splashed the waters, broken the surface of the water. So we went out and looked, and down near the rapids, we saw the snake raise its head. It had no comb on it, so it must have been a female.'

While silver or lead was thought to drive the bu-rin away, it was believed that other things, particularly rubies, would attract it. Hence the ban on wearing jewellery into the water, particularly the streams that were used for community bathing near any village.

Equally dreaded – perhaps more so, because they were more numerous – were the poisonous snakes to be found in the jungle and occasionally in villages and even houses. Back in Putao, a deadly viper had been found and killed under a bed in Robert's house; and one night a krait, also deadly, was killed under our dining-room table. And once, a seven-foot king-cobra chose my parents' wood-pile in Putao as its home.

After we moved to Zi-yu-di, our son Tom had an unforgettable encounter with a king-cobra. He was out hunting one afternoon when, just off the trail, he heard a rustling sound. Thinking it might be a deer, he decided to investigate. As he walked along a fallen log, the sound seemed closer. Just then he looked down and saw what at first seemed to be a tree branch, but when it moved he suddenly realized it was a snake – not just any snake, but a king-cobra. As this knowledge penetrated his consciousness, he froze for a moment, but then he saw that the cobra was in the process of swallowing a smaller snake, with about half the meal still protruding from its mouth!

'When I saw that,' Tom recalls, 'I knew the snake couldn't attack me and decided it was safe to try to kill it. As I stood staring, the snake began to move. I guess I must have panicked a bit, because I pulled out my knife and just started chopping at it as it slithered past me. It looked as if it might get away, so I did something that still gives me the creeps when I think about it. I reached down, grabbed it by the tail, and swung my knife real hard so as to cut clear through the body – which was about four inches in diameter – and the next thing I knew I was standing there with a foot-long piece of the snake's tail dangling from my hand. I tossed that to one side, jumped off the log, and started chasing the snake, which was heading for some bushes. I caught up with it in just the right place: its head was between two rocks, so I hit it real hard several times, until the snake was dead. I got a piece of jungle vine and tied it around the remainder of the snake near the tail end. Even after it was dead, the head kept raising up, and the hood spreading out – it was scary. And then I began to think, "What if it has a mate, and it starts after me?" I picked up the piece of tail I'd thrown away – I wanted to measure the whole thing – and started for home real fast!'

We were in the yard when Tom came back and could scarcely believe our eyes. I got out my tape-measure and found that the cobra was just over twelve feet long. That was the biggest anyone had seen in that area, and word spread quickly about the big snake that had been killed. One of the men in the village came and asked if he could have the gall-bladder – reputed to have medicinal value – and some of the fat. Tom agreed, and after the snake had been opened and the gall-bladder and fat removed, he brought his share of the fat into the house, where we rendered it somewhat like lard. Just about half the fat on the snake provided a twelve-ounce jar full of oil, which is highly prized as an ointment for jungle sores.

The Lisu who had returned home in the wake of the flag march in 1966 were, of course, curious about what had become of the friends and relatives they had left in the jungle. In the first dry season, a few of the more adventurous among them set out from Putao with items like salt and tea and cloth, which they knew would be badly needed in Hidden Valley. They were agreeably surprised to find that their 'gifts' could be exchanged for items like our aluminium pots and pans, unobtainable in Putao and thus of great value. The goods and the tales they took back to Putao stirred so much interest that more than a hundred traders found their way into Hidden Valley in the winter of 1968–69. By then we had found something far more valuable than kitchenware, or even gold. It was mushrooms.

Like many Westerners, the Lisu have a built-in suspicion of mushrooms and all other fungi. Under normal circumstances they ignore them in their diet, except for a few varieties. But, during our first two years in the jungle, driven by desperation to try anything that might vary our monotonous diet of sago and atu, most of us overcame our scruples about mushrooms. As a result, we learned to enjoy a wide variety of jungle fungi, including – as Robert and I were able to ascertain from our small reference library – such species as *galarina*, *tunaris*, *cortinarius* and the clumplike *colipia*. The mushroom we came to like best – it was also, providentially, the most plentiful in our communities – was a species for which we could find no scientific name. Known locally as *tsumu*, this particular mushroom had several qualities that distinguished it from other varieties. One was its flavour, which was more like that of a meat than a vegetable. In fact, it rather resembled tender chicken. Another was its delicate light brown colour and soft texture. A third was its peculiar habitat, which made it easy to harvest as soon as we knew the secret of where to look for it.

When we or our children first went to the jungle in

search of tsumu, we were unable to find them in the ample quantities with which our neighbours filled their baskets. We were quite disconcerted by this, at which the mushroom-pickers laughed heartily. 'Well, you have to know where to look', they explained. 'These mushrooms grow in only one place, on a dead log of chinquapin wood. If you can find a log like that and look on the underside of it, you will get all the tsumu you can carry – that is, if someone else hasn't already found the log. In the meantime, here, have some of ours!'

With this bit of lore in our possession, we became, if not the most expert tsumu-hunters in the community, at least able to hold our own with the rest. Our children learned quickly, because they had the time to gain experience with our Lisu neighbours. Robert and his family, whose house on Chinquapin Hill was in the very heart of the richest tsumu-producing region in the whole valley, soon became expert harvesters of this delicacy.

At first we were not aware of the commercial value of tsumu. We knew, as did many of the Lisu, that they were widely used by the Chinese in their cooking. But when we told some of the visitors from Putao that tsumu grew in the area, they became really excited. It seems that the price offered for these mushrooms by merchants in Putao was higher than it had been for years, because demand was great and the supply from usual sources apparently had diminished. Our visitors quickly bought up all we had on hand and promised to return for more.

Among the other special virtues of the tsumu is the rapidity with which it grows. A good, year-old chinquapin log will produce a whole new crop of mushrooms every two weeks. Our own communities could have eaten all of the local crop, but instead of doing so, most of our villagers preferred to supplement their diet with other varieties of mushroom and to collect tsumu for export only. These mushrooms were strung on thin bamboo strips and hung over and around the fireplace to dry. In this way they could be kept without spoiling for several months, while waiting for the merchants to come, and then be sold to the highest bidder. Soon the traders from Putao, who began arriving in increasing numbers, had bid up the price of tsumu in a way that had far-reaching effects on the life of our community.

At this time the official pay rate for agricultural labour in Burma, as set forth in the wage tables of the socialist government, was something like 3.15 kyats (pronounced 'jats'), or about 30 pence a day. Prices for all ordinary vegetables were likewise standardized at a proportionately modest figure. However, tsumu mushrooms were such a rarity that government commodity scales did not even include them, and their price was set by the law of supply and demand. As a result, the traders, knowing they could sell all the tsumu they could carry at a good profit in the free market, were ready to pay our villagers excellent prices for the dried ones. (They offered the equivalent of about £7 to £9 per *vis*, a unit of weight equal to 3.6 pounds; that is, up to £2 or more per pound.) During the height of the relatively brief season when the tsumu ripened, just after the monsoon, an efficient picker could sometimes harvest the equivalent of twenty pounds of dried mushrooms in the course of a single day. Thus, for a brief time, his earnings exceeded those of a successful Burmese lawyer, doctor or businessman, let alone an ordinary labourer.

Another kind of mushroom, known locally as either rat-ear or monkey-ear, and called old-man's-ear by the Chinese, had commercial value. Black in colour and much more plentiful than the tsumu, it was so easily identified that even small children could help gather it. But, then, it brought a much lower price. However, because it was easy to find, a number of the local students were able to gather and sell enough to pay their school fees and buy their school books for the year.

Most of the able-bodied male adults in our villages were full-time hunters or farmers, so the majority of mushroom-pickers were older women and young girls. The girls' slender figures made it easy for them to get into the crannies where the fungi were likely to develop. Soon many of them were earning in a few weeks' time sums that anywhere else in Burma would have been considered a splendid salary for a full year's work.

In the untamed jungles, where the trees were far apart and fell only at infrequent intervals, dead chinquapin logs were scarce. Most of them were found in old rice-fields, where the trees had been felled on purpose. Homesteads at Chinquapin Hill and other nearby areas, whose fields contained the largest number of such logs, were naturally the most efficient producers. Because visitors from other villages flocked to such areas in search of the mushrooms, notions about private property soon began to develop a new significance. Sign saying 'Outsiders not invited to gather mushrooms in this field' became a common sight around Chinquapin Hill and other mushroom-producing places. Such signs even appeared in deserted fields that contained chinquapin logs – fields owned by people who, after clearing the ground, had found more fertile plots of land elsewhere.

The mushroom boom soon resulted in the evolution of capitalistic enterprises involving more than property-ownership. Experienced businessmen in our own community – of whom our good friend Sukin was one – offered the villagers a steady price for their tsumu and bought all the mushroom-hunters could bring. Then, when the traders arrived from Putao, the businessmen exchanged their whole accumulation of tsumu for a stock of cloth, tea, salt, medicine and similar sundries, which they would then resell to our villagers. The local merchants – who, in most cases, were scrupulously fair in their dealings – could thus make a reasonable profit while providing the villagers with what amounted to a steady market in 'tsumu futures'. This spared the harvesters the necessity of waiting for the arrival of the out-of-town buyers before disposing of their produce and also tended to establish a uniform and fair price.

Actually, the tsumu mushroom was not the single most valuable item in our wide catalogue of frontier produce.

Along with the mushroom boom there developed a more specialised one in the sale of herbs for use in pharmaceutical products. In some cases, profits from the herbs proved to be even more spectacular than those realized from the mushrooms. North Burma, because of its fantastically prolific rain-forest vegetation, has always been a fertile source of medicinal herbs of many sorts, some used locally and others prized all over the world for their therapeutic qualities. Like the tsumu mushrooms, some such herbs were so rare that their price was not subject to government control, and these could be sold to exporters for whatever they would bring. Most precious of all was an alpine lily known as the *peimu*. In the Far East, the peimu is in wide demand as the basis of a tonic with medicinal properties not unlike sulpha. This tonic is regarded as a cure for all sorts of pulmonary ailments from common colds to pneumonia.

Unlike the tsumu, the peimu is extremely difficult to harvest. In the first place, it grows only above timber-line, at about twelve thousand feet, and usually in the most inaccessible, snow-covered nooks and crannies. The portion of the plant used for the tonic is the bulbous root, and the roots must be excavated one by one from rocky and often frozen soil. This arduous process destroys digging knives at the rate of two or three per day. Just finding this rare plant calls for expert knowledge, as well as climbing skills. Since a peimu-hunting expedition usually involved spending at least two weeks at a high altitude, with no guarantee of eventual success, only a very few of the hardiest hunters and explorers in our community cared to risk their time in this precarious sideline.

For those who did it successfully, the rewards were commensurate with the risks. Peimu bulbs brought considerably more per pound than the tsumu mushrooms, and so a successful foray to the mountaintops could pay off handsomely. One particularly adept peimu-gatherer by the name of Jyeba, who made one two-week trip each year, made as much as eight hundred kyats (approximately £70) from this sideline alone.

Curious about the real medicinal value of the peimu bulb, I arranged to have some sent to a major pharmaceutical manufacturer in the United States soon after our return. The report I received stated that the chemicals contained in the plant provided an antidote for tuberculosis bacilli more effective than any other single agent known. Whether the peimu can eventually be utilized to advantage in the treatment of tuberculosis (and possibly some other diseases) will require some years of experimentation to determine, the report stated.

Another herb that we found profitable as a trade crop was a rock fern of which the botanical name is *Coptis teeta*. Much hardier and more commonplace than the exotic peimu, *Coptus teeta* can readily be found growing wild in the jungle and is also easy to transplant and raise in a home garden plot. This plant is a fibrous, rooted creeper that contains a yellow dye like quinacrine dihydrochloride, used in the antimalarial drug atebrin. It has valuable properties as a germicidal lotion and, when taken internally, was found useful in reducing the fever of sufferers from malaria or dengue, although it was not a cure. This plant was by no means as precious as peimu, but was in steady enough demand by visiting traders to make a substantial contribution to the expansion of our jungle economy.

Still another product of great value that, like peimu, had to be sought at high altitudes was musk. This precious ingredient of perfume comes from a small sac under the skin of the abdomen of the musk-deer, which roams the Himalayan snowline from Tibet to north Burma. About four feet long and two feet high, the musk-deer is equipped with tusklike fangs to break the ice or snow crust that covers its food during the winter months. This small beast would long ago have been hunted to extinction except for the difficulties of tracking it down. The most adventurous of Robert's boys, his second son, Steve, learned about these difficulties the hard way, by joining a hunt.

When they are launched from a more populous base like Putao, long hunting expeditions are usually accompanied by porters to carry the camping equipment. There were no men to spare in Hidden Valley, so Steve and his companions each had to carry seventy-pound loads in addition to their weapons. Thus burdened, they found the climb to the timber-line a gruelling experience. By the second day out, Steve was beginning to feel feverish and weak, and when the party reached their camp-site – an overhanging rock shelf at about twelve thousand feet – he knew he could not go on. Steve didn't know quite what was the matter with him. He experienced alternating chills and fever and diarrhoea and concluded that he had malaria. But dosing himself with Nivaquine didn't help. Later he learned that he had been suffering from haemorrhagic dengue, sometimes known as ten-day breakbone fever. It can prove fatal, and victims who don't die often wish they could. This was Steve's feeling as he lay between bouts of fever and diarrhoea in the cavelike shelter of the rock.

'There was terrific wind – sleet storms, and wind all the time, and bitter cold', Steve recalls. 'There was a landslide that scarred the mountain for several miles, and often we would hear rocks cascading down it. Because of this, people don't go up there in the monsoon season; it's almost sure death with rocks coming down at you. To go to the toilet, I had to hang on to a root at the edge of a precipice with a drop of two or three hundred feet.

'I had told all the others to go ahead and try to accomplish the mission, but one fellow stayed with me. It was Ah-dee Wafoo's son, Ah-pu, and I had always thought of him as the ugliest fellow I had ever seen. Well, for a week, he just took care of me – cooked my food, though I didn't eat much; took me to relieve myself when I was too weak even to hang on to the root; sang to me. And a very interesting thing happened. After a week, he was just transformed! He became one of the handsomest men I'd ever seen, and even now he looks beautiful to me. I don't know how such a thing can take place.'

Just about the time Steve thought that he would surely die, he saw a great rainbow, arching from the cold mountainside where he lay, across the thick rhododendron forest below him, down through the great growths of hardwood trees below, until it touched the valley floor in a glow of gold. He yearned to follow it, to be back down in the warm valley with his family. 'All of a sudden I became determined not to give up', he says, and from that moment he began to improve slowly. By the time the others returned from the hunt, he was able to lift his pack and join them on the homeward trail, richer in everything but the musk and herbs he had gone to find.

Chapter 13

This day shall be for you a memorial day,
and you shall keep it as a feast to the Lord;
throughout your generations you shall observe
it as an ordinance for ever.

EXODUS 12 : 14

The great festival of the year, the Christmas convention,
was not always held on 25 December, but on the weekend
nearest that date. If it fell in the middle of the week, we
usually chose the weekend nearest the full moon. This was
partly because bright moonlight facilitated moving about at
night at the convention. But, even more important to people
who were camping out in the open, it was the time when
rain was least likely. The moon was our natural calendar,
just as the sun was our clock. Planting, hunting trips,
journeys and assemblies were all governed by the phases
of the moon. These natural measures of time seemed to us
much more in accord with God's plan for man than the
mechanical devices by which man drives himself in most
of the modern world. Being so in tune with the rhythms of
nature was just one more blessing of life in the jungle that
we came to miss sorely once we left.

At the convention that marked the end of 1968 and the
beginning of 1969, we tried for the first time to bring
together nearly everybody – some two thousand people in
all – from both sides of Hidden Valley. There was enough
food now, and enough leisure, to make this feasible. The
site of the convention was in some harvested rice-fields in a
flat area beside a stream, at the base of Chinquapin Hill.
We prepared for the gathering by zoning a large area so
that camping grounds would be available for each family
group. For the meeting itself we erected a great enclosure,
about two hundred feet square, by putting up poles eight
feet apart to hold crossbeams and then thatching them

over with straw and banana leaves. Under the roof we hung flowers and coloured leaves and, for a note of thanksgiving, bundles of millet or sorghum, complete with the heads of grain, as well as ears of dried corn. Along the paths leading into the village were posted signs: 'Welcome to the 1968 Birthday Convention for Jesus.'

We went early on Friday, 27 December, but most of the people began trickling in towards evening. Often we could hear them coming long before we actually saw them. Each village or family group liked to travel together. As they walked along, someone began to sing, and first one, then another, would join in until there was a four-part harmony. As we lined up to greet them, they would walk past single-file, headman first and the rest of the group strung out behind. In baskets carried on their backs and supported by straps across their heads, they piled clothes and bedding, on top of which was their food – rice, eggs, fresh pork or other meat, and flat cakes of unleavened Lisu rice bread wrapped in leaves. Some carried flutes and guitars to add to the music. Each group quickly found a camp-site, and soon the whole area was pervaded with the pungent smell of cooking fires.

Given the Lisu nature, these conventions were as much a social gathering as a religious occasion. While the women cooked, the men wandered from camp to camp comparing notes on soil conditions, crops, water and game in their respective locations. Young people began eyeing each other, for it was only at convention time that boys could get an idea of the available girls, and vice versa. Lisu sexual morality would be considered strict even by the standards of our Victorian grandparents. Men and women segregated themselves, even in church services, and boys and girls were not supposed to mingle except in a heavily chaperoned setting such as the convention. Even there, it was almost impossible for young people to establish a one-to-one relationship; there was no such thing as dating, holding hands, or moonlight walks, and even private, unchaperoned conversations were not considered proper.

Still, as Bobby recalls: 'After singing a while, the older people would get tired and go to bed, but the young ones would keep on singing. And finally some of the boys would go and sit among the girls, saying, "We need four-part harmony, and you girls are a little weak, so we have come over here to help you." The talk would be between several boys and several girls. You couldn't have one boy talking to one girl. This worked out pretty well, because the Lisu have generally what you might call an out-of-focus personal relationship – that is, they're shy of direct confrontation and kind of talk around a subject. So with this out-of-focus idea it wasn't too hard for a boy and girl to make contact with each other even in a group.'

Bobby's comments are supported by the fact that every convention was followed by a rash of proposals. Lisu tradition dictated that parents arrange marriages for their children, on the theory that love would come along as a result of being married. But among the Christian Lisu, if a boy was attracted to a particular girl and his parents agreed, he could propose to her by a letter sent through the church elders. Joni, Robert's oldest son, fell in love with the daughter of the intrepid and ingenious Boyenu, and because the feeling seemed to be mutual, Robert asked the elders if his son could write a formal proposal. However, Boyenu rejected the idea of his daughter marrying a white man, for several reasons. Pride in his Lisu heritage was probably part of it, for the Lisu do not encourage inter-marriage even with other tribes. But there were practical reasons for his objections too. Being an intelligent and perceptive man, Boyenu realized that marriage to the *hwa-pu-pa* – the white man – would probably mean that his daughter would be taken to a foreign land, and he might never see her again.

Music played a very important part in both religion and romance in Hidden Valley. The chief instrument was the guitar. An ex-soldier and carpenter's apprentice by the name of Yo-meh-zee began turning out acceptable guitars almost as soon as we were settled. As with everything else, this took patience and inventiveness. He had to make the guitars from whatever came to hand – frets and turning keys out of elephant bone, strings from the cables of downed aircraft. The bass string was the hardest, inasmuch as it took thousands of revolutions to wind it. In the end, though, the instruments were good, because Yo-meh-zee was blessed with a good sense of pitch. As money came into the valley, he began selling the guitars or trading them for labour. Bobby, for example, worked ten days to earn his guitar.

At that 1968 convention each village came with its own choir, which had been practising special songs for the occasion. Each group had an opportunity to sing in one or more of the seven services held during the convention. It was a colourful affair, because the women and girls had the time and money to deck themselves out the way they did back in Putao. Black velvet jackets made an appearance again, as did the Lisu's colourful beaded head-dresses and the long strings of beads they wore draped over one shoulder. This great service, with hundreds of joyful voices harmonizing in old hymns like 'What a Friend We Have in Jesus' and 'Amazing Grace', was a true feast to God – a feast of music.

Though we brought them hymns, we had as much to learn about music from the Lisu as they from us. Music has always been part of their lives. The Christian Lisu gave up their old folk-songs, many full of references to spirits in which they no longer believed; but, though they were very shy about it, they did not abandon their sweeter songs of love, which revealed a tenderness between man and woman that seems universal, regardless of culture or custom. Indeed, singing about love fits well with what Bobby called their 'out-of-focus' ways of courting. A favourite song of ours went this way, in rough translation:

> *I sing of a stream and the flowers all around it,*
> *The fragrance scenting the air.*
> *It reminds me of you, so it's like a dream,*

This stream that flows into the valley.
My love covers you like that stream covers rocks
And will last as long as it flows;
My love is as constant as that flowing stream,
Which means my love is for ever.

The whole spirit of that convention ratified our feeling that Hidden Valley was turning into a kind of Shangri-la, where all of us were able to pursue the free and productive life we feel God meant for man. We Morses were now fully engaged in doing the things we felt we could do best — teaching, preparing literature, preaching, healing, helping. Hidden Valley had really become home — hopefully, a permanent home.

It was immediately following this convention that Robert's family moved from Chi-cheh-do to the newly established village of Si-chuh-do (Sour Fruit Hill). The villagers, anxious to have the teacher's family in their midst, had helped them build a seven-room house. It was located on a knoll from which one could look out on a marvellous view, both up and down the valley, as well as up to the snow-covered peaks on the opposite side of the valley.

In Zi-yu-di we constructed what might be called a jungle split-level. It was, in fact, two houses, one above the other on a slope, connected by a runway. In the upper house were one large room that did double duty as kitchen and dining room, and two bedrooms for the three boys; in the lower house were one big front room, with a Lisu-style fireplace in the centre, that served as guest room, living room and study, and two small rooms that were used as bedrooms by the girls and us. These houses had thatch roofs and bamboo floors with cracks so large that if you spilled water, it would run right through. Needless to say, we hardly had to sweep the floor. Later, it took our children some time to get used to the solid floors of the West. Windows were nothing but openings with bamboo lattice-work to keep out the chickens. In winter, when the temperature might drop to thirty-eight degrees and a strong wind came down from the north, we covered them with plastic.

Furnishings were, of necessity, simple and functional. In the big room in the lower house we had a small table and another, the top of which was made of a single board, hand-hewn, three feet wide and five feet long. We also had two raised beds in the rooms and two 'easy chairs' – aluminium folding chairs we had brought with us from Putao. For beds we just rolled bedding out on top of boxes used for storage; to get at the boxes, it was a simple matter of rolling back the bedding. We made raised bamboo beds for the children, but they generally preferred to sleep on straw mats on the floor, like their Lisu friends. They said it was warmer in winter just to curl up on a mat by the fire. It was also convenient for entertaining; Lisu girls would often come to spend the night with our girls, and they would all just roll out their bedding by the fire.

The kitchen-dining area is usually the most interesting part of any house, and ours was no exeption. Our fire, in the Lisu style, was in an open pit about four feet square, at floor level, slightly to one side of centre in a room about fifteen feet by twenty feet. There was no chimney, and the smoke simply rose up to the roof and found its way out through the openings at either end of the house. Though this created some problems – there were ashes everywhere, for example – it had many practical advantages. The smoke not only helped to preserve the thatch in the roof, but served as a preservative for food in a climate where freezing was impossible. About three or four feet above the fire we placed bamboo racks with bamboo mats, on which we dried rice and other foods. We also hung corn and bacon, wrapped in leaves, in the eaves above the fire, where they would stay edible for months.

Comfortable as we were – in comparison to the camping conditions under which we had lived at first – we still, like pioneers everywhere, had to devote a good part of our available time to the essential chores of living. Despite the boom in chickens and the gradual availability of pork – it takes three years before a pig can be slaughtered for ham and bacon – a good part of our meat had to be brought in by hunting and fishing. Moreover, a great deal of time, effort and skill went into butchering and preserving meat. Fortunately, our boys became expert at this.

At first, slaughtering the pigs caused something of a psychological problem for them, because pigs were both pets and provender. Our pig population was descended from the few animals the Lisu had brought with them from Putao. To domesticate their pigs, the Lisu treat the small animals as pets, carrying them around on their backs and, in wintertime, even bringing them into the house, where the pig serves conveniently as a kind of living hot-water bottle. Our girls had followed this custom, and it was a sure indication of the boys' maturing attitude about the fundamental necessities of jungle living that they were able to face up to the job of slaughtering and butchering the pigs.

The boys felt that the most humane way to kill a pig was with a single, well-aimed shot to the head. As soon as the animal dropped, they cut its throat to let the blood run out. Then they heaved the carcass on to a slanted table made of rough boards covered with banana leaves. They had a fire going at the foot of the table to maintain a kettle of boiling water, which they poured over the carcass while they scraped it clean. Moving the carcass to a clean bed of leaves, they eviscerated and quartered it. The rest was a matter of trimming the fat and cutting the meat into various usable portions for chops and steaks and bacon. The bacon and ham were preserved by rubbing them with a mixture of salt and saltpetre and then leaving the pieces in a container coated with beeswax for approximately ten days. After this, the meat was hung to smoke above the fire. The uncured meat had to be eaten quickly, before it could spoil. Butchering for our year's supply of bacon and ham was always done in the wintertime, usually between mid-December and mid-January, at the coldest season.

While the men and boys struggled with the problem of providing food, the women and girls shared the no less arduous tasks of preparing it. They were continually experimenting with ways of making the available grains – rice and sometimes corn – into acceptable flour. One particularly difficult chore was extracting cooking oil from the tiny black seed of a plant that we cultivated around the edges of our gardens. This process involved pounding the seeds to powder in a grain-pounder, heating the powder in a steamer or in an open pan with a little bit of water, and pressing the oil out of the residue in a rather primitive fashion. The residue was placed in a small, closely woven basket, which was put between two logs; then five or six people stood on the top log to weigh it down. Another, equally primitive, method was to place the basket of seed residue in a hollow log and press a wooden bar down against it with wedges. Whatever the method, the result was an acceptable oil with an agreeable flavour, much like peanut oil. The oil had to be boiled until all traces of water had evaporated, or it would turn rancid within a week or so.

Clothes, too, were a continual problem for the women. Lisu families would often start from scratch, making thread from hemp, the plant so prized in a large part of the world as the source of hashish and marijuana. Hemp grows easily in northern Burma, and the Lisu would plant it immediately wherever they moved. They had long ago learned that eating or smoking it unbalanced a person's mind, and they treated it strictly as poison. Only the fittest survive in the jungle, and the man who would risk dulling his senses with hashish was regarded as crazy. But the man who failed to make good use of the marvellous thin bark of the stem of the hemp plant was crazier still.

In their so-called idle hours in the evening, while their men were fletching arrows or making bows for tomorrow's hunt, the Lisu women would painstakingly strip off the hemp bark, shred it with their finger-nails, and splice it to the right thickness. This fibre would then be run over the spinning-wheel to turn it into usable thread, not only for clothes, but for crossbow strings and fishing line.

Although they didn't spin thread, the Morse women

worked almost as hard on clothes as their Lisu counterparts. When the shirts, pants and dresses we had brought from Putao began to wear out, they had to be patched and finally replaced by whatever extra cloth we had brought with us and the little bit we could get from trading. Helen had a bit of mechanical help in the form of an old, hand-cranked, British-made Singer sewing-machine. But she found it an exasperating experience to try to stitch heavy cloth with only one free hand. However, she found surprising assistance in the clothes-making endeavour – as she explains it:

'I didn't have too much trouble with making shirts. I just tore apart an old one and used that for a pattern. But I couldn't take pants the boys were still wearing and tear them apart, so I just had to lay them on the cloth and make a pattern as best I could. I suppose I must have made twelve or fourteen pairs of pants that way, but they never seemed to fit quite right. Then Tommy got interested in the problem.

'Tommy figured out how to take measurements and make pants to suit the individual. Tommy's pants fitted. He got quite a reputation, and people began bringing cloth around and saying, "Please make me a pair." He must have made seventy or eighty pairs. He charged for his labour – with no back pockets, five kyats; with one back pocket, six kyats; and with two back pockets, seven kyats. At the official rate of exchange seven kyats was about sixty pence, and Tommy could make a pair of pants in a couple of days.'

While all this was hard and often tedious work, we were compensated by a pride in our own self-sufficiency that has to be experienced to be appreciated. Our lives were full and happy. We were up at dawn and, despite David's electrical wizardry, in bed early too. We usually had our evening meal at 4.30 in the winter and 5.30 in the summer, to allow some daylight hours for church services and visiting friends in the village. In short, we were settling into a routine; but, considering our past experiences, we should have known that this period of peace was too good to last.

It was Robert, our linguist and diplomat, who first began to suspect that not all of the traders coming into Hidden Valley in 1969 were pursuing legitimate business. Those interested in money would grab up all the herbs and tsumu they could carry and head back to Putao for a quick turnover. But others would linger for months, moving leisurely from village to village, spending long evenings in chitchat with the elders. Robert himself engaged these men in conversation whenever possible. He reluctantly came to the conclusion that many of them were spies, and that the Burmese government was showing a quickening interest in our affairs. Though we don't know exactly what kind of reports they took back, we do know that a bizarre story was circulated to the effect that we had set ourselves up as the white monarchs of a jungle kingdom.

Meanwhile, we heard on our transistor radio that the Burmese army was pushing forward to make a final definition of the boundary between India and Burma throughout all the hill country. This, of course, included our own area. It was partly to check on these reports, as well as for the practical purpose of getting much-needed salt, that Robert allowed his sons Joni and Steve to take part in a very risky mission into Naga territory. Their destination was a Naga village in which some of our Lisu pastors had been preaching for about ten years; and their companion was a Lisu boy, the son of one of these pastors, who was personally acquainted with some of the Naga Christians.

On reaching Naga territory after a harrowing journey down the lower Tarung Hka valley, the boys discovered evidence of a lively skirmish in progress between Burmese government troops and the Naga Independence Army. If they were captured by the Burmese government forces, the boys stood a good chance of being taken as spies and shot without trial. All three of them would have been well advised to turn back immediately and get out of the area as fast as possible. Instead, they pressed on. In fact, when they learned that their friends' village was occupied by

Burmese troops, they took the dangerous chance of sneaking in under cover of darkness.

Having located the house they wanted, and knowing they could rely on the family for protection, they crept into a back room while the members of the family were at the dinner-table. The pastor's son made his presence known by giving a low whistle as a signal to the son of the Naga family, a boy of his own age. The Naga boy lit a candle and came into the back room to investigate. When he recognized his caller, he was utterly incredulous. 'Can it really be you?' he cried. 'What are you doing here? Don't you know this town is full of Burmese soldiers?'

Speaking in hushed whispers so as not to be audible even to the family in the next room, our boys explained that their practical mission was just to bring back some salt, but that they also hoped to get a quick reading of the whole situation between the tribespeople and the Burmese government. After an uneasy night, during which a Burmese patrol actually entered the house and made a cursory search of the room in which they were hiding, the boys attained both objectives. Burdened down with a ten-pound bag of salt apiece, in addition to their original sixty-pound packs, they sneaked away before dawn, crossed the river on a 'borrowed' bamboo raft, and put two or three jungle miles between themselves and any possible pursuers by the time the sun rose the next morning.

Putting together what the boys told us with other reports and with the interest shown in us by the spurious traders, we began to realize that our days of isolation were numbered. Still, considering the difficulties of reaching Hidden Valley, we continued to hope that the Burmese officials might find it more sensible to let sleeping dogs lie, as it were, than to exert the effort to come after us. To that end, we decided to communicate with one of the Burmese civil officials, who happened to be a Christian and was stationed at the administrative centre of the North Naga Hill Tract, which apparently included Hidden Valley. The villagers not only provided this official with a complete census of the citizens of the valley, but offered to pay whatever taxes he thought we might owe. This voluntary compliance with government authority, we reasoned, might persuade the Burmese that further action on their part was unnecessary.

Regardless of unsettling thoughts about the future, we and our Lisu friends had no choice but to carry on with the lives we were making for ourselves. So, after the spring rains died down in 1969, burning and planting began again. As I have said, the Lisu made use of the strong midday updraughts as a kind of natural bellows for their fires. These winds carried sparks and fiery particles hundreds of yards into the air and then spread them harmlessly over miles of damp jungle. But this year they led to a disaster for Robert and his family.

Robert's new house had been built on a ridge where it caught the cooling breezes from every side. On 5 April 1969, while some farmers were burning their fields below, a great spark rose in the updraught and was carried by the breeze on to the roof of the house. Unlike the jungle around it, the roof of bamboo-leaf thatch was tinder-dry as a result of the heat of the sun above and the cooking fire that smouldered day and night below. No one saw the spark land, and by the time the flame was seen, it was too late. The whole house went up like a torch. All the family could save was some bedding, a radio, a typewriter, and part of Robert's translation of the New Testament. Robert's boys were out hunting when the fire occurred, so their guns and some ammunition also survived.

Despite the generosity of their neighbours, who immediately offered them a room to live in and supplied them with food and other necessities, Robert's family was stunned. This accident was particularly hard on Betty, whose life had been difficult enough between her arthritis and the constant care of a new baby. Her state of depression after the fire, though understandable, was dangerous to her health. Moreover, about the time of the fire, we were forced to admit that several of Robert's children had tooth troubles beyond their grandfather's capacity to help them.

Reluctantly the decision was reached that Betty and her children should depart for India or Thailand, where they could get expert medical attention. Thus Betty and all the children except Steve – who followed them a year or so later – crossed the border into India. They were held prisoner for about six weeks, after which they were released and deported. They went to Thailand, where they set up a home, pending developments in Hidden Valley. Robert stayed on in hopes of finishing his translation.

Once Robert's family was safely out of Hidden Valley, we began to think about the future of the Yangmi family. Jesse wanted to take advanced studies in a Bible college in the United States to equip himself better for what he hoped would be a lifetime of mission service among the tribal peoples. The fact that Jesse was a Burma national presented the distinct possibility that he would be separated from Drema Esther if the Burmese authorities should reach us. So we set about making arrangements for Jesse and Drema Esther and their children to go out, via India, to the United States. It was January 1970 before they were able to get out, and that was none too soon. Events that had been nothing but small wisps of cloud on our mountainous horizon were gathering into the dark sky of a monsoon storm.

Chapter 14

Moreover choose able men from all the people,
such as fear God, men who are trustworthy
and who hate a bribe; and place such men over
the people as rulers of thousands, of hundreds,
of fifties, and of tens.

EXODUS 18 : 21

Increasing contacts with the outside world made it plain
to us by 1970 that our valley was no longer hidden in any
real sense of the word. It became obvious that eventually
we would be brought under some form of higher authority,
either Indian or Burmese, and we were all reluctant to face
that day. We felt that a nearly ideal society had evolved
in Hidden Valley. Whether it could survive in the shadow
of the authoritarian, socialistic regimes seeking to reach an
agreement over ownership of the valley was – and still is,
as far as we know – a haunting question.

Our government in Hidden Valley was an outgrowth of
both Lisu and biblical tradition. Each village or family
group had its headman, who was not so much elected as
selected by natural processes, and who was responsible for
settling disputes, decreeing punishment, and exerting
leadership in village councils. All of us were Christians, so
the church, with its elders, teachers and preachers, served
as a kind of tribal government in which the various villages
participated. Nothing was done by decree, or even by vote.
The Lisu do not hold with the common democratic
concept of majority rule. They feel that the losing minority
is bound to be unhappy about – and possibly resistant to –
whatever decision is made in a cut-and-dried voting
process. So the Lisu rely upon consensus, in which an
important problem is discussed and discussed until an
obvious answer emerges.

It seems only logical that, in a situation where man
almost literally holds his life in his own two hands, each

individual should be granted as much participation as possible in the decision-making process. Indeed, in the jungle, life itself can well depend on the understanding that there is no set prerogative, status or authority among individuals. Many times Robert and I – and our wives as well – had to obey orders from our children unquestioningly and instantly.

The very basis of our lives required flexibility. For example, slash-and-burn agriculture simply doesn't allow for the kind of permanence so common in other parts of the world. Soil on the valley hillsides is nothing like the deep top-soil found at lower altitudes. It is just a thin layer of humus on top of clay. Though it is rich at first, it is rapidly depleted of its nutrients; moreover, it is deficient in phosphates and depends upon the ashes from the burning to make it productive. Obviously, then, the year immediately after the burning is the best for a new field. Sometimes a field can be worked a second year, too, but the profuse growth of weeds that springs up during the wet summer season makes it necessary to weed the field about four times, instead of the one time required in a first-year field. In addition, there are more leeches in an old field to make the farmer's lot more miserable, so it is understandable that the Lisu often feel it is easier to just cut and burn a new field. Because it takes about four acres to furnish a family's food supply for a year, whole villages were often required to seek new locations when they had used up the accessible land around them. It was, in fact, wisdom in making these decisions and skill in selecting proper sites that determined who became headmen among the Lisu.

Once we had churches and a school established at Zi-yu-di, however, there was a movement among the Lisu, with which we heartily agreed, to seek out flat land that would be suitable for rice paddies. This would free us all to a great extent from the slash-and-burn system and enable the three hundred or so families in the area to lead a more settled existence. The search for land was more difficult than anyone unfamiliar with the terrain might imagine.

In addition to flat paddy land, there had to be a suitable village site, with drinking water at hand and plentiful building materials, such as timber and bamboo.

The experience of Fuchyehpi, a schoolteacher and one of our more educated leaders, is indicative of the problem. Restless, and certain that somewhere in the vicinity there must be the 'promised land' – the big, flat area we were looking for – he would move his group from site to site, sometimes staying put only a month at a time. He would climb to the highest branches of a tree on top of a ridge, make a mental note of every bit of flat land in sight, and then explore it. Finally, near the junction of the Tarung and Kindring rivers, he located what he was sure was the ideal spot. Some settlers warned him against moving there, because it was the lowest point in the valley, only twenty-five hundred feet high, and was certain to be warm, swampy and full of disease-bearing mosquitoes. But he led his people there anyway. After only a year, dengue fever and malaria forced Fuchyehpi to move his village back up into the hills.

It was late in the winter of 1970 before we decided on a site for the big, permanent village we had in mind. The decision was made only after expeditions led by the most knowledgeable men in the valley had fanned out across the whole area. Their reports were examined from every angle, until the consensus held that the best place was about a mile upstream from our home in Zi-yu-di. Development began immediately. With my surveying tools, I laid out a straight central street for the village and rectangular home plots for about a hundred families, much as we had back in Putao. Work was begun on an irrigation ditch to water the rice paddies, and we started preparing building supplies.

Because this was to be a permanent village, we wanted more proper buildings than the bamboo structures we had been throwing up for quick shelter. This meant splitting boards, mostly from the hard chinquapin trees. Fortunately we had gained a good deal of experience in this art during the construction of the school. The first step was to pick a straight tree about two or three feet in diameter. This had to be chopped down with an axe, since we had no saws, then cut into logs of the desired lengths, up to twenty feet or so. To split the logs, we started with an axe-head, then replaced it with a hardwood wedge. After placing wedges in a straight line the length of the log, we whacked at each one in turn, until suddenly the log came apart with a loud crack. Using the same system, we quartered the log and split off the boards. Then the boards were trimmed with a machete. We had no nails, but I had a brace and bit, so we put the boards together by drilling holes and driving wooden pegs into them, the way they used to build ships in the Pilgrim days.

Unhappily, we were not meant to see this village rise; and, ironically, it was the village irrigation ditch that eventually led the Burmese soldiers to our doorstep. We had known for a long time that they were likely to arrive, and, apart from worship, much of our 1970 Christmas convention was devoted to arriving at a consensus on what to do about it. The issue facing the convention was highly controversial: Should we now, in view of the rumoured arrival of a border-survey party, willingly reaccept the Burmese yoke we had come so far and risked so much to escape? Or should we be prepared to make some sort of stand in defence of our newly achieved freedom?

As usual on such occasions, there were eloquent partisans on both sides. One of the leaders felt we should do everything in our power to keep free of renewed Burmese influence. He argued that we were now in an even more desperate strait than we had been in before our departure from Putao five years before: 'Then we could still flee to the west and find freedom and prosperity for ourselves in this hidden valley. But now there is no place left for us to flee to', he said. 'We have all lived under Burmese administration before – and the experience has taught us what to expect. Why should we now tamely submit to it again?'

Another leader saw things differently: 'Wait just a

minute', he said. 'What you say about Burmese authority is true. We are all agreed on that, and we hate the idea of living under it just as much as you do. But wherever we live, we will still be nominally under Burmese rule – and if we kick up a fuss and demand political freedom, the Burmese can still come after us, drag us away from the homes we have made here, and clap us all into work camps, or even jail. Suppose, instead of making a big fuss over this matter of principle, we welcome the troops when they arrive and do everything we can to prove that we have no hostility to the government and no ties with the KIA. Then the government will see that they have nothing to fear from us. We are getting along all right on our own, asking for nothing and posing no threat to their rule. Why should they then try to bother us or bring us to heel? We are too far away for them to do this without great expense and risk. We are so far away that they would surely prefer just to leave us alone!'

The debate lasted for four days, from Friday, when the convention started, until noon on the following Monday. Little by little, giving a bit here, taking a bit there, the two sides finally reached a compromise that all could accept. It was decided that our next step should be to send a delegation of elders, chosen from both sides, down to Namling to discuss the whole matter with the civil authorities there. This delegation would be authorized to take up not only the question of the tribespeople, but also that of the Morse family. The problem in our case was: Could our position be regularized so that we could stay on legally as their spiritual leaders and advisers?

One advantage of the consensus system in political affairs is that once a decision has been reached, action follows swiftly, with no delaying tactics from the losing side. Less than a week after the convention, early in January 1971, the delegation was on its way. It was a month later that the group returned with a reasonably precise course of action to recommend.

According to the civil authorities at Namling, the tribespeople had nothing whatever to fear from the army survey force, which probably would not arrive in our area before the monsoon rains put an end to their work for the year. In any case, they had no responsibilities beyond carrying out their immediate job of establishing the boundary line with India. Our villages were nominally under supervision from Namling; but, so far as the authorities there were concerned, no immediate action was likely. We had furnished proof of our readiness to accept the authority of the national government by sending in our census report with the delegation. So long as we continued to live at peace with each other and with the government, Hidden Valley would be left alone.

Much the same attitude prevailed about the members of the Morse family. If we simply stayed on quietly without demanding official permission to do so, no one was likely to bother us. However, if we insisted that our presence be officially noted and some government action be taken to legalize it, then the most likely outcome would be enforcement of the 1965 expulsion order. The choice was up to us. Our fate seemed to depend mainly on the presence of one friendly official, who might at any time be transferred. But he promised to try to visit the area after the rains, if possible, at which time our situation could be discussed.

The spring and summer of 1971 were quiet but filled with hard work for us. We were able to hold several Bible-training schools and to prepare and stencil several small booklets of study material for the preachers. But the highlight of the year came at Christmas when the convention was held at Tea Hill village. Almost five hundred people gathered there from all sides of Hidden Valley — from Binuzu on the east to Zi-yu-di and Bamboo Flats on the west.

It was just after people returned home from the Christmas convention, at the end of December, that the first contingent of Burmese troops entered our valley at Binuzu. When their commander, a polite and unassuming major, requested billets and rations for his men, who numbered perhaps thirty-five or forty, the villagers not only hastened to provide them but went beyond the call of duty in making the newcomers feel at home. This hospitality took the soldiers completely by surprise. Although friendliness to strangers is traditional in Burma, especially among the hill tribes, this attitude had been gradually changing during ten years of socialist austerity. A family on short rations that barely provide for its own needs can hardly be expected to welcome unknown guests. But, possibly spurred on by the lonely pioneer's hunger for news and variety, the Lisu of Hidden Valley had gone back to their old ways; they actually enjoyed being hosts to the troops.

What the soldiers had expected to find in Hidden Valley can only be imagined. We learned later that, having heard the rumour of our 'kingdom', they actually expected that our followers might use their weapons to protect us. Moreover, the harrowing adventures they had experienced on the way from Namling must have convinced them that they were going to face a tough people. At one point an avalanche swept ten men down a mountainside, seriously injuring five and killing two; another two men perished in an air drop; two more died of exposure; still another, while swimming in a mountain stream, was carried off by a bu-rin, the gigantic water-snake. They were thoroughly shaken by their encounter with the unrelenting jungle by the time they picked up our irrigation ditch and followed it to the first settlement.

Imagine the bafflement of these men, who broke out of the hostile jungle to find schools, churches, homes with teeming granaries, full chicken coops and pigsties. Far from encountering an armed kingdom, they discovered a peaceful community with no apparent government at all. The wealth of the Lisu quite obviously surpassed that of their own families and friends back in the so-called civilized areas of Burma. Within days the troops were so charmed by the life around them that a significant number of them wanted to lay down their arms, marry Lisu girls, and stay for ever with us in Hidden Valley. Any such defection would, of course, have caused us great difficulties with the government, and we were grateful that their orders took them back to Namling at the finish of their assignment – clearing sites for survey instruments on the mountain tops – in a couple of weeks.

Our strategy proved so successful with this first contingent of military that we began to think it would work indefinitely. The first group to visit us in Zi-yu-di was a force of Indian and Burmese engineers. We had some friendly conversation with the Burmese soldiers and expressed to their commander our desire to regularize our position with the government. We felt we had nothing to fear when, in due time, they were replaced by another Burmese army group, whose ostensible function was to gather details for army cartographers based on the data provided by the survey. What we did not reckon on was the zeal – and perhaps the ignorance – of the commander of this force.

During these successive waves of military intrusion into Hidden Valley, we Morses tried very hard to observe the spirit of the 'understanding' we had with the authorities in Namling. Accordingly, we did not personally entertain any of the troops, and we refrained from any political discussions. We didn't actually hide out; indeed, we went about our normal business of healing, teaching and preaching. But the new Burmese commander somehow came to the conclusion that he had discovered us and that he would be rewarded by reporting the presence of such illegal persons to Namling. Being conscientious, he filed an official army report, which went not only to the civil administrators in Namling, but up through the army chain of command to Rangoon.

Though the officer's report was, of course, no news to a number of people in Namling, including our Christian friend, it was evidently somewhat of a bombshell in other quarters. The Namling officials were chastised for failing to discover us earlier. They, in turn, were more than a little irritated with the officer who had caused all the trouble.

But at this point, there was nothing the government could do but take immediate steps to enforce the expulsion order of 1965. Accordingly, we were notified that our presence in Hidden Valley – or, for that matter, in any territory within the boundaries of Burma, including those most recently surveyed – was illegal, and that we were to be removed to 'headquarters', where appropriate action would be taken.

Even though the possibility of such an order was in our minds, actually to receive it was a devastating blow. It meant the abrupt end of our work in Burma; and for our parents, now in their seventies, quite possibly the end of a life's work. Besides, we had a very special feeling about Hidden Valley. The fact that the Lord had led us there, had helped us overcome so many difficulties, had guided us through so many tribulations, and had allowed us to prosper, gave us a stronger sense of belonging than we had experienced anywhere else on earth.

We continued, however, to believe in doing the will of God and sought that will once more through prayer. Of course we could have tried to cross the border into India, but it would have meant arrest and imprisonment. After all, our presence there would have been just as illegal as it now was in Burma. In our prayerful discussions, we considered this alternative very seriously, but we realized that such an escape would leave our motives for ever open to question in the minds of the Burmese. Escape would also make it more difficult, if not impossible, for us ever to return to our work in Burma, which we still would like to do some day. So we decided to throw ourselves on the mercy of Burmese officialdom, hoping thereby to get a chance to state our case in court, to prove once and for all by our words and actions that we were in no sense enemies of the state.

We knew that we were going to be leaving before long, but it was difficult to admit it, even to ourselves. Our thoughts turned to the happy gathering we had enjoyed only a few short weeks earlier at the Christmas convention.

We had been gratified by all the signs of the Lisu's physical prosperity – happy, healthy children; attractive clothes; and good food. But we were even more happy over their progress in spiritual matters. Our hearts and lives were bound to theirs with a thousand invisible ties because of all the experiences we had shared with them – all the things that go to make up life in a remote frontier area such as this had been. Leaving them would be a wrench far greater than any we had known before. Our only consolation was that we would be leaving behind us a truly viable society in the hands of proven leaders. Our pride – if we can permit ourselves a measure of pride – is that we had contributed to the work and decisions that made this possible. Perhaps the most tangible evidence of our contribution was that fruit trees were now blooming in Hidden Valley.

Chapter 15

When the king of Egypt was told that the
people had fled, the mind of Pharaoh and his
servants was changed toward the people, and
they said, 'What is this we have done, that
we have let Israel go from serving us?'
EXODUS 14 : 5

The Burmese authorities evidently gave instructions that
the Morses must not escape them again. A detail of soldiers
was assigned to bring us to Hkamti, the provincial capital,
by way of the difficult trail along the mountain ridges that
the troops had blasted out to get into Hidden Valley. We
were, in effect, prisoners, though our case had yet to be
heard. We could have told them that the march would
prove too much for our parents, now seventy-three and
seventy-four, and for the younger girls, but we had made
up our minds to comply completely with whatever orders
we were given. So we began the difficult task of sorting
out our belongings and packing in the limited time of only
a few hours.

Knowing that if we were deported our baggage would be
limited to forty-four pounds each on our subsequent
journey by air to the United States, we planned to take
only our most needed personal possessions. In addition, we
had travel clothes and bedding for use on the trail. Everything else was packed up and left with the tribespeople, to
be kept for our possible return. Some clothes and household
effects were left to various young people who had lived in
our houses from time to time and had practically become
members of our family. Books that could be of use to them
were divided up among our Lisu schoolteachers. Our farm
tools went to neighbours and companions with whom we
had worked. The disposal of our personal property, combined with our uncertainty about what lay ahead, made
the anguish of parting even more painful than it would

have been if we had known what faced us next. All we could do was pray for the wisdom to divine God's wishes and the strength to obey them.

On 6 March we set out on the trail with our military escort. The walk didn't last long. Advancing age and six years of arduous living had taken their predictable toll of my parents. Within a day and a half it was as obvious to the commander of our escort as it was to Robert and me that they would not be able to make the journey. We were important enough 'prisoners' that a serious accident or a death on the trail would be a black mark on the commander's record. So he radioed his headquarters for permission to take us back to our homes in Zi-yu-di, where he sent a full report of the situation to his superiors in Namyung and asked for a helicopter to evacuate us.

Word that we were back spread rapidly on the jungle telegraph, and before long our friends were coming by the hundreds, as they had in Putao, to help if they could, but at least to say goodbye. There was a great deal of weeping, and though we appreciated everyone's intentions, their continual presence made this period one of extreme emotional and physical exhaustion. Besides those who came just to bid us farewell, there were the pastors and church elders who gathered for last-minute conferences. Night after night, when the helicopter had not arrived that day, we would gather with them and talk about the future, theirs and ours. Because so many things were uncertain, but mostly because our hearts were going to be left in Hidden Valley, these meetings were an additional strain on all of us.

At last, at 7 a.m. on 18 March 1972, a grey day, with overcast skies, a soldier billeted in our village appeared at our door with a message from the commanding officer. Word had just come through from Namyung that the helicopter would be leaving soon and should be at our village by 9 a.m. The helicopter – a type known as the Husky, made in the United States – would land on the volley-ball court laid out next to the school-house. Our party was to be there with all our baggage by the time it arrived.

At last the moment had arrived that we had been expecting and dreading ever since that remote December of 1965 when we got our original order of deportation. On our way to the school, we stopped at the church, where we found a group of elders – among them our old guide and adviser, Khisu – awaiting us for a last prayer meeting. Once more my father chose the hymn traditional for such occasions: 'He Leadeth Me.' The tribespeople sang it slowly, with deep reverence and feeling that brought tears to our eyes.

Quite apart from our imminent departure, the arrival of a helicopter in Hidden Valley was an exciting event. The Lisu had seen planes going overhead, as disembodied as a distant star, for most of their lives, and they had learned to make wise use of the remnants of those that came to grief. In Putao, too, they had become used to the idea that these machines could actually land and take off with people dear to them and cargo useful to them. But the helicopter, which could dare the sheer mountain faces surrounding their valley and land on a handkerchief of ground, was a wonder to them. Thus, when the chopper came hopping over the trees and skidded down to a dusty landing, nearly every man, woman and child within an hour's walking distance was on hand to witness the marvel.

The pilot cut off his motor and, in the sudden silence, the door opened and two crewmen hopped out to let down a ladder. An army major in olive-drab uniform then made his appearance at the door, saluted, and stepped down to the ground. I walked forward to introduce myself and shake hands. It became apparent at once that the major was full of good nature generally and goodwill for us in particular. It was also apparent that he sensed the awkwardness of the situation in which he found himself. My first question was how many of us the helicopter would be able to carry.

'All of you, of course', he replied cheerfully. 'But you

must hurry. Is all the baggage ready? Here, boy, get cracking with Mr Morse's luggage!'

Like many Burmese in positions of authority, the major seemed to sense an immense gulf in status between himself and the willing, kindly tribespeople. At the same time he felt some diffidence towards us as educated, Caucasian foreigners. Our obvious acceptance of the tribesmen as friends and equals thus became for him a source of confusion and embarrassment. Should he follow our lead in the matter, and thus lose face with the tribespeople, or should he continue to address them in an abrupt and supercilious tone borrowed from the British raj, and thus risk losing face with us? The latter seemed to him the lesser of two evils, but his self-assurance was somewhat impaired when one of the crewmen whispered something to him in a low voice that caused him to rescind his command about the baggage.

'Here, wait a bit. Let's get all this sorted out now. How many of you are there altogether?'

'Five adults and six children', I replied.

'I see, I see. Well, now, just a minute till I find out what the position is!'

There followed another brief colloquy between the major and the crewman, a sergeant, after which the major again turned to me. 'Well, it seems I was off the mark about the capacity of the aircraft', he said. 'We can only take six of you on the first trip. Best have the women and children go first.'

But now there came another conference between the major and the sergeant, who was apparently the helicopter pilot. The gist of this proved to be that the sergeant's orders authorized only one trip. Thus, whoever did not fly out on the helicopter might well have to go out on foot after all. This presented a new problem. Obviously both our parents would have to be among the helicopter passengers, as would the two youngest girls. Helen would need to go with them, but both Robert and I felt that one or the other of us should accompany the airborne group to take care of any contingency that might arise. More discussions revealed that the helicopter would almost surely not be authorized to make a second trip to pick up the remainder of our group. So it was decided that Robert would go with the others on the Husky. The three boys, our oldest daughter, Margaret, and I would follow by land along the Hukawng valley. If there were no mishaps, we would all eventually regroup at Hkamti.

Sorting out which baskets, boxes and cases belonged on the Husky and which should stay on the ground caused more confusion and delay; but this was cut short when the major, after another whispered consultation with the sergeant, told us there was no room for anything but a little hand baggage. One suitcase was allowed, so Robert's was chosen because it contained the manuscript of the Rawang New Testament. After this we all formed a circle and bowed our heads in prayer for the last time, and then sang 'God Be With You Till We Meet Again'. By now several hundred well-wishers were on hand to see us off. Each member of the departing group shook hands with scores of these loyal followers, most of them in tears, using the double hand-clasp, which is the Lisu equivalent of an embrace.

The most memorable farewell was from Sarah, the girl who had worked for us as cook for four years. As Helen was preparing to board the helicopter, Sarah – who is afflicted with curvature of the spine – ran and threw her arms about her, sobbing pitifully and begging Helen not to go. 'Don't leave me an orphan!' she cried. 'I'll never get to see you again!' One of the Burmese soldiers present said to me later that he had never before seen such a dramatic display of human loyalty and love, and that he wished he himself could have been part of our Christian family.

Before stepping on board, my brother Robert took off his jungle boots, leaving them for me to give to one of the tribesmen, and put on an old but almost unused pair of American shoes saved from our Putao era. He and the others then boarded the Husky, each turning back in the doorway once more to wave to the crowd on the ground. The hatch then clanged shut, the motor roared into action, and the meshing windmill blades of the Husky's overhead propellers began to spin with a sudden clatter. Through a dense cloud of dust the Husky rose slowly into the air, hovered overhead for a few seconds, and then soared away over the treetops towards the west.

In the sudden loud silence that followed, Margaret, the three boys and I trudged back to our house to begin preparations for the long hike out. We had a sense of being abandoned; whatever happened now would be an anti-climax, for our days in Hidden Valley really ended with the lift-off of that helicopter. As for those aboard, we would not know their emotions until much later.

'It was a very painful, a traumatic, experience – and I've tried to avoid thinking about it, it was so painful', Robert told us. 'The fact of leaving our life's work was the big stress – and knowing that possibly this was the last time we would ever see most of the people gathered here on the school games field. We had been through so much together – starved together, suffered together, risked our lives together – that we had a very close association and identification with this particular group. The Lisu were our people, and the Kachin land was our land, our home.

'As the helicopter took off, I was watching every little scene to burn into my memory the look of the whole area. And I must admit it was a thrill, too, to get a new view of things, this 180-degree view through the bubble window. All the while I was mentally claiming the area. I kept saying to myself, "That's mine, and I'm coming back." It was a time of very deep emotion.'

For those of us who were left behind, there was no such sharp moment of departure to recall. We started out the next morning, 19 March – David's twenty-third birthday. Slowly and painfully over a period of some two weeks, we worked our way down the Tarung valley from Hidden Valley to Namyung. Though this kind of jungle trek was familiar enough to my children and me, we found it more difficult than usual, partly because Margaret was just recovering from a bout of Asian flu, and I was just coming down with the disease. At times on the trail my temperature was running at around 103 degrees, and I was too weak to carry a pack. As for the soldiers with us, they were not only inexperienced in jungle travel, but were burdened with such heavy packs and shoes that every step was painful for them.

It was only by comparing the agility of my own children with the clumsiness of the Burmese soldiers, some of whom were about the same age, that I realized how truly the young Morses had become part of the 'Monkey People', as the Lisu were sometimes called. This could hardly be surprising, since they had spent all of their lives among the Lisu and six of their most formative years in the jungle. Watching my children skip across logs and scramble around ledges that terrified the troops reminded me of one engineering project I had been forced to leave undone: the construction of a real bridge across the river that bisected the elephant trail between Zi-yu-di and all the villages to the east.

One reason the bridge had not been built was that the Lisu, and our own Morse children as well, considered the bridge they had improvised shortly after we settled in Zi-yu-di perfectly adequate. A description of this span is in itself a testimony to the surefootedness of the Lisu. While the river could be forded easily in the winter, it turned into such a raging torrent in the rainy season that some means of crossing above the flood became imperative. Searching up and down the banks, the Lisu came upon a great old banyan tree, its roots partly undercut by floodwaters, that thrust its main trunk and a head full of branches out over the stream. By cleaning off one of the branches, they found they could thread their way up the trunk and along to the end of the branch to a point above a huge rock more than halfway across the river. Because that point was a hair-raising forty feet above the water's surface, they dropped a rattan ladder from the branch to the top of the rock, which stayed dry even at highest water, and strung a narrow bamboo bridge from the rock to the far shore. Traversing this, even in wet weather, when both the tree and the rock became slippery with some kind of fungus growth, was all in a day's walk even for a Lisu grandmother. We did improve things a bit by putting up some handrails and hanging a bamboo-plank bridge from the tree on rattan cables, but more for our own convenience than for the Lisu.

I stress our children's familiarity with Lisu-style travel because it led to an incident on the road to Hkamti that I have come to regard as symbolic of the end of our somewhat idyllic life in the jungle. We had arrived at a turn in the stream bordered on one side by a high cliff above the water. A narrow ledge along the side of the cliff offered footholds of a sort to a daring traveller and led to a good path visible beyond. The only alternative – since the river here was too deep to ford and too fast to swim – would be to chop down a tree so as to make a bridge, cross to the other side, climb a high hill there, and then cross over another makeshift bridge further downstream. All this would take the better part of a day, whereas the path along the ledge could be negotiated within a few minutes by anyone with the nerve to try it. Margaret, walking a little behind the boys and myself, but ahead of the soldiers, did not even pause to consider the matter. Seeing from the tracks that the boys and I had already proceeded across the ledge, she set out along the same route and was already halfway across the cliff, clinging to handholds as she inched her way along some forty feet above the rushing current, when the soldiers, following along the trail more slowly, caught up enough to see what she was up to.

'Stop, stop!' the sergeant in charge of the troops shouted. 'You can't go on that way. Come back and wait here while we make a bridge!'

'What do we need a bridge for?' Margaret called back in Lisu. 'This ledge is plenty big enough! Just follow me!'

This blithe command from a fourteen-year-old girl was a clear challenge to the sergeant in charge. Despite whatever loss of face the failure might involve, it was a challenge that he had no intention of accepting. He remembered the fate a fellow-soldier met up with during a swim in that stream. So he raised his army rifle, pointed it at Margaret, and shouted back in Kachin: 'My soldiers have orders to keep you with us, and I will not let them risk their lives like crazy Lisu. Come back at once – or I will have to shoot!'

Realizing that he would probably do nothing of the sort, but not wishing to embarrass him further in the presence of his men, Margaret tactfully retraced her steps along the ledge, rejoined the troops, and sat down on the bank to wait while they laboriously felled a tree across the stream. She and the soldiers then crossed over, climbed the steep slope on the other side, and then crossed back over another improvised tree bridge, rejoining us only in time to make camp in the late afternoon. The wild freedom my children had learned to take for granted in Hidden Valley had suddenly been curbed by the gun of authority.

Chapter 16

The Lord will reign for ever and ever.
EXODUS 15 : 18

Arriving in Namyung after twelve days of hard travel, we could learn nothing of the fate or whereabouts of the rest of the family. All we knew was that they had been taken 'some place'. Having been told that we were to walk another twelve days to reach the district capital of Hkamti, which was where we assumed the others were, we were just setting out with a new set of military guards, after resting two days, when we were stopped outside the town.

'Plans have been changed', we were told. 'You now are to walk only two days, along the Ledo Road, to a place where there is an airstrip. There you will be picked up by a small plane and flown to Hkamti.' The reason for this change in plans became clear later, when we heard that there had been fighting between Burmese and insurgents along the road we were to have travelled.

In Hkamti all the news was bad. We learned that the rest of the family had already been sent ahead to another 'some place' and that we were to follow by plane. I was shown a copy of a statement Robert had made to the court in Hkamti and asked to subscribe to it on behalf of the rest of us. Since he had made all the points we had wanted to make, to the effect that our unorthodox departure from Putao was, in reality, an effort to comply with the law, and that neither we nor our followers had joined the KIA or other insurgent groups, I readily agreed. I was appalled, however, at the severity of the sentence that was passed: eighteen months of 'rigorous imprisonment', meaning hard labour, in a Burmese jail, after which the survivors – who,

I thought, were unlikely to include my parents – would presumably be deported.

The officials in Hkamti were as kind and as helpful as they dared be under the circumstances. They explained that their hands were virtually tied and they had no choice but to pronounce sentence. We were informed of our right to appeal, but were reminded that final disposition of the case would be, as it customarily was in Burma, up to the higher court in Mandalay. Hence the tension and the frustration that followed our arrival there to join the others.

Ten days after my parents, Helen, the two girls and Robert flew to Mandalay, we followed. The question uppermost in our minds was: Will we be reunited with the family?

As we pulled up in front of the jail, my heart sank at the forbidding appearance of the massive doors and the walls that looked so solid. Inside, we were going through the usual admittance procedures, when I heard someone call my name. I looked up, and there was Robert. Was I glad to see him! In reply to my question about the others, he said, 'They're all fine.' Then, pointing Lisu-style, with his chin, towards the door, he added, 'They're over there, just waiting for you. You'll see them in a little while.' Later, I found out from Helen why they hadn't come in with Robert.

'We had had no news of you folks after we left you', she told me. 'When we tried to find out, the prison official said, "Oh, if they're walking, it will take them at least a month to reach Hkamti!" So we weren't expecting you so soon. It was so hot that day you arrived that the girls and I went out to the water tank to bathe and cool off by pouring water over us, Burmese-style. We had just got nicely wet when someone came rushing into the yard saying, "Mrs Morse, your family has arrived. Hurry, and you can go and see them." But we couldn't go as we were! By the time the girls and I got dressed, it was too late – there was no guard to escort us through the gates. So we had to sit and wait, and an hour never seemed so long before.'

When we had finished all that was required, and all our belongings had been put away in the jail office, we were taken to the small enclosure, separate from other prisoners, where our family was being kept. As we went through the gates, the two younger girls came running to meet us. Twelve-year-old Marilyn threw her arms around me and began to weep, crying, 'Oh, Daddy, Daddy!' It brought tears to my eyes, and I noticed that even some of the guards were wiping the corners of their eyes. My reunion with Helen was less dramatic, but we both experienced a deep feeling of relief and joy that we were all together again.

The timing of our arrival was unfortunate for us because we reached Mandalay just in time for the Spring Water Festival. This festival, celebrated not only in Burma, but also in Thailand and some other parts of South-East Asia, is an ancient ritual predating the arrival of Buddhism over twenty-five hundred years ago. Nowadays it is identified with that religion, just as our Christian festivals of Christmas and Easter preserve features of ancient seasonal festivals that far antedate Christianity. Coming just before the start of the monsoon season, the Water Festival apparently had its inception in solemn rites in which priests sprinkled the heads of their followers with a few drops of water as a form of benediction. Over the centuries, however, it has assumed a much more playful character, so that now people throw cups, glasses or even pails of water at one another in a spirit of fun. Since the festival comes at the very peak of the hot season, just before the cooling rains begin, no one objects much to getting wet, and even the most dignified citizens are likely to wear clothes that will not suffer from being splashed with water. Frustrating as it may be to someone who wants to accomplish something, government and business offices are closed for a full week during the festival, and everyone, including even inmates of the jail, is expected to participate in a spirit not unlike that of *mardi gras* in Latin countries. But it was maddening to know that our letter to the American embassy would not even be sent until after the Water Festival.

In a limited way, the celebration extended even inside Mandalay Central Jail, with its thirteen hundred inmates. All of us got thoroughly drenched several times as our jailers, trying to be friendly, included us in their water-throwing. One of our warders was a young girl whose particular assignment was watching over the women and girls. To show her respect for my parents and Helen, she came to them with a small bowl of water and sprinkled a few drops on their heads and shoulders, in a touching return to the original religious tradition of the occasion.

Indeed, most of our warders were aghast that we had both our ageing parents and young children behind bars with us. In a culture that reveres the old and cherishes the young, such a thing was almost unheard of; in fact, it was normally illegal to imprison people under sixteen, but at first there was nowhere else for our children to go. So the warders went out of their way to be nice to our parents and children. Such treatment made the experience less unpleasant and traumatic for the younger children, and we began to think the jail wasn't such a bad place to serve as a sort of decompression chamber in their passage from the freedom of the jungle to the constraints and complexities of modern civilization. Their ignorance of the ways of the world was almost total: such a simple thing as a doorknob, for example, baffled them completely at first.

Once he had gained access to us in prison, almost a month after our arrival, the American consul, Carl Taylor, obtained a lawyer for us, and we made a formal appeal for reconsideration of our case. Mr Taylor suggested that he take the three girls into his home until our case was decided. We urged them to accept the invitation, but they were terrified at the idea of going off with such a huge white man. We were virtually the only white people they had ever seen, and all of us stood half a head shorter than Carl Taylor. Only when they learned that the consul's wife was a petite Chinese would they agree to go. As they were getting their few belongings together, Helen noticed little Marilyn putting one of her oldest longyis into her bag.

'Why are you taking that old thing to the consul's house?' Helen asked.

'To bathe, of course', Marilyn said.

It was only then we realized that the girls had never seen a real bathroom. In the warm months, at least, bathing for them had consisted of going to the nearest stream, where, along with the other women, they would untie their longyis from around their waist, retie them just under their arms, and hold them out like a shower curtain while they modestly sponged themselves underneath; much the same thing was accomplished from a tub at home in cold periods. Helen tried to explain.

'The consul will probably have a bathroom,' she said, 'with a bath-tub or a shower. You don't need to wear your longyi there.'

Marilyn was horrified. 'Do you mean they bathe naked!' she gasped.

It might have been their first, but we knew it would not be their last, encounter with what they would find to be shocking customs and morals in Western life, and we are thankful that thus far they seem to have taken them with the same easy stride as they took the transition to American schools. While our daughters were away getting their first lessons in adaptation, the rest of us waited impatiently and in ominous silence for the outcome of our plea.

It would be at least three weeks before the Supreme Court met in May, and we were not invited to be present at its hearing. After one initial encounter, at which we presented our case to him, we were not even allowed to see our attorney again before the hearing. He once sent his daughter, also a lawyer, to visit us, but she was turned away at the gates. The whole case would depend upon our written appeal and our attorney's eloquence. Carl Taylor would be allowed to sit in as an observer on our behalf – but not as a participant.

The only good thing that can be said about this period is that it gave Robert a perfect opportunity to continue his painstaking work of translating the New Testament into

Rawang. Robert confided that, as a Christian missionary practising in various authoritarian societies, he had always expected to spend time in some jail or other. As a result, he took the precaution of keeping with him at all times the basic materials he needed to carry on his work – the Bible and plenty of paper and pencils. By putting in as many hours as possible at his task every day, Robert completed his first draft of the translation almost on the very date, late in May, when we received word of our impending release.

As we had hoped, the consul brought with him the verdict of the court. It was probably as much as we could hope for – the sentence had been reduced from eighteen to three months, most of which we had by then already served, and we were to be deported. On 16 June, at about 5.00 a.m., we were gathered in the entry-way of the office building, awaiting the opening of the doors. A number of guards and warders were on hand to bid us farewell. As the doors swung open, we could see Mr and Mrs Taylor waiting outside with Margaret, Marilyn and Jeannette. As the female warders said goodbye to the girls, they had tears in their eyes, for they had grown very fond of the children. A few minutes later, after a short drive through Mandalay, we boarded the train for Rangoon, accompanied by armed guards. For health reasons, my parents were allowed to go by plane a little later in the day, but also under guard. At the airport in Rangoon we slept on the tables and benches in an air-conditioned waiting-room with the guard still in attendance. The next morning we were escorted aboard the first flight out to Bangkok. After nearly a quarter of a century of service, we had left Burma behind, our passports prominently stamped DEPORTED.

Though we have left our Hidden Valley in the Himalayas, it has not left us. After gazing out across the snow-capped top of the world, we find the concrete horizons of even the greatest of cities limited. After living in houses open to wind and weather, we feel stifled in the airtight boxes that are the wonder of modern architecture. After sharing a simple Christian fellowship with our Lisu friends, we are put off by the complexities of religion in the Western world. But, wherever God leads us in the future, we feel grateful to him that he gave us these years of hard but rewarding service in one of the most spectacular regions of all his creation.

We do hope that some day God's hand will guide us back into Burma. Now that I have completed this book, Robert and I and three of our sons are back in Thailand, seeking to establish a mission with the Lisu there, and hoping soon to have the rest of our families join us. We hope most of all that our parents can spend at least part of their sunset years amid the blossoming orange trees that are living witness to their fruitful lives. With God's help, it may come to pass.

EPILOGUE

When we left Rangoon airport on June 17, 1972, it was with mingled feelings of regret and relief — regret that we were leaving the land and people we loved, but relief that we were once again free.

Less than an hour later we found ourselves in Bangkok, Thailand, where Robert's son Bobby was on hand to welcome us with flowers, in the Thai fashion. As we traveled the twenty-five kilometers into town, we had our first taste of culture shock. We adults were re-entering the world of western wonders, but for the younger children it was an introduction to a totally new world, one that seemed like a fairyland. The wide roads, the rushing traffic, the tall buildings, elaborate advertising signs and other evidences of progress and prosperity were almost overwhelming after the austerity of the socialist economy in Burma.

Top priority was given to getting much-needed dental work done and having complete physical check-ups. Both Robert and I had to have hernia operations, but the rest of the family were found to be in surprisingly good health. In mid-July all of us except Robert returned to the United States. He remained in Thailand for a few months, to be with his sons Joni and Bobby, and to work with the Rawang translation assistant who had come specially from northern Burma to help check the translation of the Rawang New Testament. Bobby had been attending high school in Bangkok, but returned to the United States in September for his senior year. His older brother, Stephen, was already enrolled at Indiana University, Bloomington, Indiana. Then in November, Robert and Joni also returned to the United States.

Meanwhile, we were all getting readjusted to the American way of life. The adults were getting re-acquainted with supporters as they traveled and visited churches all over the country. Robert's three daughters (DeeDee, Camille, and Genevieve), and our three (Margaret, Marilyn, and Jeannette), were attending public schools. The boys — young men, rather — were suddenly faced with the necessity for completing their education. Our son David enrolled in two correspondence courses, one in watch-making and repair, and one in electronics. In January, 1973, Ron and Joni enrolled at Ozark Bible College in Joplin, Missouri, while Tom chose to attend Lincoln Christian College, in Lincoln, Illinois.

While in Thailand, Robert had learned that there were Lisu people living in that country also, perhaps as many as 20,000. Upon investigation he found that although another mission had been trying to reach the Lisu, they had no one available at that time to work among them, and they had no objections to our Mission working among them. While Robert and Joni were still in Chiang Mai, they had many opportunities to meet Lisu people, and before their return to the States, three men were won to the Lord. Now Robert and I and our six sons were all anxious to go to Thailand and begin work as soon as possible. But there was much to be done before that could happen.

One important factor determining our timetable was the state of Mission (and personal) finances. Because of our long, eleven-year absence, during which we were unable to communicate with supporting churches and individuals, contributions had almost stopped. Travel expenses for the eleven of us coming from Burma had been a heavy drain on resources, and Mission finances were at a very low level, insufficient for starting a new work. Our policy has always been not to make any appeals for funds, but to pray and make our needs known to God, believing that He is able, through His people, to supply our needs. God had certainly proved His faithfulness during the years in Hidden Valley. So we all prayed concerning the Mission financial needs. God answered our prayers in very unexpected ways. One was the income which came as a result of the printing of this book, "Exodus to a Hidden Valley," for all proceeds went into the Mission funds. A substantial gift of $10,000 from a family in southern Illinois was another. These, plus many smaller gifts, brought the bank balance up to the point where we felt sure it was God's will for us to go to Thailand.

By May, 1973, plans were formulated. Because none of us were familiar with the needs and conditions in Thailand, we decided that Robert and I, Joni, Bobby, Tom and Ron would go first and survey the situation. Depending on our findings, the others could join us at a later date. When we discussed our plans with Jesse Yangmi, he decided to go too. He and our sons were all intending to continue their college work in the fall, so they planned to be in Thailand just for the summer. It was a good thing that we were not able to see into the future at that point! Had we known that the "summer" was to last four to six years for some of these young men, they might have had second thoughts about going at that time.

In mid-June, 1973, we six Morse men and Jesse arrived in Bangkok, and proceeded almost immediately to Chiang Mai, about 500 miles to the north. We had had some adventures along the way, such as getting separated from some of our baggage, including our back packs, but all was eventually recovered. The bus ride to Chiang Mai was an adventure, too — a hair-raising one!

We arrived in Chiang Mai about 6:00 o'clock in the morning and found work waiting upon our doorstep in the form of an opium addict who had heard we were coming. He wanted to become a Christian, and asked us to pray for his deliverance from addiction. It had been many years since Robert and I had had an appeal for this kind of help, and for our sons it was a completely new experience, for opium addiction was not a problem in north Burma. We had no type of medication to help him, so we told him, "First Son (all Lisu are called by a name indicating their position in the family), we have no medicine, and we have no power in ourselves to help you. But God, our Heavenly Father, is able to help those who believe in Him. We will pray and ask Him to give you release from this habit which has bound you for so long. Do you believe God is able to help you?"

"Oh, yes, teachers. I believe, I believe!" he replied.

In answer to prayer First Son WAS set free from his opium habit. But he was just the first of many who were to come for help. It seemed to us that God used this first case to point out the way we were to deal with other cases of opium addiction, not using medication — other than vitamins — but depending solely on God to answer prayer. This became a strong testimony of God's power, especially when First Son went with us later and visited many of the Lisu villages in the mountains around Chiang Mai and told how God had helped him. People who had known him before could see the change in him and were willing to at least listen to the Gospel message.

The six of us stayed in a rented house in Chiang Mai, using it as a base from which to go out on trips into the villages. We found the situation in Thailand quite different from Burma. For one thing, like other tribal groups in Thailand, the Lisu were widely scattered instead of being all in one general area as in Burma. They were very suspicious of foreigners and outsiders in general, perhaps partly because many of their previous encounters had been unfortunate ones, with tourists, drug dealers, or merchants, who had tried to take advantage of the inexperienced hill people. Furthermore, because of their animist religion they were fearful of having strangers staying in their homes, especially those who practiced a different religion. They didn't want to offend their spirits by entertaining "foreign" spirits, thus possibly bringing troubles upon themselves.

But probably the biggest reason for their fear and suspicion was their belief in the stories of what would happen to those who "entered" Christianity. The most prevalent of these tales was the one that all those who became

Christians would be taken far away, to the mouth of the big river where dwelt a huge dragon. According to the rumor, the missionaries would feed the Christians to the dragon, and then its excreta would become gold and precious stones. This, they concluded, was the source of wealth of all the foreign missionaries!

When we heard this story, and some others about as strange, we understood why the women, children and even some men rapidly disappeared when we first visited their villages. No wonder we were not allowed to stay in their homes, but were sent outside the villages to stay in their field work huts! Gradually, however, they realized that we meant them no harm but truly wanted to help them. They were reassured by the fact that we all spoke Lisu, and when we invited them to visit our house in Chiang Mai, they smiled and said they would. And they did.

Our house gradually became a guest hostel, as the people from the villages came to Chiang Mai and found their way to us. Some were sick and wanted help in getting medical care, because they spoke no Thai. Some were opium addicts who had heard that the "farangs" (foreigners) could help them. And some were just curious, wondering how we lived. As they came and stayed with us, they found that we were people much like themselves, who had to eat and sleep, who got tired, and sometimes even got sick. Gradually their fears were overcome, and we were invited to several villages by people who had stayed with us, villages where we'd never been before. When we went, we were well received, and invited to stay in their homes — after all, we WERE invited guests. As they heard the message of God's love and of His Son who died for them, they slowly began to respond. Sometimes there was just one family, or even a single individual in a village who dared to openly express belief. It was as if they were testing the power of this new-found God to help them, to keep them from the power of the evil spirits they had appeased for so long.

As the response began to come, our sons all expressed their reluctance to return to the U.S. to continue their studies. As they said, "We don't know how long we might be able to stay here. If we leave while people are interested and turning to the Lord, we wouldn't have any peace. After all, there aren't very many people who already know Lisu, and can just come in and start teaching without having to spend a long time in language study. The Lord has prepared us, and we feel we should stay on for a while longer."

However, for Jesse it was different. He had a wife and four children waiting for him in the U.S., so he felt he should return. And after much prayer it was decided that Bobby, too, should go back and start his Bible College training.

In the following months we continued to visit villages, and in January, 1974, we held our first one-month Bible Training School, with about forty students. By July, the rest of my family had joined me, and we moved to a separate house. Later, different ones of Robert's family also arrived as well. And the work continued to grow.

In 1976 we received requests from some of the Lisu Christian families to allow their children to stay with us and go to school in Chiang Mai, because there were no schools in their villages. We thought there would be only six or eight children, so we agreed. Surprisingly, when school time came, there were eighteen children, too many for us to accommodate. But this was a real need, and it was decided to house them in the building we had rented as a church. Bobby, who loves children, volunteered to oversee them and their needs. This was how the Tribal Children's Hostel began. By 1979 the number of children had grown to the point where new quarters had to be found. With help from World Vision and our supporting churches, land was purchased and new facilities built which could house up to 200 children comfortably. There were 132 in residence when the buildings were dedicated in July, 1978. By 1981 it had to be expanded to accommodate the 320 children who came. All the children who come are receiving not only secular education, but also daily Christian teaching. Many of them have become Christians, but this is not a requirement for staying at the Hostel.

But the Children's Hostel was not the only area of growth. The number of Christians was steadily increasing also, and a nucleus of national leaders was being formed. Our aim has been to train people and encourage them to take responsibility, so they can carry on when the time comes that the foreign missionaries must leave. By 1983 the estimated number of Lisu Christians was about 2,300, and by mid-1985 about 3000. It is almost impossible to get an exact count because of the way whole villages suddenly decide to move, scattering out and either starting a new village or settling in already established villages.

Within a year of our arrival in Thailand, we also found ourselves again in close contact with the Christians in Burma. We began to receive letters regularly from people in various areas of the work, including some from Hidden Valley. Because of the situation in Burma, it is impossible to help them as we would like to do. But we have been able to keep in touch, to help with advice and teaching materials, and to pray for them. Also, in response to many requests, Robert has translated the Old Testament in Rawang, and the manuscript was sent to the printers in March, 1985.

In February, 1981, Helen and I, Robert and daughter Camille, and a Canadian friend, Conrad Cline, had the privilege of visiting in Rangoon for a week and meeting with about fifty of the preachers, elders, and other leaders from all the different areas of the work, including Hidden Valley. It was exciting to hear of the progress being made. For instance, the three-year Bible Seminary opened in Putao in 1968 with only a few local students. But by 1981 it had grown to fifty-three students, representing eight different language groups, who came not only from the north but also from other parts of Burma. (In 1984–85 enrollment exceeded 70). We learned of new openings on the Tibetan border, and that two families had been sent as missionaries to the Tibetan people. Also, we heard a first-hand report from a Rawang preacher who had gone across into China to visit relatives in the border areas, and he told of how the Christians there are still faithful, in spite of many years persecution and separation. Later reports have confirmed this, and told of how the Lisu Christians are now able to meet openly, and how people are becoming Christians by the hundreds. This is especially exciting because it is a spontaneous growth from within China, not as a result of foreign workers going into the area. Equally thrilling have been the reports of tremendous new opportunities among the Naga people, along the Burma-India border (but still within Burma), how they are being met, and how the church is growing.

These new opportunities in the Nagaland area have come as a direct result of the settlement of the Hidden Valley area, on which it borders. During the six years we were in Hidden Valley all the Christians were praying especially for the Naga people, that they would be open to the Gospel message. A few congregations of Naga Christians had been established along the fringe areas by Lisu and Rawang missionaries who had been working with them for several years. Some of the Christians had even made the long journey to Putao to study the Bible under my mother's teaching back in 1963. But it had not been possible to penetrate the main Naga settlements until 1980–81. After we left Hidden Valley, a large number of the Lisu Christians moved southward to an area closer to Nagaland. They established several villages along the Ledo Road, which runs along the northern edge of Nagaland. These Christian villages have served as a witness and demonstration of the Christian way of living. The years of praying and silent witness are beginning to bear fruit, as now some forty villages from the heart of Nagaland are begging for teachers. During one year alone the Lisu and Rawang churches sent about a dozen preacher/missionaries and their families to live and work in Nagaland, as well as several teams of teachers who went for two or three months at a time. At the end of 1981 there were more than 1000 new baptized Naga believers, and the number has been increasing each year.

One of the things that thrilled us most as we met with the brethren in Rangoon was seeing the missionary zeal of these Christians whom we had had the privilege of helping to train, as now they in turn reach out to others. Since our visit there in 1981, we have continued to be in close touch, so we can learn of problems and needs, and know better what type of teaching or exhortation should be given.

During the years in Thailand we have been joined by several new workers, some of whom came for a few months on a student internship, others who have stayed for longer periods of time. Among these were Marcia and Margaret King, sisters who came for a year but stayed eighteen months (both are now married and serving in other mission fields); Peggy Carter, who was with us for two years; Judy Sterling, foster daughter of a former co-worker, Dorothy Sterling; and Debbie Brown, from California, daughter of long-time friends of the Morse families. The latter two each stayed about six months. In January 1978, came Walter Ridgley, who gave up a profitable plumbing business to come to the mission field, and is still working with us. Walter helped with the Children's Hostel two years, and also carried on a ministry to foreign prisoners in Chiang Mai before returning to the U.S. for further education, and to get married. Then in March, 1978, came Norma MacKinnon, a nurse, from Prince Edward Island, Canada. Norma worked as a nurse at the Children's Hostel for a year before marrying David Morse in June, 1979. Tom Silkwood, of Danville, Illinois, came in September, 1980, and remained thirteen months before returning to the U.S. to marry Gayle Smith. Tom and Gayle returned to Thailand in July, 1982. Their son, Jeffrey Thomas was born in November, 1983. They returned to the U.S. in March, 1984 for further education, and plan to return to Thailand early in 1986. In May, 1984 Chris and Lorra Brown and son Sean joined the work, but because of health problems had to return to the U.S. in December. In August, 1984 Joel Lillie joined the work.

As we have visited friends across the United States from time to time, many have wanted to know the whereabouts and activities of the different family members. When we all returned to the United States in 1972, my parents, J. Russell and Gertrude, went to live in Tulsa, Oklahoma, their home town. They made their home with my father's older sister, Louise Whitham, but made many trips to speak to the churches about the mission work. In October, 1974, Mother had a heart attack, from which she gradually recovered and was able to resume normal activities. However, on February 6, 1977, she died very suddenly, without warning. My father continued to stay with his sister, but she too, died in December, 1978, just two weeks prior to her 100th birthday. In August, 1979, my father was married to Suwanna Leepeemis, who is a nurse, and they have continued to make their home in Tulsa. My father celebrated his 87th birthday on February 4, 1985.

Our family, Robert's family, and Jesse and Drema Yangmi and family have continued to work as missionaries in Thailand.

Jesse has spent most of his time in literature production, as he worked first on a revision of the Lisu New Testament, which was printed complete with marginal cross-references, in 1979. Continuing to work with a Lisu committee, Jesse completed an extensive revision — almost a new translation — of the Old Testament and the New Testament in Lisu. This is now being printed in Hong Kong, through the United Bible Society. Jesse and

Drema's daughter, Lucy, graduated from high school in Penang, Malaysia, in June, 1982, and is studying nursing at Mid-America Nazarene College in Olathe, Ks. In June, 1984, Mickey also graduated from high school in Penang, and is now studying Business and Marketing at Missouri Southern State College, Joplin, MO. James is in the eighth grade in Joplin. Jesse expects to rejoin the family in August, 1985, when the Bible printing and proof-reading are completed.

The Yangmi's oldest son, Samuel, has also been helping them in the mission work, primarily in evangelism. On November 16, 1978, Sam married a Christian Lahu girl, Lumae Jasai, in Chiang Mai. Interestingly, this marriage was arranged by the parents, according to local custom, although Sam and Lumae had ample opportunity to become acquainted and were in agreement. They spent three years in the U.S. while Sam completed his college studies, but they returned to Thailand in January, 1985. Sam and Lumae have three daughters, Nellie Drema (1980), Julie Esther (1982), and Samantha Lou (August, 1984).

Of Robert's children, second son Stephen was the first to marry. He and Linda Scott were married August 20, 1977, in Bloomington, Indiana. Both Steve and Linda graduated from the Oklahoma College of Osteopathic Medicine and Surgery, in Tulsa, in June, 1982, completed a year of internship in Des Moines, Iowa, and spent an additional year studying tropical diseases in Louisiana. They returned to Thailand as medical missionaries in July, 1984. Their first child, James Scott, was born March 19, 1985.

Jonathan married Nangsar Sarip, a Rawang girl whom he had known from childhood, on April 9, 1978, in Chiang Mai, Thailand. He graduated from Pacific Christian College, Fullerton, California, in May, 1982. After a year of graduate work, Joni and Nangsar returned to Thailand in January, 1984 and have been working in village evangelism, literature production, and leadership training. They have a son, Anthony Peram (1980), and a daughter, Rebecca Zemiram (1983).

Bobby chose a Chinese bride, and was married to Tasanee Cheng, February 2, 1981, in Chiang Mai, Thailand. They have a daughter, Melody Ann (1982), and a son, Robert Howe III (1983). They live in Chiang Mai, where Bobby serves as Director of the Tribal Children's Hostel.

On June 11, 1981, Robert's oldest daughter, DeeDee, married Jim Fuller in Los Angeles, California, where they are presently living. They have a son, Jeremy Nathan (1984).

Robert's second daughter, Camille, attended college first in Fullerton, CA, then in Baton Rouge, Louisiana for two years, and in February, 1984 began studying in China. His youngest daughter, Genevieve, graduated from Dalat School (high school) in Penang, Malaysia, in June, 1985. She will enter Pacific Christian College in Fullerton, CA in August, 1985.

Of my children, my oldest son, David, married Norma MacKinnon, the Canadian nurse, on June 23, 1979, in Charlottetown, P.E.I., Canada. They have two sons, Kevin Lowell (1980), and Ian David (1982). After a one-year furlough they returned to Thailand in June, 1984 to continue work in literature production, evangelistic outreach and training of nationals.

Tom, our second son, was married to Debbie Brown, of Bedford, Indiana on May 18, 1985. Debbie served for three and a half years as a missionary to Zambia before she was married. Tom also graduated from Lincoln Christian College in Lincoln, Illinois in May, 1985. Tom and Debbie plan to return to Thailand in the autumn, to continue in village evangelism and youth work.

Our youngest son, Ron, was married December 29, 1981, to Patrizia Gentile, of Rome, Italy, whom he met while attending Bible College. Ron graduated from Ozark Bible College, Joplin, Missouri, in May, 1982. He and Patrizia returned to Thailand in April, 1983, to work in village evangelism, literature production, and leadership training. Their son, Jason Daniel, was born June 17, 1984.

Our first daughter, Margaret, was married in Chiang Mai on October 10, 1981, to Anan Kasempiyarom, a Chinese Christian who is a graduate of Chiang Mai University with a degree in engineering. They are living in Chiang Mai, where Anan has his own business. They have a son, Alex (1982).

Marilyn, our second daughter, was married in Chiang Mai to one of the young Lisu evangelists, Joel Khopang, on January 20, 1979. Joel and Marilyn have been involved in village evangelism, literature production, and leadership training. They have a son, Jesse Yashien (1979), and a daughter, Saskia Louise (1981). They returned to the U.S. in April, 1984, where Joel will be continuing his studies at Ozark Christian College, in Joplin, MO.

Our youngest daughter, Jeannette, was married to Walter Ridgley on June 24, 1982. She graduated from the School of Nursing of Missouri Southern State College, Joplin, MO, in May, 1984. Walter has completed two years of studies at Ozark Christian College, Joplin, MO. They returned to Thailand in September, 1984, where they have been involved in village evangelism, living in a rural village.

The perceptive reader may have noted the international flavor added to the families by the third generation: four Americans, two Chinese, one Lisu, one Rawang, one Lahu, one Canadian and one Italian. There are already fourteen members of the fourth generation, and the prayer of all of us is that each of them will also grow up "in the nurture and admonition of the Lord" and serve Him faithfully all their lives.

Throughout the years of work of this mission group, we have tried to be available and willing to learn, adapt and serve. We feel that God has honored this and blest the work as a whole. When we left Burma, there were over 200 congregations established, each supporting its own pastor. The count now is over 400 congregations, mainly because of the continuing efforts of the national Christians. In Thailand in 1973 there were less than 100 Lisu Christians, and in mid-1985 there are around 3000. We praise God for the increase. May he continue to guide us as we strive to be faithful in doing His work.

Eugene R. Morse

Chiang Mai, Thailand
June 30, 1985

(Check and/or fill in the appropriate spaces)

___ Please send ___ copy(ies) of "Exodus to a Hidden Valley" @ $4.95 each to:

Name _____

Address _____

City _____ State _____ Zip _____

Enclosed is my check/money order for $_____.

___ Enclosed is a gift of $_____ in support of this missionary work.

___ Please place my name on the Morses' mailing list.

Name _____ Address _____

City _____ State _____ Zip _____

MAKE ALL CHECKS
AND/OR MONEY
ORDERS PAYABLE to: NORTH BURMA CHRISTIAN MISSION
MAILING ADDRESS: P. O. Box 4074
Terre Haute, IN   47804

NOTE· All income from book sales and all gifts received will be used for missionary work. Gifts are tax deductible.

(Check and/or fill in the appropriate spaces)

___ Please send ___ copy(ies) of "Exodus to a Hidden Valley" @ $4.95 each to:

Name _____

Address _____

City _____ State _____ Zip _____

Enclosed is my check/money order for $_____.

___ Enclosed is a gift of $_____ in support of this missionary work.

___ Please place my name on the Morses' mailing list.

Name _____ Address _____

City _____ State _____ Zip _____

MAKE ALL CHECKS
AND/OR MONEY
ORDERS PAYABLE to: NORTH BURMA CHRISTIAN MISSION
MAILING ADDRESS: P. O. Box 4074
                       Terre Haute, IN   47804

NOTE: All income from book sales and all gifts received will be used for missionary work. Gifts are tax deductible.

(Check and/or fill in the appropriate spaces)

___ Please send __ copy(ies) of "Exodus to a Hidden Valley" @ $4.95 each to:

Name _____

Address _____

City _____ State _____ Zip _____

Enclosed is my check/money order for $_____.

___ Enclosed is a gift of $_____ in support of this missionary work.

___ Please place my name on the Morses' mailing list.

Name _____ Address _____

City _____ State _____ Zip _____

MAKE ALL CHECKS
AND/OR MONEY
ORDERS PAYABLE to: NORTH BURMA CHRISTIAN MISSION
MAILING ADDRESS: P. O. Box 4074
                          Terre Haute, IN   47804

NOTE: All income from book sales and all gifts received will be used for missionary work. Gifts are tax deductible.

(Check and/or fill in the appropriate spaces)

___ Please send ___ copy(ies) of "Exodus to a Hidden Valley" @ $4.95 each to:

Name _____

Address _____

City _____ State _____ Zip _____

Enclosed is my check/money order for $_____.

___ Enclosed is a gift of $_____ in support of this missionary work.

___ Please place my name on the Morses' mailing list.

Name _____ Address _____

City _____ State _____ Zip _____

MAKE ALL CHECKS
AND/OR MONEY
ORDERS PAYABLE to: NORTH BURMA CHRISTIAN MISSION
MAILING ADDRESS: P. O. Box 4074
                     Terre Haute, IN   47804

NOTE: All income from book sales and all gifts received will be used for missionary work. Gifts are tax deductible.

(Check and/or fill in the appropriate spaces)

___ Please send ___ copy(ies) of "Exodus to a Hidden Valley" @ $4.95 each to:

Name _____

Address _____

City _____ State _____ Zip _____

Enclosed is my check/money order for $_____.

___ Enclosed is a gift of $_____ in support of this missionary work.

___ Please place my name on the Morses' mailing list.

Name _____ Address _____

City _____ State _____ Zip _____

MAKE ALL CHECKS
AND/OR MONEY
ORDERS PAYABLE to: NORTH BURMA CHRISTIAN MISSION
MAILING ADDRESS: P. O. Box 4074
                    Terre Haute, IN   47804

NOTE: All income from book sales and all gifts received will be used for missionary work. Gifts are tax deductible.

(Check and/or fill in the appropriate spaces)

___ Please send ___ copy(ies) of "Exodus to a Hidden Valley" @ $4.95 each to:

Name _____

Address _____

City _____ State _____ Zip _____

Enclosed is my check/money order for $_____.

___ Enclosed is a gift of $_____ in support of this missionary work.

___ Please place my name on the Morses' mailing list.

Name _____ Address _____

City _____ State _____ Zip _____ .

MAKE ALL CHECKS
AND/OR MONEY
ORDERS PAYABLE to: NORTH BURMA CHRISTIAN MISSION
MAILING ADDRESS: P. O. Box 4074
                      Terre Haute, IN   47804

NOTE: All income from book sales and all gifts received will be used for missionary work. Gifts are tax deductible.

266.0092
M88
1977

LINCOLN CHRISTIAN UNIVERSITY

76345

3 4711 00231 7701